MONROE COLLEGE LIBRARY

3 7340 01052493 9

D0918336

THE BOOK OF

BOURBON

And Other Fine
American Whiskeys

THE BOOK OF

BOURBON

And Other Fine
American Whiskeys

GARY REGAN AND
MARDEE HAIDIN REGAN

CHAPTERS PUBLISHING LTD., SHELBURNE, VERMONT 05482

TP
605
.R44
1995

Copyright © 1995 Gary Regan and Mardee Haidin Regan
Photographs copyright © 1995 Clark Capps and Becky Luigart-Stayner

All rights reserved. No part of this book may be reproduced or transmitted in any form or by any
electronic or mechanical means, including information storage and retrieval systems, without
permission in writing from the Publisher, except for the inclusion of brief quotations in a review.

Published by
Chapters Publishing Ltd.
2031 Shelburne Road
Shelburne, Vermont 05482

Library of Congress Cataloging-in-Publication Data
Regan, Gary.
The book of bourbon and other fine American whiskeys / Gary Regan and
Mardee Haidin Regan.
    p.   cm.
Includes bibliographical references (p.) and index.
ISBN 1-881527-89-1 (hardcover)
1. Whiskey—United States. I. Regan, Mardee Haidin. II. Title.
TP605.R44   1996
641.2'52'0973—dc20   95-21847

Trade distribution in the U.S. by Firefly Books (U.S.) Inc.
P.O. Box 1338 • Ellicott Station • Buffalo, NY 14205

Trade distribution in Canada by Firefly Books Ltd.
250 Sparks Avenue • Willowdale, Ontario • Canada M2H 2S4

Printed and bound in Canada by Metropole Litho Inc.
St. Bruno de Montarville, Québec

Designed by Susan McClellan
Front cover and interior color photography by Clark Capps
Front cover illustration by David Diaz
Food photography by Becky Luigart-Stayner

To our fathers, Bernard Regan, Mark Haidin and John Hilgert, ardent spirits all. And to the men and women who pioneered the American whiskey business, the people who led it back to the straight and narrow when it was in danger of straying and the distillers of our time who live the whiskey life and labor each day to keep our whiskey pure.

Acknowledgments

Touring round American whiskey distilleries to research this book has been a fascinating experience—we have been enlightened on one or another aspect of whiskey-making by each and every person we met. Our apologies go out to anyone who helped and doesn't find his or her name here. These are some of the people who went out of their way to help with our research—any errors in this book are solely ours, not theirs.

First and foremost must come Mike Veach, archivist at United Distillers in Louisville, Kentucky. Mike not only shared his data files and the vast archives he oversees, but helped us locate many of the graphics in this book, kept us informed of all new documents that he uncovered along the way and carefully checked our historical material for mistakes. Above all, however, Mike treated this book as though it were his own, and much of the historical information herein did, indeed, emanate from his sources or sources he knew to exist.

Fellow bourbon freak (and whiskey historian) Charles Cowdery of Chicago guided us through the first steps of research and was available for "brain picking" every step of the way.

Barry Estabrook, Editor-in-Chief of Chapters Publishing, who suggested this book in the first place, edited it with love and has been 110 percent behind the project. Also, Rux Martin from Chapters (who has been behind our Manhattan cocktails at every given opportunity), the ever-patient Cristen Brooks, Alice Lawrence, Melissa Cochran and this book's designer, Susan McClellan. Also, Clark Capps, who took location photographs, and Becky Luigart-Stayner, who shot studio photographs.

A special thanks to our agent, Michael Carlisle of the William Morris Agency, the man who provides us with sound advice and great Russian vodka.

The Ancient Age Distillery

Thanks to Distillery Manager Joe Darmand, Master Distiller Emeritus Elmer Tandy Lee and Master Distiller Gary Gayheart. Also to Hugues de la Vergne at the distillery's parent company, Sazerac, in New Orleans.

The Barton Distillery

Thanks to Fred McMillen, Jack Cavanaugh and Master Distiller Jerry Dalton. Jerry guided us through the intricate aspects of whiskey distillation and spent many hours of his own time poring over the technical chapters and pointing out our blunders.

The Jim Beam Distillery

Thanks to Booker Noe, a whiskey man in his own right, Jerry Summers, who "showed us around," and everyone at the Jim Beam Brands Company who went out of his or her way to make our research easier.

The Bernheim Distillery

Thanks to loveable and knowledgeable Master Distiller Ed Foote, to the all-around thoughtful, friendly efforts and objective guidance of Chris Morris and to Michael Wright, who really helped us understand the technical side of distillation. Thanks also to Martin Slattery and Renee Cooper.

The Jack Daniel Distillery

Thanks to Master Distiller Jimmy Bedford, distillery representative extraordinaire Roger Brashears and our wonderfully organized general-information-giver Nancy Holding-DeKalb.

George A. Dickel's Cascade Distillery

Thanks to Distillery Manager Jennings "David" Backus and the whole crew who showed us around the distillery.

The Early Times Distillery

Thanks to Master Distiller Lincoln Henderson and General Manager Leo Reidinger. Also to the folk at Brown-Forman and its representatives: Susan Bell, Margaret Shadburne, Barbara Waits, Stephen J. Hughes, John Vidal, Phil Lynch, Mac Brown, Robinson Brown Jr. and Owsley Brown II.

The Four Roses Distillery

Thanks to archivist Al Young, loveable Master Distiller Emeritus Ova Haney, Master Distiller Jim Rutledge and Sheila Swerling-Puritt.

The Heaven Hill Distillery

Thanks to Vice President Max Shapira, Master Distiller Parker Beam and his son and assistant, Craig Beam.

The Maker's Mark Distillery

Thanks to Bill Samuels Jr., the man responsible for piquing our interest in bourbon back in 1991. Bill held our hands every step of the way on this book; it was his passion that first led us to explore the intricacies of American whiskey before this book was contracted and his amazing objectivity that led us down many a path which might otherwise have gone unexplored. And to make everything so much easier, Bill (perhaps the most colorful character in the business) kept us smiling throughout. Thanks also to the lovely Nancy Samuels, the intrepid Melony Geary and, at the distillery, Donna Nally, Donna Miles and especially Master Distiller Steve Nally, who shared his wisdom and had great patience when we devised our recipe for bourbon.

A. Smith Bowman Distillery

Thanks to CEO John "Jay" Buchanan Adams Jr., Bob O'Halloran and Master Distiller Joseph H. Dangler.

The Wild Turkey Distillery

Thanks to the ever-smiling Master Distiller Jimmy Russell and also to Eve Gilbert and Ann T. Higgins.

At The Oscar Getz Museum of Whiskey History in Bardstown, both Mary Hite and Flaget Nally were unendingly supportive and brimming with knowledge, as was Mr. Walter Doerting, who readily made some of his family's historical documents from the Glencoe Distillery available to us.

At the wonderful Kentucky Derby Museum, Jay R. Ferguson and Candace K. Perry were unfailingly enthusiastic and helpful.

At The Filson Club, James J. Holmburg, Mary Jean Kinsman and all of the staff were very helpful in our research.

John Gunn and Larry Casey of the Blue Grass Cooperage Company in Louisville and John Boswell of The Independent Stave Company in Lebanon, Kentucky, helped us with our wood research; Dixie Hibbs, Bardstown's formidable historian, came to the rescue more than once. Joris Minne and Patrick Fitzgerald helped with information from Northern Ireland; Anthony J. Burnet and Alex G. Nicol of the Glenmorangie Distillery filled us in on the Scottish side.

On a personal note, Gary would like to thank Jim Duke and Frank Casa of Drake's Drum in New York, who helped him tremendously when he arrived on these shores in 1973; Michael Batterberry of *Food Arts* magazine, who gave him his first chance to write professionally, and Marcelle DiFalco and Kelley Regan, who edit his work there with a great deal of skill; Susan Wyler, who first approached him to write *The Bartender's Bible*; F. Paul Pacult, a good friend and fellow spirits freak; Bill Greenham and Stan Ogden, who know him well and still speak to him; and Stuffy Shmitt, whose ear is always open—and whose whiskey glass is almost always nearing empty.

Others whose names deserve thanks here are: Ralph Dupps, Bob Schecter, Louis Forman, Kay Corbett, Julian Van Winkle III, Hermann Reiner, Timothy and Gordon Hue, Patty Boston of the Kentucky Colonels, H. Edward O'Daniel Jr. of the Kentucky Distillers Association and Meg Syberg of the David Sherman Corporation. Support comes from friends and family in many ways; we'd also like to thank Vi Regan and John Hilgert, Evelyn Hackney, Pam Lockard, J. Vincent Arey, M.D., Ken and Joyce Armstrong, Michael Tanner, M.D., P.T., Louise (Loulou) Tanner, Mary Anne Pritting-Tanner Esq., Lee Bailey, Mr. Thomas Jednaszewski, Frani Shaver Lauda, Richard Sax, Roy Finamore and Darren and William Ransdell.

Contents

THE OLD PRENTICE DISTILLERY AT THE TURN OF THE CENTURY

INTRODUCTION

EEP IN THE SOUL OF AMERICAN WHISKEY LIES THE RICH PIONEER spirit that founded this nation, the steadfast determination that conquered the Great Plains and the Wild West and the enterprising attitude that made the United States a global entity never conquered by a foreign nation. Though it may sound hyperbolic to say so, we think it's all right there in a single shot of Tennessee sour mash, straight rye whiskey or bourbon.

Tennessee whiskey, that sweet, sooty liquor that bangs around your mouth shouting, "I'm a tough guy—take it or leave it," is the drink that we tend to sip on the rocks. Though a few mixed drinks work well with this stylish sour mash, it's generally best on its own. On the other hand, rye whiskey's fragrant spiciness can be very versatile— when you can find a bottle. Unfortunately, very few bars stock straight rye; take our advice and keep a supply at home. Bourbon, however, is big. Bars are now stocking more and more bottlings and the bourbon distillers are heeding the call to produce more and more brands of top-notch bourbons for our shelves. There's no doubt about it; right now, bourbon is where it's at.

Next time you are in an earthy bar—dark and dingy, with just a faint smell of stale ale and aged nicotine that's soaked into the woodwork and become part of the bar's very soul—order a bourbon. Next time you are dining on prime sirloin steak in the best steakhouse in town, try a glass of bourbon. And as you settle in to watch *60 Minutes* on a Sunday evening, the telephone turned off and the world locked out so you can savor the last few hours of the weekend, sit back and sip on an ounce or two of straight bourbon whiskey.

You can drink bourbon whether you're thirsty or not; you can drink it with your best pals, your lawyer, your mother and your colleagues. You can drink bourbon with scoundrels, and given the chance, you could have drunk bourbon with Ulysses S. Grant (who is said to have loved it a bit too much).

Bourbon, however, wasn't the first whiskey to be made in America. Though bourbon was born here and grew up here, it evolved from Pennsylvania's rye whiskeys, and it hasn't stopped yet. All of the American straight whiskeys—bourbon, rye and Tennessee—continue to evolve and change right along with the rest of us. Many of these modifications are the direct result of what makes this country unique—progress and profit motive. Just as every other American industry has struggled to become bigger, better and more profitable, so, too, has the whiskey business. However, unlike many industries, American whiskey has not lost its identity over the years; it has developed alongside the country, adapting itself to crises as they came along, evolving with technology and maturing with the nation. And though it sounds positively heretical to say so, bourbon and other sour-mash whiskeys are far more American than apple pie.

A MERICAN WHISKEY IS THE PRODUCT OF TRUE GRIT. ITS HISTORY IS TIED TO the settlers who strove to survive in a newly formed nation and have access to a slug of whiskey when they wanted it. Farmers made whiskey from the grains they grew, and later, whiskey-makers fought the government over excise taxes—sometimes winning, sometimes losing. More than a couple of political scandals reared their heads along the way, and some outrageous characters in the nineteenth and twentieth centuries campaigned to cast out the devil they called whiskey—and eventually won, albeit for a short time. Whiskey fought its way through the Civil War, struggled for recognition when short-term profiteers used the words "straight whiskey" on bottles of unadulterated garbage and, much more recently, survived the public fascination for lighter liquors such as white rum and vodka. And through it all, America's native whiskey remained a true all-American.

Don't think for a moment that the whiskey distillers of America run ahead of the pack to embrace progress and technology. Over the past 200-plus years, there has always been a solid "whiskey man" or two around, and it is these master distillers who have preserved the quality of their products and the legacies of their forefathers' peculiar customs and rituals. These whiskey firebrands have stood up to the accountants every step of the way, listened to the public's demands and fought for tradition at all costs. Bless them for that, because the result—especially in recent years—is ours to enjoy in the abundance of new, bigger-bodied, more flavorful whiskeys being released today. And more are sure to come.

Although comparisons are inevitable between American whiskey and Scotch, it is vital to understand that they are as different from each other as apples and oranges. Scotch, especially single malt, bears the smoky flavor of Scotland's native peat, utilizes large amounts of malted barley (100 percent in the case of single malts) and is much influenced by the cool, damp atmosphere of that beautiful country. American whiskey, on the other hand, is sweeter, due in large part to its recipe, and is the result of shorter aging in a considerably warmer, drier environment. If Scotch is a great Roquefort, American whiskey is the finest Brie. Both are wonderful, but each is very different from the other.

Aside from the fact that Tennessee whiskey is made only in Tennessee and just one bourbon is produced in Indiana, all of the remaining bourbons and straight rye whiskeys are presently distilled only in Kentucky (even the Virginian bourbon starts its life in the Bluegrass State), geography doesn't come into play too much when describing American whiskeys. All three states are inland, one immediately north of the other, and all are geologically similar. Scotch is made throughout a country that encompasses under 30,000 square miles of land and produces five dramatically different styles of single malts from specific areas within those borders. Combine the whiskey-producing areas of Kentucky, Indiana and Tennessee and they equal about the same area as the whole of Scotland, yet their whiskeys show little variance that can be attributed to the geographical location of individual distilleries. The variations among American whiskeys are more the product of idiosyncratic techniques and differing recipes.

Our goal is to introduce you to American whiskeys, to prove that familiarity with these distinctively American products breeds content. Getting to know bourbon, rye and Tennessee whiskey is much like being introduced to a dear friend's friend; you discover anew that the world is even smaller than you thought, that some large concepts are indeed universal and that you have remarkable experiences in common. You'll find out how these whiskeys are made, ways to taste, drink and cook with them, how to visit the distilleries in which they are made and how to let them enrich your enjoyment of life.

Finally, a word of reason: Drink in moderation. Don't drink and drive. Don't drink if it causes you to do harm to yourself or others, and above all, if you really need to drink—don't. If you can adhere to these rules, you will enjoy drinking for all the right reasons and perhaps conclude—as we have—that the effects of moderate amounts of alcohol are part and parcel of its beauty.

THE JAMESTOWN COLONY

CHAPTER ONE

THE HISTORY OF

AMERICAN

WHISKEY

THE ORIGINS OF WHISKEY CAN BE TRACED BACK TO THE monks of medieval Ireland and Scotland, who, in a quest to produce a rejuvenating "water of life," first used grains in their alchemic distillation techniques, since the grapes of warmer climates weren't available to them. Now, those two countries make their own distinctive styles of the spirit. So it is with American whiskey—the original concept was imported from faraway lands, but after some 300 years, American whiskey, which must be made with corn, an indigenous American grain, is a product unto itself.

American whiskey started its life as a raw, unaged spirit. Through the years, whiskey has developed into the complex, big-bodied, distinctively American bourbons, ryes and Tennessee whiskeys that today are savored by connoisseurs, sipped by grandmothers, tossed back by barflies and "discovered" by almost every American as he or she reaches that magical age of twenty-one. But American whiskey itself has reached maturity in relatively recent years, after spending a 300-year adolescence being molded by every major event that has affected its native country. And, at times, the reverse is true—whiskey has affected the nation itself.

EARLY COOPERS AT WORK

Whiskey-making was one of the first cottage industries in the land; it was responsible for George Washington's mustering federal troops for the first time, and whiskey went with the early pioneers as they traveled westward to explore new territories. Whiskey was a spirit of contention during the Civil War and was, in part, the reason that Grant never served a third term in the White House. Whiskey spurred the women of America to conduct a crusade that led to Prohibition and has played a part in every major war this nation has seen. In short, where America has been, so has American whiskey.

Bourbon, in fact, is so American that in 1964, Congress officially recognized it as "a distinctive product of the U.S.A." And although straight rye and Tennessee whiskeys haven't attained such a prestigious honor, they, too, have traveled the same dusty trails that led to today's superhighways and are as uniquely American as any bourbon.

When the first immigrants arrived on this continent, their fondness for alcohol in almost any shape or form led to a chain of events that would culminate in the creation of distinctive American whiskeys. By tracing the thirst the settlers wanted to slake, we can plot the development of American whiskey from the early days of the settlers in Virginia and New England all the way through to today. Furthermore, we can track the creation of bourbon and Tennessee whiskey back to their very roots—a rare opportunity when the subject is food or drink.

The Settlers' Search for a Decent Drink

BEER WAS PROBABLY THE FIRST KIND OF BEVERAGE ALCOHOL PRODUCED in the early settlements at Jamestown and Plymouth. The settlers brought quite a supply of ale and spirits with them from England, but when their supplies dwindled, they had no choice but to brew their own beer, using whatever ingredients were close at hand. By the early 1620s, colonists in Virginia were making beer that they claimed would "tide them over" until they got used to the water. But already distinctively American ingredients were being used. Captain James Thorpe, a missionary in Virginia at that time, wrote to friends in London that he had learned to make a drink from Indian corn which was so good, he sometimes chose it over English beer. Was Thorpe actually distilling corn whiskey at the time? Though that possibility is not unthinkable, it's more probable that he was making corn beer. Whatever his product, it was strong enough to get some Native Americans so drunk that they scalped and killed him in 1622.

Farther north, the Pilgrims were also making beer, and according to John Hull Brown in his book *Early American Beverages*, they weren't above adding flavorings in the form of molasses, tree barks (spruce, birch and sassafras were popular) and fruit and vegetables,

> **"In 1501 the Coopers Guild was granted a formal charter by King Henry VIII and the first cooper in the New World, John Lewis, went to work in Jamestown in 1608."**
>
> —FROM "The Williamsburg Cooper," *The Wooden Barrel*, SEPTEMBER 1968

such as apples and pumpkins, to their brews. Though many types of grapes were native to America, the wines they produced were unlike the ones the Europeans were used to. The colonists tried to cultivate European strains, but *Vitis vinifera* grapevines didn't fare well on the East Coast. Undeterred, the settlers turned their talents to fermenting other fruits—and even vegetables. They made "wines" from elderberries,

EIGHTEENTH-CENTURY STILL

parsnips, pumpkins and the like—if it fermented, they turned it into one form of beverage alcohol or another.

The first settlers imported some alcohol too—wines, brandy and fortified drinks such as Madeira, "sack" and "Canary." Although imported wines and liquors have always had that "if it comes from France, it must be good" image, the self-sufficient Pilgrims and those who followed them soon started to make all kinds of drinks from the abundant native ingredients.

As soon as beehives were located, the settlers began to produce mead and metheglin, a popular drink of the day made from a fermented mixture of honey, water and spices—most probably ginger, cloves, mace and the like. And once their orchards produced fruit, cider and perry (pear "cider") were added to the menu.

But still, these early Americans weren't content. They wanted their own liquor. Stills had been commonplace on Scottish farms since the mid-1500s, usually little more than barrel-size enclosed copper pots with a metal pipe emerging from the top and coiling down to a receptacle that caught the condensed spirit. And although some early settlers may have built their own makeshift stills from available raw materials, most stills were probably imported from Europe. Like the first beers and wines, the first liquors made here used a variety of ingredients—berries, plums, potatoes, apples, carrots and grain—anything that had the power to attract yeast and then ferment. The resultant spirits were probably not the smoothest of potions, but they were liquor all the same. Two of the more popular American spirits during the first century and a half of colonization were peach brandy, made mainly in the Southern colonies, and applejack, a brandy distilled from cider.

The still popular Laird's Applejack can trace its roots to Scotsman William Laird, who was probably a whiskey distiller in his homeland, the Highlands of Scotland. Laird settled in Monmouth County, New Jersey, in 1698 and set about applying his knowledge of distillation to apples rather than barley malt. Interestingly enough, early cidermakers who didn't possess a still would, during the winter months, leave cider outside to freeze. The following morning, they discarded the frozen portion, leaving a very strong cider—the alcohol content was concentrated in the liquid that didn't, or couldn't, freeze. Since the distillation of beverage alcohol is, in simple terms, the separation of alcohol from water, they were actually practicing a form of distillation by freezing instead of heating.

In 1640, William Kieft, the Director General of the New Netherland colony, decided that liquor should be distilled on Staten Island. His master distiller, Wilhelm Hendriksen, is said to have used corn and rye to make liquor, and since the Dutch didn't develop a formula for gin until 10 or so years later, he must have been making some form of whiskey.

But until the mid-eighteenth century, whiskey was made in relatively small quantities, mainly by farmer-distillers, and without distinctive or consistent techniques. The quality of the whiskey they were producing, however, had to have been questionable. It's interesting, though, to consider why so many farmers in the century preceding independence were also distillers. Distillation is not an easy process. Aside from having to follow a complex, multi-step recipe, distilling beverage alcohol in those days meant creating a highly flammable liquid over a heat source of open flames. Distillers always ran the risk of blowing themselves to kingdom come should a still explode. Distilling wasn't merely a case of: "Oh, I have some extra grain, might as well make some whiskey." It was a much bigger decision than that.

Think about this: Early farmers, from time to time, must have had bumper crops of grains. What could they do with the leftover grain after all their neighbors had bought or bartered enough to keep them in their daily bread? First, they made beer. Beer was produced in relatively copious quantities in the 1600s. But in those pre-pasteurization days, beer didn't keep long, so the farmers brewed only as much as could be consumed in the very near future. They used grain to feed their cattle and other farm animals—if they had them. But still, there was grain left over. The choice was simple: Let it rot or change its form, as the ancient alchemists did, and produce the "water of life." The word "whiskey" is derived from the Gaelic word *uisgebaugh* [WEEZ-ga-bochh], meaning "water of life." If you say the word quickly enough—or with a substantial quantity of whiskey in your system—it becomes, with a little shortening, "WEEZ-ga," a word that was anglicized to become "whiskey."

> **"Give an Irishman lager for a month, and he's a dead man. An Irishman is lined with copper, and the beer corrodes it. But whiskey polishes the copper and is the saving of him."**
>
> —FROM *Life on the Mississippi*, BY MARK TWAIN, 1883.

Distilling grain gives farmers two distinct avenues for profit-making: The distillate, by virtue of having a high concentration of alcohol, can be stored almost indefinitely, and liquor is relatively easy to transport—much easier than huge sheaves of corn or rye. One horse could carry about four bushels of grain or one 60-gallon barrel of whiskey—the product of 24 bushels of grain.

The farmers simply chopped down a few trees from their land, got the local cooper to make some sturdy barrels (every self-respecting settlement had a cooper or two, since barrels were used to store and transport most products, from foodstuffs to hardware, at that time), and after bartering as much as possible with his immediate neighbors, he could easily send off a wagonload of whiskey to thirsty buyers farther afield. Furthermore, the solids left behind from the distillation process were usable as cattle feed. For farmers, producing whiskey made good business sense. (A wonderful twentieth-century example of this process can be seen in the case of A. Smith Bowman, a farmer in Virginia who, in 1935, produced Virginia Gentleman Bourbon using grains grown on his farm, made barrels from the trees on his land and used the residues of his distillate to feed his farm animals—see page 189.)

But these enterprising farmer-distillers, much like the earlier distillers of plums and berries, were distilling whiskey more or less for themselves and their neighbors. Another liquor was far easier and much less expensive to produce, and it was about to become one of the first industries in America.

The Spirit of America—Rum?

THE FIRST LIQUOR TO BE MADE IN QUANTITY AND TO HAVE A MAJOR IMPACT ON the colonies was, in fact, rum. Starting in the mid-1600s, sugar and molasses were exported from the West Indies to New England, where the colonists made their very own variety of rum. Of course, settlers in the islands made their own rum, and that, too, was exported to the American colonies, ready for immediate consumption. In those days, rum was known by many different names: rumbullion, rumbustion, rumbowling, kill-devil, rhumbooze and Barbados water were all common terms for the distillate of sugarcane or molasses.

The English were going through turmoil on their home turf at this time. Cromwell had won the civil war and ruled the country from 1649 until 1660, but by the early 1700s, the monarchy had been restored, and the government was paying a little more attention to the colonies. One of the first acts to upset the American drinker, designed to raise money for the Crown, was the taxation of the sugar, molasses and rum being imported from "any of the colonies or plantations in America, not in the possession of or under the dominion of his Majesty." Although not mentioned by name, the tax was directed specifically at the main competition for British traders in the Caribbean: the merchants of the French West Indies. The same products from British colonies in the West Indies were not taxed. It was a little gentle goading to remind the colonists where their allegiances should lie. Buy British—or else. It's somewhat astounding that there was never a Boston Rum Party, but on the other hand, it's doubtful the rum-loving colonists of the time would have thrown good liquor into Boston Harbor. The Molasses Act of 1733 levied five shillings per hundredweight of sugar, six pence per gallon of molasses and nine pence per gallon of rum. The colonists, however, found an ingenious way of coping with these new taxes—for the most part, they ignored them.

In the mid-1700s, New England rum sold for around three shillings (£0.15) per gallon and was actually used in lieu of currency in what was known as the "triangle trade" with Africa and the West Indies. Here's an example of how it worked according to Martin Gilbert, author of *American History Atlas*, 1968: In 1752, by which time there were at least 30 legitimate distilleries in Rhode Island alone, a ship called *The Sanderson* left Newport with 8,220 gallons of rum on board. It isn't known how much rum remained when the ship landed in Africa, but the cargo was traded on the Gold Coast, and the ship headed for Barbados laden with 56 African slaves, 40 ounces of gold and 900 pounds of peppercorns. After trading the slaves, gold and pepper in Barbados, the ship returned to Rhode Island carrying 55 hogsheads of molasses, 3 hogsheads of sugar and over £400 in bills of exchange.

The manufacture of rum continued to be big business in America until 1808, when the United States prohibited the importation of slaves from Africa, an act that broke the triangle trade. But by that time, whiskey was well on its way to becoming the country's native spirit.

A SEVENTEENTH-CENTURY AMERICAN POT STILL

The Early Years of American Whiskey

I N 1777, THE NEWLY FORMED UNITED STATES OF AMERICA ADOPTED THE STARS and Stripes as the Continental Congress flag, and George Washington was concerned that his troops didn't have enough liquor. He actually suggested that public distilleries be constructed throughout the states, citing that "the benefits arising from the moderate use of strong liquor have been experienced in all armies and are not to be disputed."

Washington knew all about distilling liquor. He had erected stills at Mount Vernon in the 1770s in order to produce rum, and a little later on, James Anderson, his Scottish plantation manager, is said to have persuaded him to plant rye, with a mind to producing whiskey. And Washington did, indeed, make whiskey. During the year before his death in 1799, it has been estimated that he earned a considerable profit from his distillery and had upwards of 150 gallons of whiskey left in storage.

Meanwhile, during the late 1700s, the Scots-Irish, a huge group of immigrants from Northern Ireland, began arriving in the United States. These people had a long history of moving (or being moved) to new lands, coping with hardships, battling adversity and establishing thriving communities. They also knew how to make whiskey. Their arrival in America came at a time when the country was struggling to become self-sufficient. There was plenty of farmland and a demand for liquor, and the strong backs, tenacious characters and intimate knowledge of the still made the Scots-Irish perfect people to help carve out a new nation—and lay the foundations for the whiskey industry.

Over the whole of the eighteenth century, about 250,000 Scots-Irish Ulstermen and Ulsterwomen came to America. Most of them didn't linger long to mingle with the settlers on the coast—they had left Ulster to "go west," and go west they did. They settled in western Pennsylvania, western Maryland, western Virginia and the western parts of North and South Carolina. They were not, however, the only group of immigrants to have a major impact on the whiskey industry. The Germans who settled in Pennsylvania and became known as the Pennsylvania Dutch were also well versed in the use of the alembic, and by 1775, there were just as many Germans here as Scots-Irish.

LETTER FROM WASHINGTON

The Pioneer Spirit

DANIEL BOONE FIRST VENTURED INTO THE EASTERN PART OF WHAT WOULD become Kentucky on a hunting expedition in 1767, and due, in part, to his reports of its bounty, the land soon acquired an idyllic status. According to Roseann Reinemuth Hogan in her book *Kentucky Ancestry*, a churchman of the time referred to heaven as a "Kentucky sort of a place." The word "Kentucky," by the by, as translated

DANIEL BOONE DISCOVERS KENTUCKY

from Iroquoian, is proposed to have two meanings: Some say that the word means "meadowland," whereas others say that it means "dark and bloody ground" and was so called to commemorate the Native American wars fought within the area.

In 1776, Kentucky County was carved from the massive western part of Virginia previously known as Fincastle County, and a law known colloquially as "corn patch and cabin rights" was issued by the Virginia General Assembly. The law allowed settlers to lay claim to 400 acres of land, provided that they build a cabin and plant a patch of corn prior to 1778. After that time, surveyors and prospectors offered land for sale at very reasonable prices to pioneers heading west. Most settlers from Maryland and Pennsylvania started their trip in Pittsburgh and floated down the Ohio River on flatboats into Kentucky. Virginians and pioneers from North Carolina, on the other hand, usually made their way to what became the Bluegrass State through the Cumberland Gap—a route that took them over the Appalachian Mountains on the "Wilderness Trail."

Whatever brought settlers to Kentucky and however they arrived, the hardy souls who came after the "corn patch and cabin rights" deal was over bought or bartered small parcels of the large tracts of land held by speculators. The story of a fairly typical arrangement of the time is detailed in *Nelson County Kentucky: A Pictorial History* by Dixie Hibbs, a very knowledgeable Bardstown, Kentucky, historian.

She relates the story of William Bard, an agent for David Bard and John C. Owens. By 1780, partners David Bard and Owens had laid claim to 1,000 acres of land in Kentucky County. Working on their behalf, William Bard oversaw a lottery that same year in which the 33 lucky winners would be awarded lots on the land. They had no points to pay on the closing, no smooth broker taking a percentage and no rent to pay until the Revolutionary War ended (The Treaty of Paris, September 3, 1783). In fact, the lottery winners paid nothing at all for the property; the only requirement was that they clear their plot of land and build a house, at least 16 feet square, on it. The idea was that by attracting newcomers to the town, the surrounding land, owned by the same company, would grow in value. And although the town was originally known as Salem, the settlers soon adopted the name of their benefactor, and Bard's Town (Bardstown) was born. Not long after, many a fine barrel of whiskey was being made in the Bard's Town area. By the turn of the century, over 350,000 people had settled in Kentucky.

Meanwhile, the thirsty Scots-Irish and German distillers who settled in western Pennsylvania and Maryland began making rye whiskey. But why rye? Barley was the chief ingredient of European whiskey. But barley took a long time before it became acclimatized to its new home. Rye, another European grain, was a hardy crop that took root and fared well almost immediately. The Europeans, already familiar with rye, turned to it as "the next best thing" to barley. Corn, an indigenous grain, was also cultivated, and although the immigrants weren't accustomed to using it to make whiskey, it was gradually introduced to the process in small quantities.

The whiskey from the middle colonies eventually became known as Monongahela or Pennsylvania or Maryland whiskey, named for its various locations, not the grain used to make it. The farmer-distillers made a more than adequate living by raising livestock, growing grain and making rye whiskey that they could trade to fulfill their other needs. They had no ruling monarch to worry about, could practice whatever religion they pleased and didn't have to pay any excise taxes, but that wasn't going to last long. The nation had some debts that needed to be paid.

By 1790, George Washington had been inaugurated in New York City, the new country's temporary capital, and after the long years of fighting the Revolutionary War, it was time for the country to set up business. Up until this point, cultural and agricultural needs and feasibilities had dictated the production of America's whiskey, but a major event was about to occur, just a decade after the Declaration of Independence was issued, wherein whiskey would have a direct effect on the survival of the nation itself.

The Whiskey Rebellion

IN 1791, GEORGE WASHINGTON APPROVED AN EXCISE TAX ON LIQUOR. HE certainly wasn't the first politician to take out his frustrations on whiskey producers; just four years earlier, Britain had introduced a prohibitive tax on Highland stills in Scotland and declared that the whiskey produced there couldn't be distributed out-

TARRED AND FEATHERED FEDERAL AGENT: WHISKEY REBELLION

side the Highland region. Everyone seemed to have it in for the distillers.

But Washington had his reasons, and although he was himself a distiller, he listened to Alexander Hamilton, Secretary of the Treasury, who proposed that the newly formed country should pay off its debts from the Revolutionary War. To accomplish this, Hamilton persuaded Congress to introduce tariffs on imported goods, tax spirits and charter the Bank of the United States, which would hold the government's revenues and stimulate economic growth by investing in American businesses.

Hamilton had estimated the national debt at about $54 million, and on July 1, 1791, the government started to enforce an excise tax on all spirits—imported and domestic. Rates were based on the alcoholic strength of the product; spirits made from home-

grown products were taxed less than those made from imported goods. Rum, made from imported molasses, was therefore more heavily taxed than whiskey. And an annual tax was levied on each still, dependent on its capacity.

For governments in need of a few extra dollars, liquor, beer and wine have long been popular targets of taxation for two very simple reasons: Beverage alcohol is produced from food, be it fruit, sugar or grain, but it is not necessary to sustain life. Therefore, it is easy to agree that strong drink is a luxury that takes food from the mouths of all people. Add to that the fact that in some circles, drinking is also a sin, and it becomes relatively easy to convince a nation that drink should be taxed. But the 1791 tax on American whiskey was very unpopular among the farmer-distillers.

We should try to understand what these new taxes meant to the farmer-distillers of the time. It was difficult to pay because they didn't have any cash. They might have been making a decent living, but many, indeed most, transactions at that time were conducted by barter. It's a simple way to do business: Trade a quart of whiskey to the local seamstress in return for a new dress for the missus, another to the fishmonger who will supply you with dinner for a few Fridays, and when the landlord is passing by, maybe you can persuade him to take a gallon of your finest whiskey in lieu of a few months' rent. The scene and the amounts are hypothetical, but it gives a rough idea of why apparently prosperous farmers had empty pockets.

Not all farmers had stills, since stills were very expensive pieces of equipment. But "them as didn't" would bring their grain to "them as did" and have it made into whiskey. The farmer would receive a percentage of the whiskey, the distiller keeping the rest for his trouble. But no cash changed hands.

Distillers throughout the country were vexed about these new taxes, but nowhere did their anger turn to violence as universally as in western Pennsylvania. Aside from having no cash, the distillers in that area were also exasperated because, when summoned to court to answer their charges, they had to make their way to Philadelphia. For some of them, this meant traveling a couple of hundred miles through dangerous country where Native Americans were wont to attack, and it also meant leaving their farms for relatively long periods when there was work to be done—and whiskey to be made.

The Pennsylvania whiskey-makers decided to revolt. They held public meetings to discuss the matter, one of which resulted in a declaration that anyone trying to collect the taxes would be viewed as an enemy of society. According to Gerald Carson in his book *The Social History of Bourbon*, one such tax collector, who had employed the services of a dozen soldiers to guard his house, had it burned to the ground nonetheless. At one point in 1791, a mob of over 5,000 men advanced on Pittsburgh threatening to burn down the whole city, but they were met by town officials who managed to dissuade them from their mission by promising to banish certain officials and plying the mob with food and, of course, whiskey.

The following year, 1792, the government reduced the taxes a little (down to around 7¢ per gallon from 11¢, dependent on proof), and Kentucky finally became a state. Skirmishes continued between whiskey-makers and tax collectors and resulted in a few revenue agents being tarred and feathered and others terrorized into handing over their excise books to the delinquent taxpayers, but the revolt didn't really come to a head until 1794. In that year, after further reducing the taxes but still not getting cooperation from the Pennsylvanians, George Washington, for the first time in the history of the United States, rallied federal troops to quell the uprising.

Washington's proclamation, issued on August 7, 1794, offers us his views on the uprising: He claimed that the ringleaders had "encouraged the spirit of opposition by misrepresentation of the laws calculated to render them odious" and had sought "to deter those who might be so disposed from accepting offices through fear of public resentment and of injury to person and property, and to compel those who had accepted such offices by actual violence to surrender or forbear the execution of them." He went on to say that the distillers had been "inflicting cruel and humiliating punishments upon private citizens for . . . appearing to be friends of the law," and just to round out his argument, Washington claimed that "many persons in the said western parts of Pennsylvania have at length been hardy enough to perpetrate acts which I am advised amount to treason." However, several historians hypothesize that one of the goals behind Washington's rallying federal troops to quash the Whiskey Rebellion was to see whether or not the troops would muster. This was, after all, the first time that Washington had ever enforced federal law in the United States, and in order to persuade men to fight their fellow countrymen, Washington needed to prove he was a strong leader. Since around 13,000 men turned out to do battle, Washington's authority was firmly established.

Pardons were offered to anyone who agreed to comply with the law henceforth. Others—those who continued to defy the tax collectors—had their property plundered and their backs lashed and were carted off to collection centers to settle their debts. Eventually, the distillers gave in to George Washington's demands. They had fought the law. And the law had won.

During the Whiskey Rebellion, some Pennsylvania farmers fled to Kentucky, adding to the number of distillers in the new state. And many of the soldiers who had been dispatched to Pennsylvania, on hearing about the Bluegrass State's fertile soil and sweet limestone water, perfect for corn-growing and whiskey-making, decided to flee the army and settle in Kentucky. Rye whiskey had been born in Pennsylvania. Kentucky was about to give birth to a whiskey that would become known as bourbon.

Whiskey in Kentucky

WHEN THE PENNSYLVANIANS ARRIVED IN KENTUCKY, THEY WERE MET BY other masters of the still who had preceded them by a couple of decades and set up some new whiskey-making traditions. Since 1776, when corn cultivation in the area had been encouraged by Virginia's "corn patch and cabin rights" law, the pioneers had found that corn was not only a relatively easy grain to cultivate but also made a distinctive style of whiskey. Kentucky whiskey was somewhat lighter than the rye whiskey from the East, and it was a product the Westerners could call their own.

So who was the first whiskey-maker in Kentucky? We might as well ask who was the first person to bake bread. No one knows the answer. One report states that General James Wilkinson built a distillery at Harrodsburg, the earliest permanent settlement in Kentucky (1774), but that report is probably untrue, since there is no record of Wilkinson being in the area until about 10 years later. Other accounts say that Wattie

Boone, a relative of Daniel, and a certain Stephen Ritchie both made whiskey in Nelson County, Kentucky, in 1776, and this is probably accurate.

A man named Evan Williams actually built a whiskey distillery in Louisville in 1783, and this is the first recorded mention of a commercial distillery that we can find, although that doesn't mean that Boone and Ritchie weren't already selling or bartering their product. In fact, it's very unlikely that anyone with the equipment and knowledge required to make whiskey would produce only enough for himself and his family.

During the same period of time, names of other whiskey distillers crop up, and many of them have faded into obscurity. Men such as William Calk, Jacob Meyers, Joseph and Samuel Davis (brothers), James Garrard and Jacob Spear are mentioned in various documents, but either their families didn't follow in their footsteps or, if they did, their products weren't good enough to become long-lasting brand names of whiskey. One man whose name has certainly not been forgotten was the Baptist preacher Elijah Craig, who arrived in Kentucky in 1786 and was making whiskey three years later. Craig's family didn't keep up the tradition of whiskey-making that Craig started, although a whiskey has since been named for him.

A Few Other Whiskey-Makers Who Appeared in Kentucky before 1800

ALL OF THESE FAMILIES HELPED BRING THE TRADITION OF AMERICAN whiskey-making into the nineteenth and right through to the twentieth century.

• Elijah Pepper (James E. Pepper and Old Crow Bourbons) settled in Old Pepper Springs, Kentucky, in 1776. Within four years he was selling whiskey.

• Robert Samuels (Maker's Mark Bourbon) arrived in Kentucky in 1780 and probably set up his still shortly thereafter.

• Jacob Beam (Jim Beam Bourbon) came to Kentucky in 1785 and reportedly built his first distillery three years later. Beam family members, however, not being the sort to lay claim to falsehoods, say that their records indicate it was 1795 before their forebear actually sold his first barrel of whiskey.

• Basil Hayden (Old Grand-Dad Bourbon) settled in Kentucky in 1785.

• Henry Hudson Wathen (whose family kept the Old Grand-Dad label alive in the late nineteenth century) began distilling whiskey in Kentucky in 1788.

• The Brown family (Old Forester Bourbon) settled in Kentucky in 1792.

• Daniel Weller (W. L. Weller Bourbon) floated into Bardstown on a flatboat in 1794.

The Very First Bourbon Whiskey

BY 1786, THE WHISKEY THAT WE NOW CALL BOURBON WAS KNOWN AS "Kentucky" or "Western" whiskey—just so people could distinguish it from Pennsylvania, Monongahela or Maryland rye whiskey. Also in that same year, Bourbon County was created from a large chunk of what was previously Virginia's Fayette County, and around this time, when Spain permitted it (Spain still had control of the Mississippi), Kentucky whiskey first started being shipped downriver to thirsty people in St. Louis and New Orleans. Bourbon whiskey was about to acquire its name.

For some reason, everyone seems to want to know the name of the very first person to make bourbon. The truth is, no one knows. The Reverend Elijah Craig is often recognized as being the "inventor" of bourbon, but that claim is completely unsubstantiated. Craig was definitely a whiskey distiller in the late eighteenth century, and his whiskey was probably known as Kentucky whiskey or maybe even bourbon, but there's no real evidence to prove that he was the first person to make bourbon. In fact, according to most people familiar with the subject, it is more probable that Elijah Craig's name was used to fight the Prohibition movement in the late nineteenth century simply because he was a Baptist minister. Smart marketing has been around for millennia—what could be better than declaring a good Christian as the "inventor" of bourbon when the distillers had to argue against temperance forces that quoted the Bible to further their cause?

Another bone of contention about the Craig theory is the fact that since Craig never actually lived in Bourbon County (he was based slightly to the west of the county border), some people claim that this discredits him completely from ever having made a whiskey known as bourbon. However, just to give Craig the benefit of the doubt, if "bourbon" whiskey had a good reputation down South (he *did* ship his whiskey down there), he may have called his product "bourbon" even though he didn't live there. At the time, the town of Limestone, located in Bourbon County at the point where the Kentucky River flows into the Ohio River, was the main port for central Kentucky.

Any search for the first bourbon whiskey should begin with a look at what made Kentucky so perfect for such a whiskey to have been created there. Kentucky had plentiful hardwood trees (17 varieties of oak are native to the state), pristine limestone-filtered water and arable land—it was a perfect place to make whiskey. The cultivation of corn was encouraged, and it was, therefore, the predominant grain. The water was ideal for distillation, and the settlers had plenty of wood with which to make barrels.

All the ingredients needed for whiskey-making were available to these early Kentuckians, but in a quest for the origins of a specific style of whiskey, it's necessary to work backward. Before 1800, Kentucky whiskey was *known* as bourbon, but the chances that we would recognize it as bourbon today are very slim indeed. To match today's style of bourbon whiskey, we must use today's standards as our guide. In order to be called bourbon, a spirit must be aged for at least two years in charred new oak casks and contain more corn than the sum of all other grains used. Therefore, to find the creator of bourbon, we must search for the person most likely to have put the standards all together. The corn question is relatively easy; since corn was the predominant grain within the state, the majority of distillers in Kentucky most likely used corn to make their whiskey. The aging factor needs a little more investigation. Whiskey has always been stored in wooden casks, but not always for very long and not always in *charred* new barrels. Finally, there's the sour-mash component to consider.

Who Burned the Casks?

THE STRAIGHT WOODEN STAVES THAT ARE USED TO FORM A BARREL MUST BE heated in order to bend the wood into the familiar barrel shape. This shape is used primarily so that the bands that hold the barrel together can be tightened around the wider midsection, thus pushing the staves closer together and forming a watertight—or whiskey-tight—seal. From time immemorial, coopers have been forming barrels over fire, and therefore "toasting" the staves while they were making them bow. Wine is aged in toasted barrels, and indeed bourbon casks are toasted *before* they are charred. A popular anecdote has it that a careless cooper accidentally let his staves catch fire and conveniently "forgot" to tell the distiller who bought the barrel about the mishap. The whiskey man noticed an improvement in his liquor and figured out what had happened, and from that day forth, charred barrels were preferred by whiskeymakers. It's just an old story, but there could be a grain of truth in it.

The distillers needed to store their whiskey in "tight" or leakproof barrels, and at that time, tight barrels were used to store just about everything from water to molasses to linseed oil to tar. Tight barrels were valuable and recyclable, and used barrels were less expensive than new ones. Maybe as a matter of routine, distillers who invested in used cooperage would set fire to the interior of the barrel to rid it of any lingering odors or dirt, and once again, at some point, charred barrels were recognized as having a good effect on whiskey.

A book in the United Distillers' archives in Louisville mentions charred barrels, but unfortunately, the cover is missing and there is no date printed on its pages—just a handwritten note that includes a reference to the year 1854. The book is full of questions and answers on many different subjects, one of them being: "Q: Why are water and wine casks charred on the inside? A: Because charring the inside of a cask reduces it to a kind of charcoal; and charcoal (by absorbing animal and vegetable impurities) keeps the liquor [liquid] sweet and good." But this document, assuming the 1854 date is within 50 years of the publication date, is from the nineteenth century. Were charred barrels being used before that date? Most probably, but the chances of their being used *exclusively* by one distiller are very remote.

Down the River in Flatboats

IN THE LATE 1700S, WHEN A DISTILLER MADE WHISKEY, HE WANTED TO SELL IT AS quickly as possible. The distiller needed money, and the rest of the town needed whiskey to take the edge off the hazards of living in a new territory surrounded by natives who seemed to think they had every right to live on their own land. So when did the whiskey-makers start aging their products? When whiskey spends time in a barrel, it may seem to be sleeping, but in actuality, it is growing up. Its body gets bigger, its soul develops character, and the sharp, childish bite of young, raw whiskey becomes a deep, somber declaration of maturity. There must have been cases of individuals who stored whiskey and realized that it tasted better as time went by, but nevertheless, the practice of choosing to keep whiskey "in the wood" so that it would mature didn't become commonplace until sometime during the early to mid-nineteenth century.

The theory that whiskey improved with age was proved once a whiskey-maker tasted his product after its journey downriver to New Orleans. In his 1804 book *Voyage à l'ouest des monts alléghanys, dans les états de l'Ohio, du Kentucky, et du Tennessee,* French botanist François André Michaux explained that since he had missed the spring season when the water was high, he had to travel some 80 miles on land before boarding a boat in Pennsylvania to take him to Kentucky. This was typical of the time. Boats from Pennsylvania, Kentucky and Tennessee would wait for the rivers to rise before embarking on their journey downriver. In those days (and right up until fairly recently), most distilling was done during the cool autumn months, right after the crops had been harvested. But the whiskey-makers would have to wait until spring before they could launch their flatboats. So if the whiskey was produced in, say, September or October, and it couldn't begin its trip to the Big Easy until, say, April, by the time it made its way to Bourbon Street, it could have been eight to nine months old. Certainly that was not enough time in the wood to soothe its soul completely, but it was undoubtedly long enough for the whiskey to have gained some color and mellowed sufficiently for quaffers to notice the difference.

In the latter part of the eighteenth century, both John Ritchie and Elijah Craig were shipping whiskey by flatboat to New Orleans, and they probably weren't the only ones. But whether or not they were shipping their product in charred casks is highly debatable; we know only that this particular practice became popular in the 50-odd years that followed.

A FLATBOAT ON THE OHIO RIVER

There is solid evidence, however, that by the mid-1800s, some whiskeys were being aged long enough to give them a decent amount of color. In *The Lincoln Reader*, 1947, editor Paul M. Angle included a personal recollection of one James S. Ewing, who was an eyewitness to an 1854 meeting between Abraham Lincoln and his formidable debating rival, Stephen A. Douglas. In Ewing's account of the event, he referred to a decanter of "red liquor"—a term for bourbon that would become widely used by the end of that century. When whiskey is first distilled, it is clear—it looks exactly like vodka. Only time in wood gives it color, and only time in charred wood results in the crimson-hued tint that is peculiar to bourbon. So we can draw from Ewing's reference to red liquor that in the mid-nineteenth century *some* whiskey was being aged in charred casks, and it was aged long enough for it to gain bourbon's characteristic crimson hue.

Some canny souls of the period between 1800 and 1840 must have noticed not only that this aged whiskey was smoother than the raw product straight from the still but also that the stuff that came from expensive brand-new casks didn't have quite the finesse of that from the used casks that had been charred to clean them up. Was it a specific person on a specific date? It's doubtful. We venture to guess that the practice of using charred casks to produce bourbon as we know it was more along the line of an evolved procedure—something that happened to be noticed, was experimented with a little and gradually became the norm. We're left with one nagging factor: the sour-mash process.

Every straight bourbon produced today is a sour-mash whiskey, in which a portion of the residue from one batch of mash is used to start the next, much as sourdough starter is used to start more batches of dough. Therefore, if we want to know who first produced bourbon whiskey *as we know it*, sour mash must enter the picture. Dr. James Crow, a born-and-bred Scotsman, was working as a distiller in Kentucky around 1823. Crow was a man of medicine and science, and it was he who experimented scientifically with using setback (sour mash) to control certain aspects of his whiskey-making methods. His whiskeys, Old Crow and Old Pepper, were very popular during the Civil War, and he has always been hailed as a man who not only made good bourbon but also knew exactly *why* his bourbon was good. He had the scientific knowledge to be able to tinker intelligently with various aspects of his processes in order to make a better whiskey. He made whiskey using corn as the predominant grain, he insisted on aging it in charred casks, and he used a sour-mash starter. For those who insist on having a name, we say James Crow "invented" bourbon sometime between 1823 and 1845.

The Formative Years

IN THE YEARS BETWEEN THE SETTLING OF KENTUCKY AND THE CIVIL WAR, many minor and a few major events started to affect the whiskey business in America. While the United States was searching for an identity, certain families were forming the basis for what were to become major whiskey empires.

The Pepper family was one of the few Kentucky distillers who could afford the taxes that spurred the Whiskey Rebellion. Many others were hauled into court and fined for their lack of cooperation. In 1798, almost 200 Kentucky whiskey distillers were found guilty of making whiskey without a license (Elijah Craig—a Baptist minister, no less—among them). Others began to supply grain to families like the Peppers rather than distill their own products. It was the beginning of the American way of doing business, and many small concerns combined and consolidated into larger companies.

In 1816, a company registered in New England incorporated in Kentucky under the name of the Hope Distilling Company; it was a very big venture—many years before its time. The company had $100,000 in capital and bought 100 acres of Louisville land, where a huge distillery was built. Grain-handling machinery that would do the work of 30 men was installed; the company's two gigantic stills, one of them "erected on an entirely new principle," about which we can find no details, contained 10 tons of copper and produced enough "used grain" to feed 5,000 hogs. These guys meant business. The distillery operated for a few years, but Hope was shattered and forced to

AN EARLY-NINETEENTH-CENTURY DISTILLERY

close when all of the capital was spent. They had the right idea, and if they just could have waited another 50 years or so, they might have made a fortune. The story is documented in *A Memorial History of Louisville*, 1896, edited by J. Stoddard Johnston, and includes the comment that the New Englanders went back to their rum, leaving the Kentuckians to their whiskey. The fact was, at that time the public wouldn't buy whiskey that wasn't made in small, old-fashioned pot stills. It just didn't taste the same.

Another major development of this era was the 1825 invention of the Lincoln County Process by Tennessean Alfred Eaton. This is the all-important filtration system in which whiskey is dripped through a minimum of 10 feet of sugar-maple charcoal before it is put in barrels for aging. The process is still used today, and it distinguishes Tennessee whiskey from bourbon and all other straight American whiskeys. Tennesseans, however, were not the only ones to use charcoal filtration; one pre-1820 document in the Filson Club, a Louisville historical society, describes filtering whiskey through layers of white flannel, clean white sand and pulverized charcoal made from "good green wood such as sugar tree hickory." However, the Kentucky distiller who detailed these instructions used only 18 to 20 inches of charcoal—nothing close to the 10-plus feet used in Eaton's process. Since Eaton is said to have noted that his Lincoln County Process took a long time, some historians have taken his words to mean that he was aging his whiskey as early as 1825. But since it takes between a week and 10 days for the whiskey to travel through all of the charcoal, we think he was referring to his new, though slow, method of filtration.

It's important to remember that the Industrial Revolution in the United States was well on its way at this point. The first cotton mill in America had opened in 1789, and when America signed a treaty with Spain in 1795, the Mississippi River became the old man whose back would carry goods for sale or trade with no hindrance from the Iberians. The Louisiana Purchase of 1803 added Missouri, Arkansas and parts of Louisiana to the United States, as well as a huge expanse of land that would eventually become Iowa, North and South Dakota, Nebraska, Oklahoma, most of Kansas and parts of Montana, Wyoming, Minnesota and Colorado. The adventurous and the curious started moving farther away from the East Coast, boosting the whiskey business as they progressed westward. Fact was, the farther away from the coast people traveled, the more expensive it was for them to make rum from imported molasses; in reaction, more people turned to whiskey for solace.

Even before the turn of the century, the rum business had been winding down. Frenchman Jean Pierre Brissot wrote of his 1788 trip to Boston (*Nouveau Voyage dans les États-Unis de l'Amérique septentrionale*, 1791): "The rum distilleries are on the decline since the suppression of the slave trade, in which this liquor was employed." Then, in 1807, the Embargo Act restricted the importation of molasses from British ports, and the following year, the importation of slaves was made illegal altogether, completely destroying the "triangle trade" among the United States, Africa and the West Indies. The rum business in the United States was doomed. Its demise created plenty of room for the up-and-coming whiskey industry.

The Industrial Revolution, both in the United States and Great Britain, saw inventors and inventions coming out of the woodwork, and more than a few people tried their hands at devising new types of stills. None, however, were as successful as Aenaes Coffey, who patented his perfected continuous still in Britain in 1831. In time, Coffey's invention would greatly affect the whiskey business worldwide, but its effect on the American whiskey industry would have to wait until after the Civil War.

In fact, although pot stills were used by most of the legitimate distillers, some poorer folk were still "running it on the log." This was a backwoods method of distillation that seems rather convoluted—but it worked. The process is partially described by Gerald Carson in *The Social History of Bourbon*. A distiller would take a log, split it lengthwise, hollow out each half and bind it back together. The log was then stood upright and filled from the top with fermented mash. A lid of sorts must then have been fitted onto the top of the log. It was probably similar in shape to a Hershey's Kiss, with the "top knot" narrowing into a pipe that would carry the vapors to a vessel, where they would condense. Somewhere, close to the top of the log or in the lid itself, must have been a hole fitted with the copper pipe that carried live steam into the still from a nearby kettle. The steam would, in time, heat the mash and vaporize the alcohol. Carson does mention, however, that the log stills were used only for a primary distillation, and the spirit would then be redistilled in a pot still. The final product was called "log and copper whiskey." Joseph Dant, whose family would later be responsible for giving Yellowstone and J.W. Dant bourbons to the world, was using the "log" method in 1836 to make his first Kentucky whiskey.

During the first decades of the new century, science began to play a part in the manufacture of whiskey, due to a large extent to James Crow's sour-mash methods. But Kentucky whiskey-makers had already started refining and improving their methods. They had found that by using only the "center cut" of their distillate and returning the "end of the run" back to the still for redistillation (a method still practiced today), they could remove unwanted bitter flavors from their whiskey. Bourbon was becoming a little more sophisticated.

Other major changes that affected the whiskey industry in the early 1800s included the actions of that marvelous gourmet President Thomas Jefferson, who in 1802 repealed the excise tax that had caused the Whiskey Rebellion and thereby lightened the financial load on the distillers. Not that Jefferson was a whiskey man; he was much more enamored of imported wines. At one point, he advocated reducing taxes on such products, saying that nations where cheap wine was available for the common man did not suffer the same insobrieties as those where whiskey was the least expensive beverage alcohol. Jefferson once asked, "Who would drink whiskey if wine were cheap enough?" Well, those who lived in the Bluegrass State might have argued the point. In 1804, François André Michaux wrote: "Kentuckians have preserved the manners of the Virginians. They carry the passion for gaming and for spirituous liquors to an excess. . . . The public houses are always crowded, especially so during the sittings of the courts of justice." However, Jefferson did stop the excise taxes on American liquor, and apart from the few years between 1813 and 1817, when taxes were levied in order to pay the costs of the War of 1812, whiskey wouldn't be taxed again until 1862.

By 1820, over 25 percent of the total U.S. population lived west of the Appalachians, and by that time, steamboats had replaced the flatboats and were plying the Mississippi laden with Kentucky whiskey. New markets were opening up, and the whiskey business was becoming more and more profitable. Over 2,000 barrels of whiskey were shipped out of Kentucky in 1820, and it was widely known as bourbon. In *Kentucky*

AN "IMPROVED" WHISKEY DISTILLERY

Bourbon—The Early Years of Whiskeymaking, Henry G. Crowgey describes an 1821 newspaper advertisement for bourbon whiskey, so it's fairly safe to assume that the distiller of that time knew that the readers would understand what it was he had for sale. Bourbon was here to stay. Here's a list of prominent whiskey-makers whose products hit the shelves between 1800 and 1860:

• Abraham Overholt (Old Overholt Rye Whiskey) established his distillery in western Pennsylvania in 1810.

• J.W. Dant (Yellowstone and J.W. Dant Bourbons) set up his still (the famous log) in 1836.

• Oscar Pepper (James E. Pepper and Old Crow Bourbons) built the Old Oscar Pepper Distillery in 1838.

• George T. Stagg (the Ancient Age Distillery) opened his first distillery in 1840.

• Taylor William Samuels (Maker's Mark Bourbon) was operating a commercial distillery in Deatsville in 1844.

• W.L. Weller (W.L. Weller Bourbon), whose grandfather, Daniel, had owned a distillery in 1800, formed a wholesale whiskey business in 1849, using the slogan "Honest whiskey at an honest price."

• David Beam (Jim Beam Bourbon) was working at the Old Tub Distillery in 1850, and his son, David M. Beam, became distiller there in 1853.

• John H. Beam (Early Times Bourbon), David's other son, was co-owner of the Early Times Distillery in 1860.

• Henry McKenna (Henry McKenna Bourbon) started making whiskey near Bardstown in 1855.

What's in the Bottle?

D URING THE PERIOD LEADING UP TO THE CIVIL WAR, SOME BRAND-NAME WHISKEYS gained in popularity. Distillers whose whiskey had a good reputation started to give their product a name, and deserving of mention here is Oscar Pepper who, in 1838, built the Old Oscar Pepper Distillery, hired James Crow as master distiller and marketed their whiskey as Old 1776—Born with the Republic. The name referred to Oscar's father, Elijah, who settled in Kentucky in 1776 and made whiskey shortly thereafter; it's one of the earliest references to whiskey men "marketing" their product.

Most whiskeys of this time were sold in barrels to retailers. The distillers supplied bars and saloons with decanters and bottles that bore the distillers' names and could be used to pour their product, but it wasn't at all uncommon for cheap whiskey to be poured from its cask into decanters that advertised a more expensive product. A bottle exists today, produced in 1848, that bears the word "bourbon" and the distiller's name, M. Bininger and Company of New York. Bininger, as far as we are able to ascertain, was a dealer in bulk whiskey who bottled some of his product. But not until 1870 would the company headed by George Garvin Brown (Old Forester) sell its whiskey only in sealed bottles. Brown's goal was to assure the public that they would finally know exactly what whiskey was in the bottle.

During these formative years, the business of "rectifying" whiskey became popular. Most rectifiers were—and are—reputable wholesalers who bought whiskey from different distilleries (or a selection of casks from just one distillery) and mingled them together to arrive at a consistent product they could call their own. Some of them filtered the whiskey they purchased in bulk in order to rectify it, taking out some impurities and rendering the whiskey somewhat smoother. However, there was yet a third group of so-called rectifiers who had an eye on a fast buck. These scalawags blended small amounts of straight whiskey with huge quantities of flavorless neutral grain spirits and a few flavorings, then sold their product as "straight whiskey."

These days, what they produced is called blended whiskey, and we would be remiss if we didn't mention just how good blended whiskeys can be. Not only are blends, in many cases, less expensive than straight whiskeys, but the act of blending whiskey has now become an art form and results in a softer dram that is ideally suited for use with mixers, with some of the more expensive blends being complex enough to be savored for their own intricacies. However, most of the first blended-whiskey producers were merely trying to pull the wool over the public's eyes.

Although these rogues would grow more prevalent during the latter part of the century, by 1860 there was already at least one book on the market that gave instructions on how to make imitation liquors and wines. *A Treatise on the Manufacture, Imitation, Adulteration, and Reduction of Foreign Wines, Brandies, Gins, Rums, Etc. Etc.* included instructions on how to make imitation whiskeys such as "Old Rye," "Old Rye Monongahela" and "Old Bourbon." The author, John Stephen, M.D., who billed himself as "A Practical Chemist and Experienced Liquor Dealer," noted that his methods, known as "the French System," were almost unknown in this country and accused previous rectifiers of adulterating liquors with "poisonous and deleterious compounds."

Stephen's "French System" of making imitation whiskey, was, as he predicted in his book, to become the standard method of making less expensive whiskey. There are three recipes for making imitation "Old Bourbon" in Stephen's book. One calls for 20 gallons of "proof spirit" (neutral spirits diluted to 100° proof), five gallons of pure bourbon, one pint of simple syrup (sugar water), one ounce of spirits of niter and some burned sugar for coloring. The other two formulas use less straight whiskey but add flavorings such as tinctures of cloves and allspice. The book also gives recipes for the various tinctures and instructions on how to make a "Bead for Liquors," calling for a two-to-one mixture of vitriol and sweet oil, one drop of which is sufficient to put a bead on a quart of liquor. (If you shake a bottle of whiskey, the bubbles that form on top, known as the "bead," are an indication of the amount of alcohol in the whiskey.)

The book serves as an indication that a number of cheap whiskeys were being produced just before and after the Civil War. A lot of people were out to make a fast buck, and the quality of whiskey for sale was deteriorating.

Trains and Boats and a New Look at Drinking

THE WHISKEY BUSINESS IN THE UNITED STATES WAS GREATLY AFFECTED BY the advent of the railroad—wherever people roamed, they needed red liquor to help them along, and when the railroads began expanding, it became easier, and quicker, to get whiskey to new markets. In 1830, fewer than 50 miles of railroad tracks existed in the United States; 10 years later, there were almost 3,000 miles of railroad; and by 1850,

THE BIRTH OF TEMPERANCE IN AMERICA

you could travel over 9,000 miles on steam-engine trains. So along with the steam-boats on the Mississippi, the whiskey industry now had railroads to take its product south. And west. And north. And even east—to exotic ports such as New York City where, according to Luc Sante, author of *Low Life, Lures and Snares of Old New York*, for under a nickel, you could drink all the whiskey you could manage by sucking it through a rubber tube until you had to stop to take a breath.

And telegraph wires were all the rage during this period too; by 1850, more than 50,000 miles of wire had been strung. So if a saloon owner in the West needed whiskey in a hurry, he could now order by telegram and have a few barrels on the way to him the very next day.

But while all this technology was helping people reach out and touch someone, other events were starting to bode badly for the whiskey men of America. In 1826, The American Temperance Society was founded in Boston, and it was a society that distillers would come to dread.

Nineteenth-century America was anything but temperate. According to an "approximate" guide in the *Dictionary of the History of the American Brewing and Distilling Industries* by William L. Downard, the consumption of pure alcohol (200° proof) in 1825 was seven gallons per person over the age of 15. This figure, of course, is somewhat difficult to comprehend until you learn that the *same* table estimates that in 1970, consumption was at 2.5 gallons. Americans in 1825 were drinking almost three times as much alcohol as the people living in the somewhat wild days of 1970.

During the first half of the nineteenth century, America also saw a vast increase in immigration from England, Ireland, Scotland and Germany—all countries whose inhabitants are generally regarded as being fond of a drink. According to Oscar Getz in *Whiskey—An American Pictorial History*, by 1860, on a per-capita basis, Americans were drinking over 28 percent more spirits than they had consumed just a decade earlier.

Lest you suffer under the misapprehension that Prohibition didn't rear its ugly head

GREATEST TEMPERANCE ADVOCATE ON EARTH

P.T. BARNUM, THE MAN WHO STARTED HIS CAREER BY EXHIBITING A WOMAN WHO claimed to be George Washington's nurse and went on to produce The Greatest Show on Earth in 1870, was also a vociferous advocate of temperance. After touring Europe with General Tom Thumb and introducing Jenny Lind, the "Swedish Nightingale," to the American public, he personally presented free-for-all temperance lectures for an entire season.

WHISKEY ON A NINETEENTH-CENTURY BATTLEFIELD

until 1920, you should know that various states introduced the noble experiment, in statewide or local-option form, well before then. Maine was made dry in 1846, Vermont in 1852, New Hampshire and Massachusetts in 1855, and New York in 1854. In Europe, the first temperance organization had come into being in Ireland in 1818 (later known as the Ulster Temperance Society), and similar organizations sprung up in Scotland, England, Norway and Sweden in the first half of the nineteenth century. In the United States, almost one million people had signed the pledge by 1840, and the angst about "overconsumption" continued to grow.

For many proponents of temperance, however, the word meant "moderation," not complete abstention. One such society in New York State allowed its members to choose between swearing off liquor only—giving them ample leeway to get rip-roaring drunk on wine or beer—and signing the pledge to abstain from any and all beverage alcohol—total abstinence. Those choosing to give up all forms of booze had their names marked in the register with a capital "T" for "total"—they were the world's first tee-totalers.

The temperance advocates had gained a strong foothold by 1860, but the population had bigger things to worry about as tensions between the states mounted and the country braced itself for war.

An Uncivil War and Its Aftermath

THE CIVIL WAR TORE THE WHISKEY-MAKING STATES APART. PENNSYLVANIA was solidly in the Union, but Kentucky and Maryland were two of the four border states in which slavery existed and was legal, yet whose political leanings were mostly with the Union. However, many of the residents of these states sided with the Confederate cause—states' rights. Since the late 1700s, when whiskey was first shipped down South, a number of Kentucky's whiskey-makers had come to rely heavily on the southern states' demand and market for their products. Hence people such as John Thompson Street Brown, father of George Garvin Brown (Old Forester), and the Weller brothers (W.L. Weller's sons), along with many other Kentuckians, served in the Confederate Army.

Over the course of the war, some distilleries were destroyed, some distillers died, and the rest survived as best they could. But in 1862, President Abraham Lincoln was forced to reintroduce the excise tax on whiskey to help pay for the Union war effort. Once again, just as in the Revolutionary War and the War of 1812, whiskey was made to help finance the armed forces.

Whiskey had great value during the Civil War. It had the power to soothe men's souls, to make them forget the carnage of the battlefield, and perhaps most important, whiskey often acted as the only anesthetic available. A paper written in 1993 by Mervel V. Hanes, M.D., of Louisville, points out that although quinine and laudanum were used medic-inally in the mid-1800s, few other medicines, apart from whiskey, were available. Even as-pirin, which was discovered in 1849, wasn't used medicinally until the end of the century.

> The term "bootlegger" most probably dates to the Civil War when peddlers who sold illicit bottles of booze to soldiers are said to have hidden the bottles in the tops of their boots.

So during the Civil War, more than a little red liquor was poured over a wound to clean it and much, much more was poured down parched throats to depress awareness and ease the pain of countrymen fighting countrymen on their own land.

According to Gerald Carson, in his book *The Social History of Bourbon*, the Northern soldiers had more money than their adversaries and could buy more whiskey. But although Union officers were allowed to buy whiskey, enlisted men had to rely on rations as their legitimate source of liquor. Needless to say, soldiers on both sides were, for the most part, hungry, cold, frightened and sorely in need of solace wherever they could find it. If temporary refuge from their plight lay in a slug of whiskey, they would find a way of getting it.

YOUNG ABE

Although he was known as a temperance proponent as an adult, Abraham Lincoln might have been involved in the whiskey business when he was growing up in the backwoods of Kentucky. According to an article that appeared in *The Nelson County Record* in 1896, Abe's father, Thomas Lincoln, worked for a while at a distillery (established in 1780 by Wattie Boone) close to Knob Creek, one of Abe's childhood homes.

The story goes that Thomas Lincoln worked at the distillery shortly before the family moved to Indiana, and since he found it inconvenient to walk home for meals, his young son, Abe, would hike the mile or so to the distillery carrying food for his father. Eventually, the boy was given some work at the distillery, and Wattie Boone reportedly predicted that young Abe would one day be a great man no matter what path he chose in life, "and if he goes into the whiskey business, he will be the best distiller in the land."

The Union troops procured their whiskey from wherever they could: having it sent by their families, dodging the guards and finding their way to a local grogshop and, in the case of one whole regiment during the Christmas celebrations of 1864, making a full 15 gallons of bad whiskey all by themselves. The Confederate troops, on the other hand, didn't get their fair share of whiskey, not only because of their lack of hard cash but also because the South couldn't afford to use what valuable grain there was to make such frivolous stuff as whiskey; people were wanting of the basic necessities just to exist.

Not all Northerners believed that their soldiers were drinking more than the Southern troops. When recording the 1863 arrival of the Sons of Temperance at the White House, Lincoln's secretary, John Hay, noted that the group blamed the defeats of Union troops on intemperance among the soldiers. But Hay could not believe it; "the rebels drink more and worse whiskey than we do," he wrote.

Whatever the reality of who was drinking more, the Southern populace needed food more than they needed whiskey. The Confederacy, therefore, declared prohibition on a state-to-state basis and tried to buy up all the available whiskey to use as medicine, for Navy rations and, in certain instances, for soldiers who needed a "medicinal" boost. States reacted to the prohibition with varying degrees of complicity. Carson states that one colonel from Georgia was actually making whiskey himself—prohibition be damned. The fact was that since Jefferson Davis had made whiskey hard to come by, its value had increased by leaps and bounds. The black-market price for whiskey was, in 1863, about $35 per gallon, compared to about 25¢ for the same amount at the end of 1860. Black marketeers who had the means to make whiskey simply couldn't restrain themselves.

Overall, the Civil War's effect on the whiskey business, by no means negligible, was to whittle down the number of whiskey distilleries and distillers—a fact that probably didn't upset temperance advocate Abraham Lincoln.

The Boy From Kentucky

DID LINCOLN ENJOY THE WARMTH OF AN OCCASIONAL GLASS OF WHISKEY? More than a few accounts suggest as much, but as far as can be ascertained, it just isn't true. Two quotes from Lincoln are often used out of context and make him sound like a drinking man; both are taken from a speech he made to the Springfield, Washington, Temperance Society in 1842. The first cites Lincoln's saying that intoxicating drinks were commonly the first draught of the infant and the last draught of the dying man. Indeed, Lincoln said just that; but he was not applauding the use and enjoyment of liquor. Instead, in the context of the speech, he was merely describing a common practice of the times, implying that if people were made aware of the evils of alcohol, such foolishness would stop. In effect, Lincoln was urging the temperance group to enlighten the public.

In the second example, Lincoln is often erroneously quoted as saying that injury from alcohol arose from the abuse of a good thing rather than from the use of a bad thing. Again, the quote has been twisted over the years to make Lincoln sound as though he were defending drinkers. What he actually said was that although many people were injured by alcohol, *they* didn't seem to believe that it was from the use of a bad thing and *they* thought it merely from the abuse of a good thing. Lincoln himself implied that he believed the injuries were a direct result of the use of liquor—a bad thing.

In this same speech, Lincoln stated his belief that people would be more likely to stop drinking if, instead of being preached to about the evils of alcohol, they were shown examples of how sobriety would enhance their lives. In the twentieth century, Alcoholics Anonymous went on to prove his point.

To cap off the Lincoln question, two more instances give insight into his views: In 1854, after Lincoln refused to partake of whiskey on a particular occasion, Stephen A. Douglas asked him if he were a member of a temperance society. Lincoln replied that although he wasn't a member of any such society, he personally didn't drink. Later, in 1861, he did, however, add his signature to a temperance declaration that already bore the names of earlier Presidents, including John Quincy Adams, James Buchanan, Martin Van Buren, Millard Fillmore, Andrew Jackson, James Madison, Franklin Pierce, James K. Polk, Zachary Taylor and John Tyler.

Whiskeygate

W HEN RECONSTRUCTION BEGAN, PRESIDENT ANDREW JOHNSON FACED huge problems. His policies were bitterly opposed by the Republican majority in Congress, which unsuccessfully initiated impeachment proceedings in the Senate, and he was chided for supporting Seward's Folly, the purchase of Alaska (and its yet undiscovered gold) from Russia for $7,200,000. When Ulysses S. Grant was elected U.S. president in 1868, the country's relief was palpable.

Grant's military experience, however, didn't prepare him for the presidency. After taking office in 1869, he was plagued by the politics of Reconstruction, and his administration was beset by scandal after scandal. One embarrassment came in 1869 when speculators Jay Gould and James Fisk attempted to corner the gold market. They had "conned" Grant into becoming an ally, and the scheme backfired into one of the worst panics in American financial history. Another humiliation occurred after Grant's re-election in 1872, when Vice President Schuyler Colfax was investigated for accepting bribes. But perhaps the worst was a whiskey scandal.

The Whiskey Ring, as it became known, involved some cohorts of President Grant's skimming more than a few tax dollars from the whiskey producers—and the country. However, to some extent, Grant was directly involved with this scam. One of its main culprits, who was never convicted of any wrongdoing, was protected by Grant, and rumor at the time had it that Grant's son Fred and brother Orvil had directly profited from the fraud. These were to be trying times for the President.

The major players in the Whiskey Ring were General Orville E. Babcock, Grant's secretary; General John McDonald, the regional superintendent of the Internal Revenue Service, headquartered in St. Louis; and Benjamin Helm Bristow, the man who initiated the investigation into the affair when he became Secretary of the Treasury in 1874.

Here, in very simple terms, is how the scam worked: Sometime around 1870, government agents, charged with keeping an eye on how much whiskey was being made, arranged to ignore a certain percentage of the distillate in return for cash in the amount of roughly half the money the distillery would have paid in taxes. When "straight" tax collectors who were not part of the ring were due to call, the distillers were forewarned to "play safe" and pay up.

The Whiskey Ring agents claimed to have a "higher" purpose in their treachery; they told distillers that the dollars they collected were going into a special fund to help reelect Grant. Was this Whiskeygate? Although we can't say for certain how many people actually believed their claim to be patriotic party do-gooders, evidence points to up to 15 million gallons of whiskey a year, which would have generated a cool $7.5 million in taxes—an extraordinary amount of money at the time—going untaxed between 1870

ULYSSES S. GRANT

and 1874. And Grant *was* returned to office in 1872.

Due to his incompetency and the number of other scandals within his administration, Grant was not a popular man by the end of 1874. He was thinking of running for a third term—even though he had once told Congress that he was not prepared for the office at all—and people within his administration despaired of some of the people he had chosen to work alongside him. Rumors of the Whiskey Ring were rife at this point, and many upstanding aides at the White House breathed a sigh of relief when Benjamin Bristow was appointed to the Treasury—he was a very well respected man. One of his first acts was to convince Congress to grant money to investigate the alleged corruption within the Internal Revenue Service. With the help of some newspapermen in St. Louis, Bristow was about to crack the ring wide open.

The first money used for the investigation went to reporter Myron Colony, who was hired by the Treasury Department to gather evidence against whoever was responsible for misdirecting the excise taxes. Colony did a very thorough job and accumulated enough data to place John McDonald (the St. Louis-based superintendent of the IRS) at the head of the Whiskey Ring. First off, McDonald was confronted with the evidence, and he did indeed confess to his crimes. However, McDonald had a few cards up his sleeve, and although he offered to replace the money in return for immunity, claiming he would get it from the distilleries, he also mentioned Grant's name to add weight to his plea for clemency.

DRINKING HABITS

ALTHOUGH ABRAHAM LINCOLN was not himself a drinking man, he did once admit that for others, whiskey sometimes had its uses. During the Civil War, people in high places took to criticizing General Ulysses S. Grant, and they often picked on his drinking, which was, at times, considerable. Lincoln is said to have inquired as to what brand of whiskey Grant preferred, saying that he would like to send some to his other generals.

McDonald was somewhat of an old pal of the President, having been recommended for his position by more than a couple of friends of Julia Grant's family. Even so, Grant made it clear that he wanted to clean up the whole mess and prosecute whoever was responsible for stealing the money. The following month, over 300 distillers and government employees were arrested for their involvement in the Whiskey Ring, and everyone was certain that justice was being served. But Grant was soon to have a change of heart, one that would rock his aides and affect the outcome of the whole affair.

Further investigations implicated Babcock, Grant's personal friend and trusted secretary, in the ring—but Grant refused to believe the evidence. And while Grant had originally claimed to have been "grievously betrayed" by McDonald, he now said that

GRANT HEAD OVER HEELS IN A WHISKEY BARREL

McDonald was a reliable friend and cited McDonald's friendship with Babcock as good enough reason to believe that he was innocent of the charges. However, some potentially damaging documents had been discovered that pointed to reasons other than friendship for Grant's change of heart.

A series of cryptic telegrams in the Treasury Department's possession tied Babcock to the affair. Not only did they suggest that Babcock had warned McDonald of the impending investigation, but they bore a strange signature—"Sylph." Was Sylph the Deep Throat of the day? No, not really. It turns out that Sylph was a White House sexual dalliance rather than an anonymous inside source. It was Babcock who wired the warning and added the odd signature. According to most reports, Sylph was a woman said to have had an extramarital affair with Grant, and she had pestered him ever since. Rumor had it that McDonald had helped Grant by making sure Sylph left him alone, and if the rumors were true, it was no wonder that Grant allied himself with McDonald. Why did Babcock use the name Sylph on the telegrams? Well, he certainly didn't want to use his own name on them—they were, after all, fairly incriminating—and it seems that Babcock and McDonald used Sylph's name as a kind of inside joke when exchanging correspondence. If trouble occurred, perhaps the name Sylph could help secure a show of friendship from the President. The ploy seems to have had the desired effect.

From there, things went from bad to worse for the investigators. According to William S. McFeely, author of *Grant, A Biography*, although both Grant and Babcock were confronted with this very damning evidence, Babcock insisted that the telegrams were about something other than the Whiskey Ring, and Grant sided with him. However, the Treasury was not to be deterred. Even though some documents pertaining to the case were stolen (allegedly by a man in the employ of Grant himself), in due time Babcock was indicted.

Grant's actions in this sordid affair can be interpreted in several ways: Grant was trying to help some old friends; he was afraid that his alleged affair with Sylph would be revealed; or members of Grant's family—and maybe even Grant himself—were implicated in the Whiskey Ring.

Babcock was finally brought to trial in 1876, and due in large part to testimony from Grant in the form of a deposition, he was acquitted of all crimes. Although Grant allowed Babcock to return to his job at the White House, officials made sure that he was replaced just a few days later. Babcock became an Inspector of Lighthouses and drowned in 1884; McDonald was found guilty of his crimes in 1875, fined $5,000 and sentenced to three years' imprisonment but was pardoned, less than two years later, by President Hayes.

Upon his release from jail, McDonald accused Grant of taking part in the Ring in his book *Secrets of the Great Whiskey Ring,* 1880. In it, McDonald maintains that his actions in the Whiskey Ring were a direct result of instructions from Babcock. And since, according to McDonald, Babcock was widely regarded as being "the President's chief advisor," he regarded any requests from Babcock as having "emanated from the highest authority." Sylph, again according to McDonald's book—and we should take into consideration that he wrote the book to throw most of the blame for the Whiskey Ring scandal on others—was a woman with whom he had arranged a liaison for Babcock, not Grant. He described her as "unquestionably the handsomest woman in St. Louis" and went on to say, "Her form was petite, and yet withal, a plumpness and development which made her a being whose tempting, luscious deliciousness was irresistible." Obviously, McDonald was quite taken with the woman, although a sketch of Sylph in his book reveals her to have been more homely than irresistible.

Reconstruction—of the Whiskey Business

WHILE PRESIDENTS JOHNSON AND GRANT WERE GOING THROUGH THEIR personal and political strifes, the excise tax that Lincoln had been forced to impose in 1862 had taken a heavy toll on the whiskey industry. The tax was due upon production, as soon as the whiskey ran out of the still, and after the Civil War, many of the smaller distillers just didn't have the capital to comply with the law. By this point in time, aged whiskey was preferred by far over the raw spirit that had been acceptable some 60 years previous. Reconstruction marked a time in the whiskey business that really sorted out the men from the boys; unfortunately, many of the boys were the ones who made great whiskey, and many of the men were more concerned with business. Quantity mattered more than quality. Luckily for us, a few of the business types had deep pockets and a long-term view, and these were the distillers who continued to make good whiskey.

During the postwar years, when many distilleries were being built or rebuilt, Aenaes Coffey's continuous still became commonplace in the American whiskey business. The death knell was tolling for the slower, more work-intensive, old-fashioned pot stills. Many of the larger distilleries built massive continuous stills between 1865 and 1900; whiskey was becoming big business, and continuous stills were more economical. We wouldn't, however, see the very last of the pot still until Prohibition, and one die-hard distillery in Pennsylvania was using a pot still for a secondary distillation until it closed in the late 1980s.

Not everyone was enamored of this new method, however, and some forward-thinking individuals took to actively advertising the fact that they continued to use "old-fashioned methods." Even as late as 1891, James E. Pepper was proclaiming in print that he distilled twice over open fires, signifying the use of pot stills.

In the years between the Civil War and 1900, the very ways in which whiskey was packaged and marketed were also updated and modernized. Though the first glass factory in American was built in Jamestown, Virginia, in 1608, it would be 1903, when Michael J. Owens invented the first automatic bottle-making machine, before selling whiskey in bottles was financially viable for most distillers. Until then, glass bottles remained fragile, expensive hand-blown vessels that were very dear in every way. Decorative glass and ceramic bottles containing whiskey were a novelty that had been around since the early 1800s. Some depicted Benjamin Franklin, George Washington, Grover Cleveland and Carry Nation, while others pictured tableaux, such as a jockey on horseback or a Continental soldier. One late-nineteenth-century whiskey bottle was shaped like a baby's bottle and bore the words, "Here is the Milk of Human Kindness."

Bottles, however, were the exception rather than the rule—they simply added to

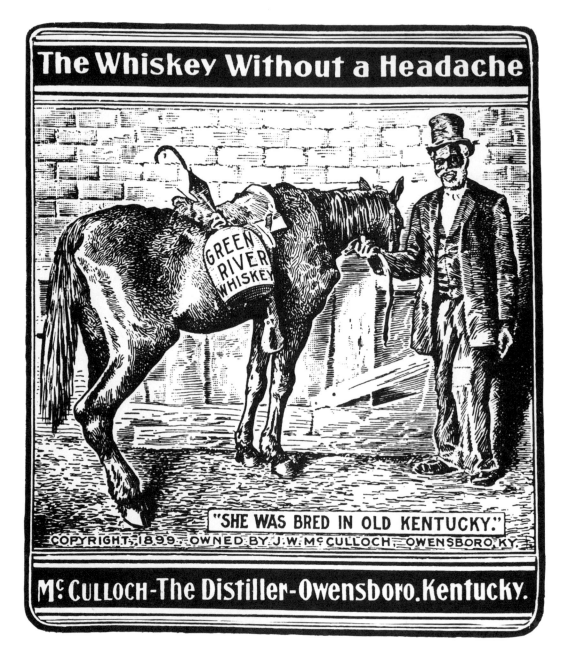

The Whiskey Without a Headache

GREEN RIVER WHISKEY

"SHE WAS BRED IN OLD KENTUCKY."
COPYRIGHT, 1899. OWNED BY J.W. McCULLOCH, OWENSBORO, KY.

McCULLOCH-The Distiller-Owensboro, Kentucky.

MARKETING REFINEMENTS COME TO THE WHISKEY BUSINESS

the price of whiskey. Most goods at this time were sold locally by portions—the buyer knew to bring his or her own flour sack, barrel, tub or jug to the purveyor, who filled it with flour, oats, lard or whiskey. The jugs most often were glazed stoneware in sizes ranging from one pint to five gallons. But in the late 1860s, the use of hinged metal molds made it easier to make glass bottles in greater numbers and at far more reasonable prices. These bottles were too costly for many distillers, but some, at least, took advantage of the invention. This date coincides nicely with George Garvin Brown's 1870 decision to sell his Old Forester bourbon exclusively in sealed bottles.

With the advent of the glassmaker's hinged mold came incised molds that could act as labels to display the distiller's name, address, brand name or another designation. Most of these were of the plainest design, though handsome in their simplicity. The advantage of this new type of packaging was that the potable became more portable.

During the years of Reconstruction, more and more people, most of them experienced whiskey drinkers, went West. When they arrived, they needed whiskey, and distillers rushed to meet the demand. They were shipping whiskey to all sorts of colorful Western towns—Laramie, Tombstone, Dodge City—but it wasn't always good; much was completely unaged and cut with water. When a movie cowboy orders "three fingers of red-eye" (although a dictionary will tell you that "red-eye" is cheap whiskey), he is actually demanding the "good stuff"—it doesn't get red until it's aged. By the 1880s, however, when some of those travelers had amassed small fortunes, decent aged whiskey was at last being shipped to the Wild West.

During the postwar period, the distillers were busy either going broke or going for broke. Here's an update of a few significant people and events in the years between 1860 and 1900:

• In 1864, David M. Beam, owner of the Old Tub Distillery, was blessed with a child—the one and only Jim Beam.

• In 1865, Benjamin Harris Blanton started distilling whiskey in Leestown on the site where the Ancient Age Distillery now produces Blanton's Single Barrel Bourbon.

• J.B. Dant, son of J.W. Dant, built the Cold Spring Distillery in 1865 and would soon produce Yellowstone Bourbon.

• Jack Daniel opened his Tennessee distillery in 1866.

• George A. Dickel, that other great proponent of Tennessee whiskey, started a very respectable rectifying and bottling operation in 1866. The Cascade Distillery in Tullahoma, Tennessee, was founded in 1877 and later purchased by Dickel's company. Dickel died in 1894 from injuries sustained in a fall from a horse in 1888.

• In 1867, the Chapeze brothers founded their first commercial distillery and gave birth to a whiskey that would become known as Old Charter.

• Thomas B. Ripy, whose sons would build a distillery that is known today as the Wild Turkey Distillery, opened his first whiskey distillery in 1869.

• George Garvin Brown (Old Forester) and his half-brother, J.T.S. Brown, went into the wholesale whiskey business in 1870.

• Irishman James Thompson joined George Garvin Brown (his second cousin) in the whiskey business during the mid-1870s. Thompson later formed his own company and bought the Glenmore Distillery in 1910.

- Frederick and Philip Stitzel built their first distillery in Louisville in 1872. Their company would later merge with the Weller company and become known as Stitzel-Weller.

- John E. Fitzgerald, whose Old Fitzgerald Bourbon would become the joy of the Stitzel-Weller brands, built a distillery in 1870.

- Isaac Wolfe Bernheim and his brother, Bernard, started a wholesale whiskey business in Paducah in 1872. Their whiskey would eventually be known as I.W. Harper.

- In 1876, Tom Moore and Ben Mattingly bought their first distillery. The plant produced Tom Moore Bourbon in 1879 and Mattingly & Moore Bourbon by 1896.

- James E. Pepper built the James E. Pepper Distillery in 1879 and soon produced a whiskey that bore his name.

- In 1882, a distillery by the name of R.B. Hayden and Company fired up its stills to make the first bottles of Old Grand-Dad Bourbon.

- Old Taylor Bourbon first hit the shelves in 1887.

- Paul Jones introduced his Four Roses whiskey to Kentucky in 1888.

- Jim Beam joined with Albert J. Hart to run the Old Tub Distillery in 1892.

- In 1893, one of the most colorful characters ever to grace the whiskey industry, Julian "Pappy" Van Winkle, entered the whiskey business as a salesman for W.L. Weller and Son.

- The distillery that made Old Grand-Dad whiskey was taken over by the Wathen family in 1899.

A Matter of Trust

THOUGH THE WHISKEY INDUSTRY MIGHT HAVE STARTED ON A SMALL SCALE, during the years following the Civil War, it developed into a form of commerce in which a substantial amount of money was to be made. Major distilleries had been founded, whiskey families had staked their claims, and the foundations for many a whiskey empire had been laid. There was, however, yet another whiskey scandal looming, later in the 1800s. This time it came from within the industry itself and had a direct effect on which brands of whiskey are available to us today.

You would think that you could trust something called the Whiskey Trust. But, no, this grand-scale scam featured characters whose aim was to control production and prices in the whiskey industry. John D. Rockefeller Sr., had paved the way with Standard Oil, and all it took after that was a few clever men in Peoria, Illinois. These men created the Distillers' and Cattle Feeders' Trust, unofficially known as the Whiskey Trust, with an eye to buying up small-scale distilleries—whether or not they wanted to be bought—and thus controlling the price and quantity of whiskey on the market. Once a small dis-

A LATE-NINETEENTH-CENTURY DISTILLERY

tillery became part of the Trust, it was either closed down or production was cut back, the aim being to control production at as many distilleries as possible.

Other such organizations within the industry existed in various parts of the country around this same time, but the distilling industry in Peoria, having started with one distillery in 1844, had actually outgrown its counterpart in Kentucky by 1880. According to William L. Downard, author of the *Dictionary of the History of the American Brewing and Distilling Industries*, Peoria's whiskey business was an offshoot of the city's active grain mills—surpluses were used to make whiskey. And although distillation of many different spirits continued in Illinois right up until Prohibition, the years that followed Repeal saw Kentucky, once again, become the whiskey center of America.

Greed, of course, was the motivating factor in all of these shenanigans, and what the Whiskey Trust didn't count on was that some of the smaller distilleries within the Trust would make as much whiskey as they desired and simply lie about their production figures. The Trust had effective ways of dealing with these offenders and with those who wanted to remain independent—they destroyed their distilleries. Russian businessman Peter A. Demens wrote about their nasty business in *Sketches of the North American United States*, 1895, "Several weeks ago the Illinois whiskey trust by hired

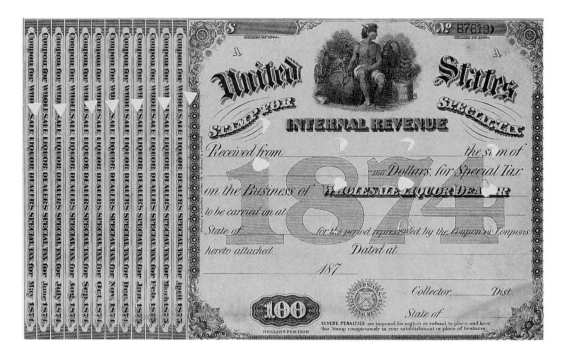

A WHOLESALE LIQUOR DEALER'S PERMIT

agents dynamited a distillery in Chicago that refused to enter the combine."

Federal and local investigations into the Trust, which changed its name to the Distilling and Cattle Feeding Company in 1890, finally forced the company into receivership in 1895. It was split into many smaller entities, but some of these companies then joined together again as the Distilling Company of America, and in 1899, *that* company found itself under federal investigation. To cut a long, complicated story down to a minimum, the company finally gave in to legal pressure and dissolved in 1902. A similar "trust" of that time was the Kentucky Distilleries and Warehouse Company (KDWC), formed in 1899.

The most unfortunate outcome of the Whiskey Trust was that many small distilleries simply disappeared, while others were left under the control of large concerns. Back in 1850, both Old Pepper and Old Crow whiskeys were made at the same distillery. Whether or not they were one and the same whiskey, bottled under different labels, is not known—but is certainly possible. By the end of the century, however, because of the consolidation of so many distilleries during the days of the whiskey trusts, many different whiskeys emanated from relatively few distilleries, a practice still common today. We should mention, however, that some modern distillers go to great trouble to differentiate their various bottlings, by using different recipes and/or by selecting whiskeys that have developed particular styles during aging.

Bonding

TAXES HAVE LONG BEEN THE BANE OF THE WHISKEY BUSINESS'S EXISTENCE, and toward the end of the nineteenth century, demand was high for a fair policy that would benefit the country without crippling the entire liquor industry. The taxes, when they were reintroduced in 1862 to help pay for the Civil War, had been set at 20¢ per "proof gallon" (one gallon at 100° proof), but by 1865, they had risen to a whopping $2 per gallon, the exact same amount that would be levied after Repeal, almost 70 years later. It was too much for the industry to bear. Fact was that when the taxes were passed on to the general public, whiskey became too expensive for the common man. But, as we well know, if the public wants whiskey, it shall jolly well have it, and the people who profited most from this very high tax were none other than the moonshiners.

The term "moonshine" was probably coined by the Scots when new laws introduced in 1781 drove them to establish stills way up in the hills of Scotland that could be operated surreptitiously, literally by the light of the moon. There are still "shiners" in America today, and apparently, the greatest concentration of such people is probably in the Carolinas. But back when the government's excise tax was raised to $2 in 1865, the moonshiners of Kentucky and Tennessee began making white lightning in abundance and cashing in on the woes of the legitimate distillers. Fortunately, however, government officials rethought their actions when they realized that much of the whiskey being consumed at the time wasn't being taxed at all. If they couldn't get the public to pay high prices for legitimate whiskey, they would have to reduce the tax and help the whiskey business back onto its tax-paying feet. While they had the government's attention, the distillers took the opportunity to point out the fact that paying taxes on unaged whiskey, a product that couldn't yet be sold, was another problem that should be dealt with.

In 1868, Congress passed a bill that reduced the excise tax to 50¢ per gallon, required a tax stamp to be put on all American-made spirits and gave distillers a grace period—known as the "bonding" period—of one year before having to pay taxes on liquor that was aging. During this time, the liquor was kept under governmental supervision in "bonded" warehouses. Bonding helped the whiskey producers a little, since it meant that they didn't have to pay their taxes as soon as the spirit ran out of the still, but 12 months wasn't a very long grace period considering that whiskey under two years old isn't worth drinking and that it doesn't really gain much character until it has been in the wood for three to four years. So although the new law did help somewhat on the financial side, the distillers still paid taxes on their product considerably before they could sell it at a decent price.

Still, the government had made some changes and provided a modicum of relief for the whiskey industry, and the years that followed were to shape the business into what it has become today. The bonding period was increased to three years in 1879, and in 1894, after the nation had just suffered a massive depression known as The Panic of 1893, it was increased again, this time to eight years. This time period remained in effect until the Forand Act of 1958 increased it to 20 years. To help the distillers further, the government agreed that stores of whiskey could be used as collateral for taxes when they came due. Whiskey bonds became a very valuable commodity.

However, much whiskey was being sold in bulk to rectifiers and bottlers of the time, and the problem of unscrupulous wholesalers (and retailers) adulterating good whiskey had to be tackled. Enter Colonel Edmund Haynes Taylor Jr.

Taylor, the man responsible for giving us Old Taylor Bourbon in 1887, was known as a discerning distiller who focused on the high quality of his products. Along with many other reputable distillers and rectifiers, Taylor was worried that the bad whiskey in the marketplace would reflect on the whole industry. Thus he teamed up with Secretary of the Treasury John G. Carlisle, and together, they lobbied for the Bottled-in-Bond Act of 1897.

This act stipulated that bonded whiskey must be made at one distillery in one batch, aged for at least four years in warehouses supervised by the government and bottled at 100° proof (50 percent alcohol.) It also stated that only *straight* whiskey could be bonded, although distillates other than whiskey—rum, for instance—that met the requirements could also be Bottled in Bond. The act gave legitimate distillers the ability to prove the quality of their products, and though it was a step in the right direction, the fight for honest labeling was only just beginning.

In Britain at the turn of the century, blended Scotches were the cause of much controversy when single-malt-Scotch producers sued certain retailers of blended Scotch for selling "an article not of the nature and substance demanded." Blended Scotch, they said, was a "silent spirit," whereas a pure malt "went down singing hymns." The Distillers Company, a group of blended-Scotch producers, fought back, claiming that because single malts contained many more impurities (flavor-giving congeners) than blends, theirs was the purer spirit. The battle eventually was won by the blenders, and the word "Scotch" was legally allowable on bottles of blended Scotch whisky. Back on this side of the Atlantic, similar battles were being waged.

In the early years of the twentieth century, large food companies had started shipping foodstuffs all over the country, and there was growing concern about the preservatives and dyes being used as well as the sanitary conditions in the packaging and processing plants. Laws that would properly define foodstuffs and pharmaceuticals and help protect consumers were, therefore, presented to Congress; luckily for us, whiskey was one of the items under discussion. Just as their counterparts in Scotland had done, American producers of blended whiskeys argued that their products were purer than straight whiskeys, since they contained fewer impurities. They didn't seem to care that these very "impurities" were responsible for the distinctive flavor of the whiskey. However, the blenders had to contend with a certain Dr. Wiley, head of the Bureau of Chemistry, a part of the Department of Agriculture, and a true believer in straight whiskey.

At one point, Wiley is rumored to have taken a bottle of bad whiskey to President Theodore Roosevelt, who examined the product and declared that if people could no longer get a decent glass of whiskey, it was time something was done about it. Well, something was done, and when the law was enforced in 1907, all grain spirits other than straight whiskey had to be labeled "compound," "imitation" or "blended." Consumers interpreted this language to mean that the only true whiskey was straight whiskey. This wasn't entirely fair to the producers of blended products, so when Taft took office in 1909, he decided to establish further standards of identity and clarify the definition. All whiskeys were, once again, whiskeys—some were blended, and some were straight—but the label had to declare which type was in the bottle.

It's tempting to think that with that law under their belts, Grant out of the way and a somewhat standardized method of production, the whiskey distillers of America were able to sit back and make some money. However, those nineteenth-century temperance movements had been gaining momentum, and the whiskey industry was about to confront its most formidable enemy. Here's what was happening to the brand names at this time:

• I.W. Harper Bourbon won a gold medal at the Exposition Universal, in Paris, France, in 1900, and another at the Louisiana Purchase Exposition in 1904.

• J.T.S. Brown and Sons (J.T.S. Brown Bourbon) bought the Old Prentice Distillery in Anderson County sometime during the early 1900s.

• Cabin Still and Kentucky Tavern whiskeys were both trademarked in 1903.

• Old Fitzgerald whiskey started being marketed in Europe in 1904.

• In 1904, the Cascade Distillery (George A. Dickel) was enlarged, making it the largest distillery in the whole of Tennessee at that time.

• Jack Daniel's No. 7 whiskey won a gold medal at the Louisiana Purchase Exhibition of the 1904 World's Fair in St. Louis, and the brand would soon be marketed overseas. The following year, Jack Daniel injured his toe while kicking a safe, and strange as it may sound, the wound led to his death in 1911.

• The Ripy brothers opened a distillery in 1905 that would later be known as The Wild Turkey Distillery.

• Lem Motlow, who took over the Jack Daniel Distillery when Jack retired in 1907, introduced Lem Motlow's Tennessee Sour Mash, Jack Daniel's No. 5 whiskey and Lem Motlow's Peach Brandy shortly after gaining control of the distillery. Lem's peach brandy was made in an old pot still. He died in 1947.

• Tennessee enforced statewide Prohibition in 1910. Jack Daniel's whiskey continued to be distilled in St. Louis and Alabama, while George A. Dickel's whiskey transferred to Louisville, where huge leaching vats to facilitate the Tennessean Lincoln County Process of charcoal mellowing were erected at the Stitzel distillery.

• J.B. Dant (Yellowstone Bourbon) built a distillery at Gethsemane, Kentucky, in 1912.

• Colonel Albert B. Blanton became plant manager at the George T. Stagg Distillery in 1912.

• In 1913, an article appeared in *The Louisville Courier-Journal*'s special "Southern Prosperity" edition wherein whiskey dealer S.C. Herbst proclaimed that his Old Judge and Old Fitzgerald brands of bourbon were the last "Old Fashioned Copper Pot Distilled Whiskeys."

Hymns to Be Sung and Axes to Be Wielded

ACCORDING TO PATRICIA M. RICE, AUTHOR OF *Altered States*, IN 1873 Eliza Jane Thompson, a woman with a passionate distaste for the drinking classes, led 70 women to drugstores and bars in her hometown of Hillsboro, Ohio, where they stood outside and sang hymns and prayed. After news of the occurrence reached the ears of similar-minded women around the country, over 50,000 promoters of temperance followed suit. The movement became known as the Women's Crusade and led to the 1874 formation of the Women's Christian Temperance Union (WCTU) in Cleveland, Ohio.

One of the women who had joined the Women's Crusade—and was president of the WCTU from 1879 until her death in 1898—was Frances Elizabeth Caroline Willard, born in Churchville, New York, in 1839. Willard fought for more than temperance; she was also involved in other "women's issues," such as suffrage and civil rights, and she had some further attributes that frustrated the antitemperance folk. At that time, women involved with women's rights often were characterized as "plain," but Willard was anything but plain. Indeed, not only was she a very attractive woman, she was also known as an effective speaker who was "soft-spoken and womanly."

The antics of the famed Carry Nation, who was also a member of the Women's Christian Temperance Union, are recorded by Oscar Getz in his book *Whiskey—An American Pictorial History*. No tale of Prohibition would be complete without a few words on this colorful woman. Carry Amelia Moore, who stood almost six feet tall and weighed around 175 pounds, was born in Kentucky in 1846 and raised there, in Missouri and in Texas. In 1867, she married a physician and alcoholic, Dr. Charles Gloyd and was widowed when her husband, despite her remonstrations, reaped the

CARRY NATION WITH HER HATCHET AND BIBLE

IF BY WHISKEY . . .

DURING THE YEARS PRECEDING PROHIBITION, DEBATES BETWEEN THE "WETS" AND the "drys" raged fierce. Some politicians, however, cagily hedged their bets by delivering speeches that proclaimed the rights and wrongs of both sides of every issue.

One such oration is the "If by whiskey" speech, printed in William Safire's "On Language" column in *The New York Times Magazine,* December 21, 1991. It was found by Mr. Norman L. Simpson of Fayetteville, New York, in the archives of his wife's family business, a company that sold advertising space on billboards.

Probably because the upcoming Volstead Act was threatening to take away a huge chunk of his profits, Simpson's father-in-law collected newspaper clippings, during the years when the debates were still raging, that related to the growing Prohibition movement. Although this particular speech was not dated or attributed, surely it was delivered by a born politician:

I'll take a stand on any issue at any time, regardless of how fraught with controversy it may be. You have asked me how I feel about whiskey; well, Brother, here's how I stand.

If by whiskey, you mean the Devil's brew, the Poison scourge, the bloody monster that defies innocence, dethrones reason, creates misery and poverty, yea, literally takes the bread out of the mouths of babes; if you mean the Evil Drink that topples men and women from pinnacles of righteous, gracious living into the bottomless pit of despair, degradation, shame, helplessness and hopelessness—then I am against it with all my power.

But if by whiskey, you mean the oil of conversation, the philosophic wine and ale that is consumed when good fellows get together, that puts a song in their hearts, laughter on their lips and the warm glow of contentment in their eyes; if you mean that sterling drink that puts the spring in an old man's steps on a frosty morning; if you mean that drink, the sale of which pours into our treasury untold millions of dollars which are used to provide tender care for our little crippled children, our pitifully aged and infirm and to build our highways and schools—then, Brother, I am for it. This is my stand.

rewards of drinking too much. He was buried in a drunkard's grave. Less than 10 years later, Carry married David Nation, a lawyer and minister, who eventually divorced her because of her slightly insane ways of demonstrating her distaste for alcohol. Not that she hated only alcohol; Carry also hated sex, tobacco and Teddy Roosevelt.

Nation believed that she had conversations with Jesus and that He had directed her

CARRY NATION AND TEMPERANCE ADVOCATES SMASH A BAR

to destroy saloons. And that is exactly what she set out to do. In 1900, she gathered a group of supporters, stormed a drugstore in Kansas, rolled out a cask of brandy and smashed it to smithereens with a sledgehammer. Not content with that, she then set fire to the contents. Later that year, she actually smashed up an entire saloon in Kiowa, Oklahoma. We must give a little credit here to the lady; her tactics certainly had an effect on the illegal bars at the time—many of them closed. But it wasn't until the following year that Carry Nation actually wielded the hatchet that became her trademark when she destroyed a saloon in Wichita. In her spare time, Nation published a newsletter called *Hatchet* and another known as *Smasher's Mail*.

Of course, her actions weren't without drawbacks; Nation was jailed in Wichita and a few other towns, but it never stopped her from going out and smashing more saloons whenever she was released. Her ways became too radical for the WCTU, which eventually rejected her, leaving her without financial support. Not one to be sidetracked for long, Carry Nation took to lecturing on the vaudeville circuit to raise money and traveled to every state in the country, breaking up bars as she went. In 1908, she even ventured to Britain and Ireland, where she spread the word of Jesus and His dislike of neighborhood taverns. Carry Nation died of a stroke in 1911.

The Noble Experiment

"**I** DO NOT CARE TO LIVE IN A WORLD THAT IS TOO GOOD TO BE GENIAL; too ascetic to be honest, too proscriptive to be happy. I do not believe that men can be legislated into angels—even red-nosed angels." Henry Watterson, owner and editor of *The Louisville Courier-Journal*, wrote those words in 1913. The country could have used a few more men who weren't afraid to voice their antiprohibitionistic opinions at the time. Decrying Prohibition during the first two decades of this century was somewhat akin to promoting cigarettes in 1995—although it doesn't amount to treason, it just isn't very acceptable.

Though temperance societies had sprung up at the beginning of the nineteenth century and had grown stronger, larger and more adamant about their quest after the Civil War, gone were the days of espousing moderation. By the turn of the century, total abstinence was the goal. The cause for concern was understandable; the liquor industry was growing very quickly, and it wasn't well regulated. In 1874, more than 200,000 retailers sold liquor in the United States, a whopping 120,000 more than just 10 years earlier.

By 1900, many of the smaller temperance societies had either given their support to or had become part of the Anti-Saloon League, founded in 1893. Their mission was to fight for the death of the saloon. The most influential group on the other side of the Prohibition debate was The Wine and Spirits Association, formed in 1891 to counter the propaganda of the many temperance societies. The biggest problem that faced the "wets" was that not enough people in the beverage alcohol business took the "drys" seriously—most people thought that if they ignored the drys, they would go away. However, since the majority of brewers and distillers thought of the drys as not much more than religious fanatics, they not only chose to ignore them but foolishly carried on doing business as usual—a bad move and one that would eventually lead to their downfall. In fact, the drys had some very serious legitimate issues that needed to be addressed.

Around the turn of the century, most saloons were unruly places that served liquor, wine and beer to almost anyone: young or old, sober or drunk, morning, noon or night. George Ade, author of *The Old-Time Saloon*, noted that in Chicago, once a saloon

HISTORICAL MISQUOTATION

HERBERT C. HOOVER IS frequently miscredited as having said, "Prohibition is a noble experiment." In fact, what he said was that Prohibition was " . . . a great social and economic experiment, noble in motive and far-reaching in purpose."

A DEPICTION OF THE WOMEN'S CHRISTIAN TEMPERANCE UNION

keeper got his license, he would throw the key to his bar into Lake Michigan so that his doors could never again be locked. It was common practice for corrupt local officials to accept bribes to assure lenient treatment of wayward tavern keepers and drunken customers alike. A good number of bars were dens of iniquity where one could buy drugs, consort with prostitutes, hire strong-armed boys to do a little dirty work or bribe voters with a few shots of whiskey. In New York, when a law was passed that made it illegal to sell drinks on Sunday except when they were accompanied by a meal, many hotels took to placing a sandwich on each table. The sandwich was never eaten—but many drinks were sold.

Of course, many respectable bars existed in the pre-Prohibition era, and one such establishment was the Old Waldorf Bar in Manhattan. The bar opened in 1897 and closed its doors when Prohibition was enacted. Albert Stevens Crockett, historian for the Waldorf-Astoria Hotel, detailed some of the colorful history of the bar in *The Old Waldorf-Astoria Bar Book*. By his accounts, it was indeed a bar worth frequenting.

Crockett paints a picture of a fancy saloon filled with power brokers being served by no less than a dozen white-coated bartenders who were "busy all afternoon and evening ministering to an endless array of thirsts." Respectable as this bar may have been, Crockett does mention customers who were "filled to overflowing and had to be either carried or led away."

Crockett also mentions a tradition of this era that was never properly reestablished after Prohibition ended—the free-lunch table. Precursor to modern "happy hours,"

CITIZENS SEEKING REPEAL OF THE VOLSTEAD ACT

the Waldorf's feast included caviar, Virginia ham, canapés and "thirst-provoking anchovies in various-tinted guises." The idea, of course, was to lure men there for a free lunch and sell them as much beer and liquor as possible in the interim. These tables were not just offered in the posh bars; working-class saloons served similar meals, but the fare on their tables—pickled eggs, frankfurters, stews and thick, hearty soups—was not nearly as sumptuous as that at the Waldorf.

There is no doubt that liquor was being abused, and one fellow, George Garvin Brown, creator of the Old Forester brand and a founding member of The Wine and Spirits Association (WSA), *did* take steps to counter the Prohibition movement. The WSA tried to dissuade politicians and churchgoers from taking the Anti-Saloon League's mission to its logical conclusion. Members lectured and wrote to prominent people on both sides of the issue, trying to bank the fire a little. But Brown also had some priorities of his own, and he decided to take on the religious fanatics who he felt were hiding behind the skirts of the pulpit.

In 1910, Brown published a booklet, *The Holy Bible Repudiates Prohibition*, in which

he quoted passages from the Bible that showed divine approval of the consumption of beverage alcohol. One such quote was from Deuteronomy 14: "And thou shalt bestow that money for whatever thy soul lusteth after, for oxen, or for sheep, or for wine, or for strong drink, or for whatsoever thy soul desireth; and thou shalt eat there before the Lord thy God, and thou shalt rejoice, thou and thine household."

After quoting the passage, Brown commented, "The context shows that for the convenience of those living at a distance from the place appointed by God for feasts in His honor, authority was given to sell for money that which was required for tithes and feasts and provide the same at the place appointed by God for His worship. This passage shows the fallacy of the position taken by some agitators that even though wine was used authoritatively in Bible times, it was homemade wine only, and not bought and sold."

For Brown, this book was more than his way of countering the drys' movement; it

> **"Give strong drink unto him that is ready to perish . . . Let him drink and forget his poverty, and remember his misery no more."**
>
> PROVERBS 31, 6-7

A PRE-PROHIBITION SALOON

was a personal mission. He was a deeply religious man whose association with his church had been threatened because of his involvement in the whiskey business, and he honestly deplored the drys using the "word of the Lord" to promote their quest. And he was right; the Anti-Saloon League was doing just that.

The Anti-Saloon League's 1910 yearbook contains a declaration signed by the League's fearless General Superintendent, Reverend Purley A. Baker, D.D.:

"The Anti-Saloon League is not, strictly speaking, an organization. It is what its name indicates—a League. It is a league of organizations. It is the federated church, and under all circumstances loyal to the church. It has no interest apart from the church. It goes just as fast and just as far as public sentiment of the church will permit. It has not come to the kingdom simply to build a little local sentiment, or to secure the passage of a few laws, nor yet to vote the saloons from a few hundred towns. These are mere incidents in its progress. It has come to solve the liquor problem."

The yearbook goes on to note the progress that the drys had made since the League's inception in 1893. According to this booklet, over 12,000 saloons had been closed "by various means" in the year 1909, and over 41 million Americans were living in "dry" territory. The U.S. population in 1909 was about 90.5 million; therefore, if the League's statistics were accurate, over 45 percent of the country already was dry in 1910.

Actually, by that year, every state in the union had some form of Prohibition. It was statewide in some instances and under various forms of local option (towns, counties, municipalities or city districts having the right to legislate and enforce Prohibition) in others. It's easy to see that national Prohibition was inevitable sooner or later. Five years later, and five years before the whole country had to seek solace from illicit stills and bathtub gin, 20 states were dry: Alabama, Arizona, Arkansas, Connecticut, Georgia, Illinois, Iowa, Kansas, Kentucky, Louisiana, Maine, Minnesota, Mississippi, Missouri, North Carolina, North Dakota, New Hampshire, Oklahoma, Tennessee and West Virginia. The Anti-Saloon League had structured its tactics to make sure that a number of individual states went dry before lobbying for national Prohibition, and they were succeeding at an alarming rate.

While all this was going on, the whiskey industry had been making good use of a loophole in the law by selling liquor by mail. It was a grand system that had actually been around since about 1870, when bottles became more common as a way of packaging whiskey. As local prohibition spread, drinkers in dry areas began writing away for whiskey as never before, and they were treated to some marvelous offers and premiums.

Advertisements in magazines and newspapers of the time gave consumers the chance not only to buy whiskey at reduced rates but also to receive special offers such as an "elegant gold-filled watch" sent free to "all who influence ten new customers to each order one gallon or more of our goods." If you had only four friends, you could receive "the most beautiful set of Limoges China Dishes you ever saw" for persuading each of them to order a gallon of spirits from the Security Distilling Company of Chicago.

Rye whiskey was still very popular during the early twentieth century, and the number of bottlings of Pennsylvania rye or Monongahela rye whiskey generally outnum-

---

THE DEATH OF JOHN BARLEYCORN

During Prohibition, a tombstone was erected in Meridian, Connecticut, that read:

In Memoriam John Barleycorn
Born B.C.   Died Jan. 16, 1920
Resurrection?

Take Your Choice

1 Quart $1.00 or 4 Quarts $3.20

WE PAY EXPRESS CHARGES IN EITHER CASE

For years we have been telling you about the goodness of **HAYNER WHISKEY.** Now we want you to **TRY IT.** We are willing to lose money to get you to do so, for we know if you only try it you will always buy it, just as our half-a-million satisfied customers are now doing. Remember, we have one of the largest distilleries in the world. We are the largest bottlers of whiskey in the world. We have more whiskey in our eight Bonded Warehouses than any other distiller in the world. There is more **HAYNER WHISKEY** sold than any other brand of whiskey in the world. We have been in business for over 37 years and have a capital of $500,000.00 paid in full so you run no risk when you deal with us. Your money back at once if you are not satisfied. Don't forget that **HAYNER WHISKEY** goes direct from our own distillery to you, with all its original strength, richness and flavor, thus assuring you of perfect purity and saving you the enormous profits of the dealers. You cannot buy anything purer, better or more satisfactory than **HAYNER WHISKEY** no matter how much you pay.

Don't forget that a **HAYNER** quart is an honest quart of 32 ounces, 4 to the gallon. It takes 5 of the ordinary so-called "quarts" to make a gallon. We give one-fourth more in every bottle, reducing our price just that much.

Direct from our Distillery to You

HAYNER WHISKEY

Saves Dealers' Profits — Prevents Adulteration

Send us **$1.00** for **ONE QUART** or **$3.20** for **FOUR FULL QUARTS** of **HAYNER SEVEN-YEAR-OLD RYE** and we will pay the express charges. We ship in a plain, sealed package; no marks to even suggest contents. When the whiskey reaches your home, try it, sample it thoroughly. Then, if you don't find it all right, perfectly satisfactory in every way and better than you ever had before or can buy from anybody else at any price, ship it back to us at our expense and your money will be promptly refunded. Isn't that fair? We stand all the expense if you don't wish to keep the whiskey. **YOU** risk nothing. We ship one quart on your first or trial order only. All subsequent orders must be for at least 4 quarts at 80 cents a quart. The packing and express charges are almost as much on one quart as on four, and even at $1.00 for one quart we lose money, but we want you to try it. **We would prefer to have you order 4 quarts for $3.20, for then we would make a little profit and you would also save money.** But take your choice. $1.00 for 1 quart or $3.20 for 4 quarts, express prepaid. Your money back if you're not satisfied. Write our nearest office today.

FREE IF YOU MENTION THIS PAPER WE WILL SEND YOU A GOLD-TIPPED GLASS AND CORKSCREW **FREE**

Trial Orders for Arizona, California, Colorado, Idaho, Montana, Nevada, New Mexico, Oregon, Utah, Washington or Wyoming must be 1 QUART for $1.35 by EXPRESS PREPAID. Subsequent orders on the basis of 4 QUARTS for $4.00 by EXPRESS PREPAID, or 20 QUARTS for $16.00 by FREIGHT PREPAID.

ESTABLISHED 1866

THE HAYNER DISTILLING COMPANY

DISTILLERY TROY, O.

DAYTON, OHIO   ST. LOUIS, MO.   ST. PAUL, MINN.   ATLANTA, GA.

A MAIL-ORDER WHISKEY ADVERTISEMENT

bered the bourbons in advertisements of the time. America was still producing "Pure Malt" (presumably 100 percent malted barley) whiskeys at the time—in 1913, a dozen bottles of Regan's Pure Malt Whiskey would cost a mere $6, whereas four quarts of I.W. Harper Bourbon brought $5 on the mail-order market. A bottle of Old Crow in 1916 would have cost $2 to $3, depending on its age (the $3 bottling was distilled in 1884, the less expensive one in 1904), and rye whiskey at the time was being sold at similar prices.

Trade was brisk for the mail-order whiskey suppliers, but the Prohibitionists did not stand idly by while thousands of gallons of whiskey were mailed to their hard-fought-for dry states and counties. In 1913, the Webb-Kenyon Interstate Liquor Act was passed, effectively preventing the traffic of liquor from wet to dry states. The mail-order business continued, but with not nearly as much spirit as before.

In Europe, the "Great War" broke out in 1914, and although President Woodrow Wilson initially declared that the country would remain neutral, on April 6, 1917, the United States declared war on Germany. Along with

---

WHOSE LIBERTY?

FAMED LAWYER AND ORATOR Clarence Darrow (1857-1938) offered this legal opinion on the Noble Experiment: "Prohibition is an outrageous and senseless invasion of the personal liberty of millions of intelligent and temperate persons who see nothing dangerous or immoral in the moderate consumption of alcoholic beverages."

---

the rest of the country, the whiskey industry braced itself for more setbacks. The Lever Food and Fuel Act was enacted later that year; designed to preserve food supplies during World War I, it made all distillation of beverage alcohol illegal. Drinking was still legal in some areas of the country—but not for much longer.

Just over two years later, on January 17, 1920, after the Volstead Act that enabled the National Prohibition Law had been passed by 287 votes to 100, the nation was officially dry. That year saw the birth of yet another organization, The Association Against the Prohibition Amendment, made up of many brewers, distillers and some very wealthy and influential people, DuPont family members among them. The association felt compelled to keep the government informed of the drawbacks of Prohibition, stressing mainly that without taxes from alcohol, the economy was suffering, that farmers had lost a market for their grains and the subsequent surplus had brought grain prices down and that unemployment in related industries was rising steadily. It was partially due to these efforts that Prohibition would be repealed some 13 years later.

The Roaring Twenties

BY MOST ACCOUNTS, PROHIBITION WASN'T SO DRY AFTER ALL. THE YEARS between 1920 and 1933 are usually associated with speakeasies, bootleggers, bathtub gin and gangsters, and for some, those were the highlights of the decade. If you were part of the relatively small percentage of the population who frequented speakeasies, the nightlife was sparkling, and it was in the fun-filled, mobster-run clubs of this era that the twenties roared with a hoarse throat, worn dry by bad liquor.

One of the strangest effects of Prohibition, however, was this: Hard liquor actually became more popular. Why? Simply because it packed more alcohol into a small quantity of liquid than wine or beer and was therefore easier to transport and hide from the authorities. People who had once enjoyed a few beers at the local saloon were now tossing back shots of whiskey and drinking fanciful cocktails made with poor-quality booze. It is estimated that although relatively little wine or beer was poured during Prohibition, consumption of the hard stuff actually *increased* by more than 15 percent per person. It then declined by about 25 percent after Repeal.

Felix graf von Luckner, a visitor to America during Prohibition, painted a marvelous scene of the effects of the experiment in his book *Seeteuful erebert America*, 1928:

"Prohibition has created a new, universally respected, a well-beloved, and a very profitable occupation, that of the bootlegger who takes care of the importation of the forbidden liquor. Everyone knows this, even the powers of the government. But this profession is beloved because it is essential, and it is respected because its pursuit is clothed with an element of danger and with a sporting risk. Now and then one is caught, that must happen pro forma and then he must do time or, if he is wealthy enough, get someone to do time for him.

"Yet it is undeniable that prohibition has in some respects been signally successful. The filthy saloons, the gin mills which formerly flourished on every corner and in which the laborer once drank off half his wages, have disappeared. Now he can instead buy his own car, and ride off for a weekend or a few days with his wife and children in the country or at the sea. But, on the other hand, a great deal of poison or methyl alcohol has taken the place of the good old pure whiskey. The number of crimes and misdemeanors that originated in drunkenness has declined. But by contrast, a large part of the population has become accustomed to disregard and to violate the law without thinking. The worst is, that precisely as a consequence of the law, the taste for alcohol has spread ever more widely among the youth. The sporting attraction of the forbidden and the dangerous leads to violations. My observations have convinced me that many fewer would drink were it not illegal."

Since, as von Luckner noted, the sleazy gin mills had disappeared and much drinking, therefore, occurred in swank nightclubs and the homes of the wealthy, Prohibition's other weird effect was that drinking became more socially acceptable than it had been prior to 1920. Speakeasies weren't the only places you could buy booze during Prohibition. In his book *The Great Illusion*, Herbert Asbury quotes a 1929 telegram that listed over 30 people and places that supplied liquor in Manhattan. The locations included delicatessens, shoe-shine parlors, barbershops, delivery agencies, paint stores, taxi drivers, moving-van companies and, of course, newspapermen's associations. Many stories might never have met their deadlines if the hard-drinking journalists of yesteryear weren't able to knock back a shot or two. And although the Governor of New York's office wasn't mentioned in the telegram, it is said that even during the dry years, Franklin D. Roosevelt was wont to serve cocktails from his desk every afternoon at four.

MEDICINAL WHISKEY

The Noble Experiment also helped the drug industry of the time inasmuch as some city folk who didn't want to risk flouting the law simply went down to their local teahouse (a euphemism of the time) and smoked marijuana, which remained legal until 1937. But these were also the days when many people were stricken with a variety of weird and wonderful maladies that needed regular treatment with frequent tots of decent, aged "medicinal" whiskey.

Six distilleries were given permits to sell medicinal whiskey during Prohibition—A. Ph. Stitzel, Glenmore, Schenley, Brown-Forman, National Distillers and Frankfort Distilleries—and these companies were allowed to store whiskey and sell it to licensed druggists, who in turn could mete it out to customers who had a doctor's prescription. In his book *Nothing Better In The Market*, John Ed Pearce says that only 10 such medicinal whiskey permits were applied for, and although the reasons for such a small number aren't quite clear, it was possible that most people in the industry simply thought the permits not worth the bother. Further amendments to the law made it possible to distill whiskey (during "distilling holidays") that would be used for medicinal purposes.

GOVERNMENT AGENTS DESTROY STILLS DURING PROHIBITION

This legitimate whiskey was prized for its high quality, since unless people could get smuggled Scotch, most of the other available whiskeys were roughly made and seldom aged by the moonshiners who produced them.

Horrible stories about people going blind after drinking bootleg liquor are true. Some bootleggers took a shortcut and produced highly toxic methyl or wood alcohol instead of ethyl (beverage) alcohol. Methyl alcohol has a direct effect on the optic nerve, and as little as one ounce has been known to cause death. Others—either those not versed in the art of distillation or those too concerned with time and money—would not adhere to the art of the distiller wherein only the center section of the whiskey is deemed suitable for consumption. Instead, they would sell the entire batch of spirits, and the resultant whiskey, although it wouldn't make drinkers blind, was a far cry from the pure, bold red liquor that the distillers had fought for at the turn of the century. All sorts of ploys were used to make this rotgut at least look good. Bootleggers colored their white lightning with ingredients such as iodine and tobacco to make it look as though it had been "in the wood" for a few years.

The Volstead Act all but destroyed many of the legitimate whiskey distilleries. Most of them were dismantled, and of the 17 plants operating in Kentucky prior to Prohibition, only seven were making whiskey in 1935. Yes, all sorts of deals were going on

throughout this period—distilleries without a "medicine" license were selling their stocks to those who had a license, others maintained warehouses where those with licenses could store their whiskey under government supervision, and an unofficial cartel sent Owsley Brown of Brown-Forman to Europe to try to sell over 20,000 barrels of bourbon—a mission that was only partially successful. But toward the end of Prohibition, those who were still producing whiskey were busy making plans for Repeal.

The Reawakening of the American Whiskey Business

WHEN PROHIBITION ENDED, NOT EVERYONE WAS HAPPY ABOUT IT. DRY Senator Morris Sheppard of Texas, one of the authors of the Eighteenth Amendment, had delivered a speech on January 16, the eve of the date that Prohibition went into effect, every year since 1920. In February 1933, he conducted what *Time* magazine described as "a pathetic one-man filibuster against Repeal." His oration lasted over eight hours, but nonetheless, the Senate voted the following day to take up the Repeal resolution by 58 votes to 23. Prohibition finally ended at 5:32 P.M., Eastern Standard Time, on December 5, 1933.

During the months preceding Repeal, speculation was rife about how the liquor industry would handle the expected new business. One thing was certain: There would be major changes in the way the industry conducted itself. Once again, it would be those with deep pockets who could afford to cope with the new regulations that came with Repeal.

The whiskey producers of America were somewhat nervous that much of their audience was gone. Since good straight whiskey was hard to come by during the dry years, the public had become accustomed to gin. Why gin? Mainly because gin was what the bootleggers had decided to make, with good reason: It is relatively simple to take unaged spirits straight from the still, add a little oil of juniper and create gin—not London Dry Gin, a distinctive spirit with a host of natural flavors lovingly distilled into it, but a very crude form of what is now called "compound" gin, a less expensive substitute. During Prohibition, not only did the aromatic juniper help disguise just how poorly the liquor had been made, it also gave the drinking public what they wanted—a highly flavorful spirit. Since most people were used to the bold body and heady flavors of good whiskey, gin was far preferable to vodka, a spirit that was virtually unknown in America at the time. Even by 1939, when Charles H. Baker Jr.'s excellent book *The Gentleman's Companion* was published, the author noted that vodka was "unnecessary to medium or small bars."

There was, however, another factor that worried the post-Prohibition whiskey men: their supplies of aged whiskey were critically low. December 1933 saw an America with only about 20 million gallons of whiskey on hand, compared with the more than 60 million gallons of surplus whiskey when Prohibition began. Most of what there was had been distilled just the previous year or so during the "distilling holidays" allowed by the government once Repeal was in sight. The Canadians and the Scots, on the other hand, had plenty of aged whiskey, and they were champing at the bit to ship it into the United States. One immediate solution to the American distillers' problem was to sell blended rather than straight whiskey, thereby "stretching" the good stuff with neutral spirits and flavorings. The hope was that it would tide them over for a few years until they had enough aged straight whiskey to please the public. What they weren't considering, of course, was that once the public grew accustomed to blended whiskey, chances were they would never return to the "pure" stuff. Here's a list of the whiskey distillers still remaining in the game after Prohibition ended:

• The biggest whiskey company was the National Distillers Products Company, a reputable company formed in the 1920s that was an indirect offshoot of the disreputable Whiskey Trust of the late nineteenth century. In 1933, National owned approximately 50 percent of all of the whiskey in America along with a number of notable distilleries, such as the Wathen Distillery (Old Grand-Dad, Old Taylor and Old Crow), the Overholt Distillery (Old Overholt) and three other distilleries that produced straight whiskey. The company was acquired by the Jim Beam Brands Company in the 1980s.

• The James B. Beam Distilling Company was formed in 1933. It was purchased in the 1960s by what is now the American Brands Company and is currently called the

A SALOON REOPENS FOR BUSINESS AFTER REPEAL

Jim Beam Brands Company. It now owns the Old Taylor, Old Crow, Old Overholt and Old Grand-Dad brand names, in addition to four small-batch bourbons—Booker's, Baker's, Knob Creek and Basil Hayden's—and its signature Jim Beam whiskeys.

• Schenley, under the guidance of its owner, Lewis Rosenstiel, had acquired a number of distilleries, brand names and quite a stock of whiskey during Prohibition. By 1934, his company owned the George T. Stagg Distillery (Ancient Age) and the James E. Pepper Distillery (James E. Pepper whiskey) among others. I.W. Harper, Old Charter and Cascade (George A. Dickel) brand names were purchased by Schenley in the late 1930s, and Schenley itself was later acquired by United Distillers.

• The George T. Stagg Distillery went on to become the Ancient Age Distillery and was sold before Schenley was taken over. The plant is now owned by the Sazerac Company and produces Ancient Age, Eagle Rare, Benchmark and a range of single-barrel bourbons—Blanton's, Rock Hill Farms, Elmer T. Lee and Hancock's Reserve.

• The Stitzel distillery joined forces with the Weller company to form Stitzel-Weller. The company bought the Old Fitzgerald brand name in 1933 and went on to become part of United Distillers in the 1980s.

• Glenmore Distilleries (Kentucky Tavern, among others) survived Prohibition well and went on to become a major producer and importer of a number of liquors and liqueurs. The company was acquired by United Distillers in 1991.

• Brown-Forman (Old Forester, Early Times) had a supply of aged whiskey on hand to kick off the 1933 celebrations. After the company's 1934 fiscal year didn't turn out to be as profitable as predicted, its president, Owsley Brown, did the honorable thing and offered half of his stock to his disappointed investors in lieu of a dividend. The company went on to buy the Jack Daniel Distillery in the 1950s.

• Frankfort Distilleries (owners of the Four Roses brand) survived the dry years and was bought by the Seagram company in the 1940s.

• Leslie Samuels (Maker's Mark) reopened his Deatsville distillery in 1933 and sold T.W. Samuels Bourbon (named for the first Samuels to open a commercial distillery). His son, another T.W. Samuels, took over the operation after Leslie's death and ran it until 1943. After taking a 10-year sabbatical from the industry, he returned to his whiskey roots, bought a plant in Loretto that he named Star Hill Farm and started to produce Maker's Mark Bourbon in 1953.

• The Tom Moore Distillery was reopened as the Barton Distillery after Prohibition. It was later taken over by Oscar Getz and is now owned by Barton Brands. Whiskeys made at this distillery include Very Old Barton, Ten High, Kentucky Gentleman, Colonel Lee, Tom Moore and Barclay's.

• A. Smith Bowman, a farmer in Virginia who had been in the whiskey business prior to Prohibition, started making Virginia Gentleman Bourbon in 1935.

• In 1935, a group of investors opened the Heaven Hill Distillery in Bardstown. The Shapira family, owners of this distillery, now produce Heaven Hill, Evan Williams, Elijah Craig, Henry McKenna, J.T.S. Brown and Mattingly & Moore bourbons as well as Pikesville Supreme Rye Whiskey.

• Also in 1935, the Austin Nichols company, previously concerned solely with the food business, took an interest in whiskey and other liquors. In 1942, they introduced Wild Turkey bourbon to the marketplace.

The New Deal

ON MAY 29, 1933, FRANKLIN ROOSEVELT DECLARED A NATIONAL EMERGENCY that had been brought about by a series of events that culminated in the stock market crash of 1929 and the massive unemployment that followed. In order to "put people to work," Roosevelt proposed a "New Deal" for the country. As part of this deal, Congress passed his National Industrial Recovery Bill that effectively suspended anti-trust laws and compelled industries to write their own fair trade codes. The idea, in general terms, was to make each industry share the available work among as many people as possible. Just over six months later, when Prohibition was repealed, the beer, wine and spirits industries had to devise codes of their own.

Owsley Brown (Brown-Forman), Frank Thompson (Glenmore) and a group of other concerned distillers met with attorneys from the Wholesale Liquor Dealers Association in Washington, D.C. Their aim was to unite the entire distilled-spirits industry, write a code of conduct that would be acceptable to all and convince everyone to sign it. The idea was that the distillers would show their willingness and ability to police themselves from within and prevent post-Prohibition bars from becoming the seedy, unregulated dives they had been prior to 1920. To a large extent, it worked.

In December of that year, the Distilled Spirits Institute (DSI) was formed in the New York offices of the Schenley Products Company. DSI went on to merge with the Licensed Beverage Industries (formed in 1946) and the Bourbon Institute (formed in 1958) to become the Distilled Spirits Council of the United States (DISCUS) in 1973.

> **It is estimated that the United States derives about $5 billion each year from taxes paid on the manufacture and sale of beverage alcohol.**

Also in December 1933, President Roosevelt formed the Federal Alcohol Control Administration (FACA), an agency charged with establishing codes to which any company in the beverage-alcohol business was legally compelled to adhere. Luckily for the distillers, the FACA was controlled by Joseph Choate, a man who had been against Prohibition from the outset and who said that he intended to use "as little external control as possible." The FACA became the Federal Alcohol Administration in 1935, and the following year, it issued updated classifications of all liquors. This agency eventually became part of the Bureau of Alcohol, Tobacco and Firearms.

America "Lightens Up"

ALTHOUGH MANY PRE-PROHIBITION BRANDS OF WHISKEY MADE THEIR way back to the shelves after Repeal, they weren't always identical to their older namesakes. One example was Schenley's Golden Wedding rye whiskey, a very popular brand before Prohibition. During the dry years, Seagram had used the same name in Canada, but American bootleggers sold an inferior whiskey that they called Golden Wedding, and thus the public was still very aware of the name. When wet days returned, Schenley, which was in the same boat as most other whiskey producers who did not have enough aged product on hand, decided to mix some of their good aged whiskey with some younger straight whiskeys and market it as Golden Wedding—the first "blend" of straight whiskeys on the market.

The upshot? Public confusion. Was this a blended whiskey? No; it didn't contain neutral spirits or added flavorings or colorings. And though Schenley tried to make that point very clear by printing on the label "It's ALL Whiskey . . . No Alcohol or Spirits Added," the result was the wrath of blended-whiskey producers who said that the words were a put-down of their products. Schenley changed the wording on the label to "Whiskey—A Blend—All Straight Whiskeys," but it was too late. The brand died.

> Another White House dweller who enjoyed a tot of red liquor was Harry Truman. He played poker (in his pajamas and an old robe) with journalists when he was campaigning around the country, had no airs or graces and enjoyed bourbon with ginger ale.

Many of the other straight whiskeys on the market at this time were merely young—they were bottled at 12 to 18 months and sold under familiar labels. Meanwhile, Seagram introduced its "Five Crown" and "Seven Crown" blended whiskeys to the American public, and they were an unmitigated success. We are willing to bet that if you had to choose between a one-year-old straight whiskey and a well-made blended whiskey, you, too, would pick the latter.

By the early 1940s, however, the distillers had managed to age sufficient quantities of straight whiskey to have an appreciable amount of good aged bourbon and rye back on the shelves. But 21 years had passed since Prohibition had taken such wonderful, big-bodied, rich, flavorful whiskeys away from the public. Tastes had changed, and blended whiskeys had become increasingly popular.

All was by no means lost, however. Nobody stopped making bourbon, rye or Tennessee whiskey simply because sales weren't as good as expected; they dealt with the

WHISKEY GOES TO WAR

situation as best they could. In some instances, distillers ventured into importing, exporting and distilling different products to diversify their lines. Meanwhile, across the Atlantic, the storm that would become World War II was brewing.

During the war, American distilleries were enlisted to produce industrial alcohol (beverage alcohol at 190° proof) for the war effort, and once again, the whiskey supplies began to dwindle. Even the whiskey bottles had to be made to new government standards that called for thinner glass and no unnecessary designs. Strangely enough, one of the major beneficiaries of World War II was the rum industry, the very enterprise that had fallen at the heels of the whiskey business some 150 years previous. Since rum was made nearby, in the Caribbean, and therefore was easy and relatively inexpensive to transport to the United States, it became the drink of choice of many Americans beleaguered by both the shortage of whiskey and a lack of money. By 1945, Americans were consuming about three times as much rum as they had in 1941. Wartime dance bands didn't just sing *Rum and Coca Cola*; they drank it too.

Whiskey was rationed during the war, and some brands were discontinued. Some distilleries installed newer versions of the continuous still so they could produce industrial alcohol, and others simply sent their low-proof alcohol to distilleries that could redistill it until it was strong enough for the war effort. The government did allow a couple of "distillation holidays" toward the end of the war, but it would be the late 1940s to early 1950s before most distilleries were once again up and running full force with a decent supply of aged whiskey on hand.

It's interesting to note just how much the whiskey business helped the war effort at this time. Indeed, had Prohibition not come to an end, the government would have had enormous difficulties fulfilling the need for industrial alcohol. And according to various industry documents of the time, it was used in a variety of astounding ways:

• In the manufacture of rubber, antifreeze, tetraethyllead (used in the production of aviation gasoline), rayon for parachutes and ether, among other things.

• 23 gallons of industrial alcohol were required in the manufacture of a Jeep.

• 19¾ gallons were needed to produce one 16-inch naval shell.

• 1 gallon was needed in order to make 64 hand grenades or two 155mm Howitzer shells.

A by-product of making any form of beverage alcohol from grain is the leftover mash, which is dried and used as feed for farm animals. Here again, the whiskey business contributed to the war effort by keeping cattle and pigs well fed when food for the general populace was at a premium. Indeed, for every 1,000 bushels of corn used to make alcohol, the leftover mash could feed 30 head of cattle and 15 pigs for 112 days, thus producing 1,000 pounds of beef and 240 pounds of pork.

So although the public was protected and fed, in part, by the whiskey producers of America, they just didn't have enough decent whiskey to drink. And don't think they didn't complain. An editorial in *The New York World Telegram* in 1944 stated, "Public and official alarm over the shortage of liquor is pathetic in a people who are supposed to be adult."

It's clear that the whiskey business had its problems. The swingers of the twenties preferred gin to whiskey; post-Prohibition whiskey drinkers got used to blended whiskeys; and then the demon rum reared its head during World War II. Demand was diminished—and things didn't change a great deal until some learned spirits aficionados decided that whiskey wasn't getting enough attention and started to shed some light on the intricacies of single malt Scotch in the 1980s. The timing was brilliant. America had just come through two decades of decadence and was primed to get serious about over-consumption and take a hard look at what it was drinking.

Whiskey at the Close of the Twentieth Century

IN THE 1960S AND 1970S, AMERICANS REVELED IN ALL OF THE GLORIES OF the barroom; cocktails were served in myriad pastel hues and in copious quantities. The country drank and drank. Suddenly, though, Betty Ford, Ringo Starr and Liz Taylor came clean and publicly said goodbye to John Barleycorn, and a new interest in sobriety was born. When groups such as Mothers Against Drunk Driving (MADD) sprang up, the whole country started talking, once more, about the evils of drink. Happily, the atmosphere was nowhere near as oppressive as it had been for our forefathers at the beginning of this century. These groups took aim at irresponsible drinking. They were out to prevent accidents and to help those with a drinking problem take better care of themselves.

But this new batch of concerned citizens not only did what they set out to do (for which they deserve much accolade); they also paved the path for a return to the bold, rich flavors of straight American whiskey.

Sometime during the mid-1980s, people who were wont to throw $20 on the bar and stay there until it was gone were no longer able to spend it on four or five screwdrivers or seven or eight beers. It wasn't socially acceptable, it wasn't good for the body, and it was no longer a laughing matter. But these people still had the same amount of money to spend. How did they spend it? They spent it on the "good stuff." Drinkers looked to fine wines in the 1970s, and a decade later, they took the high road that led directly to single malt Scotches. And these were not the bygone days when men were the sole decision makers; by this time, women, too, had buying power—and they were discriminating consumers. The most avid of these budding aficionadas and aficionados worked at learning about their drinks. Some sat alone

> In a 1991 interview, Phil Donahue asked Katharine Hepburn about Spencer Tracy's drinking habits. Ms. Hepburn's reply was typically sage: "I have known several men who drank too much—and they were all extremely interesting."

at the bar taking notes on the malt they were sampling; others assembled in groups, experienced a few different drams and discussed and compared each one's particular intricacies. And so it was that whiskey, albeit Scotch whisky, was once again given the attention it deserved. The American whiskey distillers took note.

Suddenly, liquor store shelves were filled with new bottlings of old brands of fine American whiskey and old-looking bottlings of new brands, and new terms were being bandied about. Finally, "small-batch whiskey," "single-barrel whiskey" and "wheated bourbon" were getting their fair share of attention. Once again, people were demanding straight rye whiskey—not the blended product that had been poured as "rye" at many a bar since as far back as the 1950s.

Some distillers were resting comfortably, knowing that they had been producing fine heavy-bodied whiskeys all along, while others who had "lightened" their products in an attempt to compete with gin, vodka and rum were now, thankfully, rethinking their position. We will not be surprised to see one or two pot-still American whiskeys on the market within the next five years or so.

As consumers, we are lucky that so many good straight American whiskeys are still left in the marketplace. The whiskeys—and the people who make them—deserve a place in our hearts. We raise a glass to the pioneers and heroes of the American whiskey industry: Jacob Beam, I.W. Bernheim, Colonel Blanton, Wattie Boone, A. Smith Bowman, George Garvin Brown, the Chapeze brothers, James Crow, Jack Daniel, J.W. Dant, George Dickel, Basil Hayden, Paul Jones, Henry McKenna, Tom Moore, Elijah Pepper, T.B. Ripy, Robert Samuels, the Shapira brothers, E.H. Taylor, Pappy Van Winkle, W.L. Weller and Evan Williams.

CHAPTER TWO

HOW TO
TASTE
WHISKEY

T HE FIRST RULE OF WHISKEY TASTING IS: IT'S YOUR OPINION that counts—if you like it, it must be good. The second rule of whiskey tasting is: Whiskey is not wine, and therefore, it should not be judged in the same way or by the same standards. Eighty-proof whiskey is more than three times higher in alcohol by volume than most wines. Whiskeys are also drunk in much smaller proportions; six ounces of wine is a reasonable serving, but six ounces of whiskey is in no way normal. Because wines are more dilute than whiskeys, their flavors are generally softer; whiskeys, with their higher concentration of alcohol, have sharp points that needle the palate, pepper the nose and warm the throat with much more ferocity than wine. Put simply, forget most of what you have learned about tasting wine—a whiskey-tasting experience is different.

The third rule of whiskey tasting is: Never taste just one. Start off with a minimum of three bottlings; by assembling at least three, you create a broader basis for comparison. The aim is not necessarily to determine which is the "best" bottling; the goal is to learn about the whiskey so that you'll have a better idea of how best to use it.

Tasting is different from drinking. In tasting, the intention is to concentrate on both the whole and its parts. The parts might include subtle nuances, usually referred to as "notes," and some tasters simply won't experience them. Much of tasting is dependent on sense memories—especially the sense of smell—and everyone's experiences and sensory organs are different. So though it's worth trying to identify specific flavors and aromas when tasting whiskeys, don't be chagrined if your experience is different from someone else's. If you don't taste a particular flavor, say, the chamomile or orange zest or basil that someone else records, that's okay. Indeed, many of us can profit most by trying to detect exactly how the whiskey makes us *feel*. What does it bring to mind? A scent? A place you've been? An experience from your childhood? Sometimes, you'll get a faint whiff of the attic at Grandma's house or that blend of tea you sipped at a Japanese restaurant. At times, whole experiences from the past will come rushing through your brain, and from time to time, the images will be mixed—you'll remember the leather jacket you bought when you were sixteen, your Latin teacher's meerschaum pipe and the peppermints that a favorite aunt always had on her breath.

How to Taste American Whiskey

TASTE YOUR WHISKEY NEAT—NO ICE, NO WATER, NOTHING. YOU CAN ALWAYS add a drop of water if the spirit is intrusively strong—many tasters insist on adding water—but we believe that, in the case of these American products, the aroma of room-temperature whiskey and the flavors on your tongue will be truest when taken neat. Adding ice to American whiskey when the aim is to determine its intricacies is self-defeating—coldness numbs the palate and disguises some of the nuances of any food or beverage. Yet it's worth taking the "ice factor" into consideration when evaluating these spirits—their flavors can be quite intense at room temperature—and many are "designed" to suit the American predilection for ice and mixed drinks.

Hosting a whiskey tasting can be a fun and enlightening way to while away a couple of hours with a few good friends. The session can occur after dinner, but tasting on a full stomach doesn't produce precise results. It is far better to arrange a complete evening of tasting that leads into a small get-together or hold the tasting before presenting the food or snacks.

It pays to have certain aspects in place before you begin:

• If possible, set up the tasting at a large table. Choose a white table covering, or use white place mats at each seat. (A white table covering is ideal, since it allows the best background for viewing the color of the whiskey.)

• If there are any aromatic flowers, plants or candles nearby, remove them from the area until after the tasting.

• Set out a glass of chilled, but not iced, water for each taster. This will be used to

A Tasting Vocabulary

SKEPTICS THINK THE WORDS THAT TASTERS USE TO DESCRIBE foods and beverages are absurd. They almost always object to such descriptions as "the florid rush of overripe wild strawberries," and if they've never experienced those conditions, who can say they're wrong? Palates differ tremendously, and so do people's abilities to describe feelings and flavors. However, some of the fancier words used in tasting descriptions are founded in reality and shouldn't be discounted simply because they sound a bit over the top. A bourbon can be woody (it ages in a wooden barrel), smoky or sooty (the barrel is charred), feature oaky flavors (from the charred barrels and the oak they're made from) or be grain-y (whiskey is made from grain, after all). Rhododendron might be difficult to track, and the scent of lilies of the valley during a spring thunderstorm might not apply to all tasters' sense memories, but for some people, at least, it's real.

The following words are commonly used to describe flavors and aromas that can be found in bourbons and other American whiskeys. Read them over to get a feel for what you are looking for, and then ignore them completely. You're the taster, and you're right.

banana	honey	perfume-y
blackcurrant	leather	plum
burnt sugar	lemon	sharp
caramel	maple syrup	smoky
cereal-y	mint	smoldering wood
cherry	must	sooty
cinnamon	new-mown grass	tar
clover	new-mown hay	tobacco
earth	nutmeg	vanilla
grain-y	oak	violet
grassy	orange	walnut
hazelnut	peach	woody

Over the years with Old Overholt

Just as the whiskey distilled by Abraham Overholt was pronounced *different* by his friends and neighbors in Broad Ford, Pennsylvania around 1810 —so do those who prefer a good, honest, straight rye whiskey today find Old Overholt *different*—and for the same reason. Its inviting amber color—its robust flavor of the grain—still add up to "the good taste that always stands out." And it is still being made on the site of that little log cabin distillery on the Youghiogheny.

This whiskey is 5 years old

Many a pioneer neighbor said,"I don't know why—but Abe Overholt's whiskey is <u>different</u>."

Its good taste always stands out

Straight Rye Whiskey — Bottled in Bond — 100 Proof
NATIONAL DISTILLERS PRODUCTS CORPORATION, NEW YORK

rinse the mouth between whiskeys. If some tasters will be spitting instead of swallowing, make sure that each of them has an opaque container as a spittoon.

• Set out one or more baskets of bite-size pieces of crusty white bread or plain crackers, such as water biscuits or matzoh. Good plain bread, however, tends to do a better job of cleansing the palate and is generally more enjoyable than a dry cracker.

• Set out one glass per person for each whiskey that will be tasted; arrange them in a pattern that will help the tasters keep track of which is which. Ideally, the glasses should be glass; plastic or paper will bring their own flavors and aromas to the tasting. But don't think the glasses have to match. If you have a choice, go with any glass that is relatively narrow at the rim—a brandy snifter is fine, many white wine glasses are good, the sherry glasses called *copitas* are perfect. Make sure that the glasses are clean and free of any soap residue.

• Plan to include at least three but no more than six different whiskeys in your tasting. More than six becomes just too much for a single tasting session. Don't pour the whiskeys ahead of time unless you have the means to cover each glass to prevent its aromas from dissipating. It's preferable to pour them immediately before tasting them.

• Set out a few bottles of uncarbonated bottled water; a brand with as little flavor as possible is best. These may be used for diluting the whiskey after an initial taste; many of the higher-proof whiskeys could be too strong without some dilution.

• Provide the tasters with paper and pens for scribbling their notes. You might want to run off a simple version of a tasting sheet. It can include a list of some of the various aspects—aroma, body, finish—that might be considered, or it could offer a list of words to trigger descriptions. Don't overdo it—blank paper is fine. The idea is to make it possible for tasters to record their impressions at the time of tasting. The last thing you want to do is intimidate.

Choosing Which Whiskeys to Taste

CHOOSING AN INTERESTING MIX OF WHISKEYS FOR THE TASTING IS IMPORTANT, and many possible themes can be followed. You might want to have a "battle of the brands," in which each guest brings a personal favorite bottling and you declare a "winner" at the end of the evening. However, although that type of tasting can be fun, it will rarely be very productive. "Blind tastings," in which the whiskeys are poured from decanters or identical unlabeled bottles, can be fun and very interesting. No one (or at most just one person) knows what product is being poured, so the tasters have nothing to go on but the liquid in the glass. Be warned; some tasters don't enjoy the "helplessness" they feel at the lack of all information. Others welcome the chance to taste without any prejudice at all. And it's worth stressing that what you taste today probably should be tasted next week or next month. As human beings, we bring the baggage of our lives and habits to our tastings, and sometimes what we do or don't discern is merely a matter of mood or sleepiness or a lack of concentration. The whiskey you disliked last week could please you no end this week.

Here are some suggestions for the types of American whiskeys you could group together for an informal tasting:

• A selection of three wheated bourbons and three bourbons made with rye as a small grain, say, Maker's Mark, Old Fitzgerald and Van Winkle wheated bourbons together with Old Grand-Dad, Evan Williams and Old Forester.

• A simple tasting of one bottle each of bourbon, straight rye and Tennessee whiskey. Choose from any bottlings; the differences in style will be apparent.

• A selection of different brand-name whiskeys that are marketed as collections or that emanate from the same distillery. You could select the four small-batch whiskeys from the Jim Beam Brands Company along with a couple of its regular bottlings; the five whiskeys put together as The Bourbon Heritage Collection by United Distillers; a selection from The Wild Turkey Distillery, Heaven Hill or Barton; or maybe a group of the four single-barrel bourbons that are produced at the Ancient Age Distillery.

It is not generally recommended that you taste different bottlings of the same brand-name whiskey that differ only in proof; the difference between 80 and 100 proof at the same age usually is negligible. But it can be interesting to taste the same whiskey at different ages—to see how much flavor it develops during a few extra years "in the wood." The final selection is your choice; you could even decide to taste American whiskeys alongside some Irish whiskeys or Scotch. Just remember that a tasting is not necessarily a competition among the whiskeys—it is a method of becoming familiar with the various styles available to you.

Determine the order of the whiskeys you will taste. Generally, it's best to start with the ones that are bottled at lower proofs (80°) and leave the higher proofs, which are usually bigger in the mouth, until later.

Conducting a Tasting

BEFORE YOU START, LAY OUT THE GROUND RULES FOR YOUR TASTING. Sometimes, it's most interesting to go through all the samples without discussing them until afterward. Most often, however, you'll want to discuss them as they are tasted. Warn people not to drain their glasses; it's best to leave some there for comparisons later on. Be sure to stress that a tasting is not a competition in any way. There is no winner, no prize for the person who can list the most flavors. The tasting is an opportunity to experience some different whiskeys side by side to find out which particular bottlings best suit each person's individual taste buds and preferences. The second half of that aim is to enjoy doing it. Warn the tasters to maintain the order of their glasses so they can go back to, say, #2 after they've tasted #4 if they want to.

• Pour about ½ ounce of whiskey into the first glass.

• Note the whiskey's color. When you observe the deep, coppery tones of some lush, heavy-bodied straight whiskeys, you are peeking at their souls. What you see is often what you literally will taste.

• Nose the whiskey: Without swirling the liquid, stick your nose as far into the glass as possible and inhale deeply. What did you smell? Did you "taste" anything? When nosing liquor, most people tend to swirl it around the glass—just like wine—before they lean their nose into it to detect the aromas. But swirling liquor can release too much alcohol to give you a full picture of the whiskey. Initially, just hold the glass steady and allow the aromas to float up to your nose; open your mouth just a touch and breathe gently through your nose and mouth at the same time. You will set up a circulation of aromas that buzz through your entire head, and this way, you get a *feel* for the whiskey at the same time as you search for aromas and bouquet. Many tasters like to nose whiskey twice: Once with the nose in the glass and a second time with the nose held just above the rim of the glass. The first set of scents is the aroma, the second the bouquet. Don't forget to keep notes of your impressions.

GLASSES FOR TASTING

IF YOU INVEST IN *copita* (SHERRY) glasses for tasting purposes, you'll never regret it. All of the pros use them because the shape is just right for cupping the bowl in the palm of the hand to bring the whiskey to body temperature, and the gradual inward slope of the glass that widens into a nose-size rim keeps the aromas buzzing around in the glass waiting for you to inhale them.

• Taste the whiskey: Take a sip that's enough to partially fill (but not overfill) your mouth. If you like, part your lips slightly and draw in some air over the whiskey. Hold it there for a moment, swish it back and forth, and let it flow around your whole mouth, bathing your tongue and swirling over your gums. How does the whiskey feel in your mouth? Is it velvety smooth, or is it a little rough around the edges? Does it seem to fill your entire mouth (big body), or is it just tracing lines around your cheeks and tongue (light body)? The body of a whiskey can also be referred to as the "mouthfeel," a term commonly used by tasters. Is it thin? Thick? Neither thick nor thin? Is it hot and stingy or mellow and smooth or an odd combination of both? Does its taste go along with the way it smelled? Swallow the whiskey, and pay attention to how that feels and tastes—all the impressions that come from the experience. This is the part of tasting referred to as the "finish." How long does the flavor stay with you? Does it warm your stomach? What else happens? Do whole new flavors crop up? Anything is possible. Keep taking notes—don't rely on your memory.

In 1969, President Richard Nixon gave Soviet Premier Nikita Khrushchev a glass of I.W. Harper bourbon. "This is very good whiskey," said Khrushchev, "but you Americans spoil it. You put more ice in there than whiskey."

• Taste the whiskey a second time, if desired. If the proof is high, diluting it slightly can release flavors that weren't there for the first go-round.

• Discuss the results with your fellow tasters.

• Move on to the next whiskey.

• After everyone has tasted each whiskey and jotted down his or her findings, go back through the bottlings, one by one. Compare all the impressions, and after listening to everyone else's opinions, taste the whiskeys again to see whether or not you can detect any flavors or aromas that previously evaded your palate. This is the most educational part of a tasting, and you shouldn't be shy about adding someone else's findings to your own notes just so long as you agree with them. You will find that often someone else's description can trigger something that you couldn't name. Indeed, sometimes you'll learn a new flavor from someone else's description.

In Conclusion

AS YOU READ THROUGH THE TASTING NOTES FOR THE VARIOUS WHISKEYS in the next chapter, there are certain aspects of tasting—and of American whiskeys as a whole—that bear keeping in mind: If you find that reading about individual flavors—chamomile, leather, etc.—is nothing more than confusing, go straight to our "Overall" section, which includes suggestions for the best way to use or serve each bottling. Though some whiskeys are prime for savoring in a snifter and some make marvelous Manhattans, still others are perfect to drink on ice, with a splash of water or club soda or even a heavy dose of ginger ale.

Some of us drive Cadillacs, while others swear by Hondas. The lucky ones among us drive the Honda to work and bring out the Cadillac only on the weekend. And so it is with whiskey—some of the whiskeys discussed here are very inexpensive—produced and marketed toward people who enjoy mixed drinks—while others bear a hefty price tag and should be reserved for special occasions. It is futile to compare these whiskeys to each other for quality. They are birds of a different feather.

JACK DANIEL

CHAPTER THREE

BRANDS & BOTTLINGS

AN A TO Z GUIDE
TO AMERICAN
WHISKEYS

PEER INTO A GLASS OF BOURBON, AND LET IT SING TO YOU. We think most good bourbons sound like Tom Waits; their harsh-sounding voices belie their caring hearts and deep, deep souls. At certain times, you can actually hear a few Sinatra-like notes from a glass of bourbon, and occasionally, you just might catch the strains of both Joplins (Scott and Janis) or feel the rich, reverberating voice of Casals' cello playing a Beethoven sonata. Oh, yes, bourbon can sing alright. And it's worthy of any time you care to spend in discovering its harmony.

Whether your style is modern, Baroque or somewhere in between, choosing a favorite whiskey is a very subjective, very personal adventure. Some of us like whiskey to be smooth and round, some want a broncobustin' bourbon with a capital *B*, some of us will never drink it straight, and others will have it no other way. Some of us are drawn to the aesthetics of the bottle or label or presentation, others seek a "generic" look, refusing to be influenced by fancy marketing, while still others require a highly esteemed "status" name. Sometimes price makes the big difference, and some people are convinced there's a genetic component: "I drink what Mom and Dad drank."

If you're a one-brand whiskey drinker with no interest in anything else on the market, you are missing out on some wonderful bottlings. And if the history of your particular brand of choice is the only one that holds any interest for you, you won't learn about some of the illustrious characters who helped forge the industry. But if you want adventure, if you want to risk falling in love with Pappy Van Winkle, misting up at the thought of James Crow reciting the poems of his native Scotland's Baird Burns, or giggling over financier Andrew Mellon's "public perception" problems when he mixed being in the whiskey business with being Secretary of the Treasury, read on. If you look at the tasting notes for the 10-year-old Eagle Rare Bourbon, you may find yourself a new whiskey to savor after dinner. If you are a staunch drinker of Jack Daniel's and never look at another label, read this chapter and meet his erudite cousin Gentleman Jack. And if you think that single-barrel and small-batch bourbons are mere marketing ploys, this chapter might just open your eyes—you have been missing out on some very special whiskeys.

Indeed, whether your interests lie in Americana or you're simply looking for a guide to what to try, chances are good that you'll find a couple of lively yarns and at least one new brand from the over 100 American whiskeys included here.

Confronting Whiskey Confusion

NEARLY EVERY AMERICAN WHISKEY CAME FROM HUMBLE ORIGINS, AND THE majority of them have had to struggle to survive. Most of the brand names have changed hands over and over again; sometimes the original recipes and techniques have been preserved, but not always as the same brand. If automobiles worked the way whiskey works, Cadillac might well have produced the Edsel and the Pontiac Grand Prix might have been retired in the 1960s—by Rambler. For the most part, the whiskey industry was completely revamped after Prohibition, and even since then, many brands have been bought and sold several times.

Many whiskey families, however, have preserved the integrity of American whiskey as a whole. And although some brand names have changed ownership through the years, traditions have been passed down from father to son, from distiller to distiller and sometimes from one distillery to a different one. A few of these families—the ones who make Maker's Mark, Old Forester and Jim Beam, for example—have gone and still go to great lengths to maintain those early traditions. Consider W.L. Weller Bourbon: it is made in the exact same style that Pappy Van Winkle preferred when he took over the brand name during Prohibition. Wild Turkey has been with us only since the 1940s, but the master distiller at the plant worked with a member of the Ripy family, whose father had helped establish the Ripy way of making whiskey 40 years before.

Some whiskeys have very sparse histories because they are relatively new on the shelves or have names that were simply conjured up by marketing departments. Other whiskeys, mostly those introduced since Repeal, bear the names of illustrious historical whiskey-makers but don't accurately represent their methods or products.

The fact that so many whiskeys have been bought and sold over the years is, in part, what makes them so very American. Don't despair that you can't taste the same whiskey that Ulysses S. Grant drank after the Civil War ended; few spirits of any kind that are available today are made in precisely the same way they started out. Single malt Scotch, for example, hasn't been aged in bourbon casks for very long; its style has changed along with time and market preferences.

A few of the brands and bottlings that follow do not list a site for their distillery or production. These brands are sold by companies designated as "producers," "merchants," "marketers," "rectifiers and bottlers" or whatever title they prefer; they are concerns that buy whiskey, aged or unaged, in bulk from a dis-

PAPPY VAN WINKLE

tillery and then keep the name of the distillery secret. Indeed, sometimes the company name suggests that they are distillers, but unless we list them under the heading of "Distillery," they do not actually make the whiskey themselves.

Historically, "rectifying" referred merely to the filtration of whiskey, but eventually, the term became tied to the production of blended whiskey. Times have changed; now, rectifiers also deal in straight whiskey that they purchase from distillers and bottle under their own label. Here's an example: A company enters into a contract with a distillery and orders a certain amount of a particular whiskey. The contract can specify production details—what recipe is used, length of aging, barrel proof—or not; those decisions are for the seller and the buyer to decide. Bear in mind that only 12 operating distilleries produce straight American whiskey and that most all of them do a superlative job. Therefore, these products are being made by masters of the craft.

In most cases, the whiskey is aged by its distiller for at least four years. At that point, it is shipped to the purchasing company, which then rectifies and bottles it. Bottling is fairly self-explanatory; the whiskey is put into bottles bearing the company's own label—but rectifying can be somewhat confusing. Rectifying straight whiskey, in liquor-industry terms, can mean anything from filtering to chill-filtering to mingling together various barrels of straight whiskeys to bringing the whiskey down to a certain proof by the addition of demineralized water. The distillers themselves utilize all of these processes to produce their own brands of straight whiskeys. Each rectifier has his or her own procedure.

Many inexpensive bourbons are marketed by rectifiers and bottlers, mostly in small quantities under all sorts of different names. They fill the need for "well" whiskey, the less expensive brand that a bartender pours when the customer doesn't specify a name brand. However, although most are fairly insignificant and not of the same high standards that the more well-known brands demand, there are exceptions—don't discount any whiskey until you've tried it. Indeed, some of these bottlings are noteworthy and of historical importance, produced or marketed by companies such as the David Sherman Company of St. Louis, Missouri (Ezra Brooks and Yellowstone); Van Winkle and Son of Louisville, Kentucky (Old Rip Van Winkle) and Cork n Bottle of Covington, Kentucky (A.H. Hirsch). Several of these whiskeys are included here, though not all of them; there are too many brand names and their distribution often is limited.

In one case, confusion is caused because a single distillery goes under three different names. The Ancient Age Distillery in Frankfort, Kentucky, is often referred to and is also known as the Blanton Distillery or the Leestown Distillery.

When the name on the label of any bottling is consistent with the names of the other bottlings from that distillery, all of those whiskeys are reviewed in the same section. For example, all three bottlings of George Dickel's whiskey are reviewed under the George Dickel heading. If, however, the name on the label differs from the other whiskeys from the same distillery, that whiskey is reviewed under its own name; for example, Gentleman Jack Rare Tennessee Whiskey is reviewed separately from the Jack Daniel's bottlings.

About the Ratings

WHEN TWO OR MORE BOTTLINGS OF THE SAME BRAND DIFFER ONLY IN proof and are similar to each other in style, we have combined their tasting notes to reflect their qualities as a group. However, if the whiskeys differ greatly in style or if there is an age difference in the bottlings, they are reviewed separately.

Bottlings that do not bear an age statement are a minimum of four years old; we have noted the bottling's age only when an age statement appears.

The Specialty Listings

Some whiskeys fall into special categories or designations:

SMALL-BATCH BOURBONS

Baker's
Booker's
Basil Hayden's
Knob Creek
Wild Turkey Rare Breed

SINGLE-BARREL BOURBONS

Benchmark XO *(for export only)*
Blanton's
Elmer T. Lee
Evan Williams Single Barrel
  Vintage
Four Roses Single Barrel Reserve
  (for export only)
Hancock's Reserve
Rock Hill Farms
Wild Turkey Kentucky Spirit

WHEATED BOURBONS

These bottlings use wheat rather than rye in their mashbills:
Kentucky Tavern
Maker's Mark
Old Fitzgerald
Rebel Yell
Van Winkle
W.L. Weller

VINTAGE BOURBONS

Evan Williams Single Barrel
  Vintage

POT-STILLED BOURBON

A.H. Hirsch

THE BOURBON HERITAGE COLLECTION

United Distillers put these five bottlings together in 1994 so that whiskey lovers could taste superlative samples of an assortment of American whiskeys with differing styles. The collection contains:
George Dickel Special Barrel
  Reserve Tennessee Whisky
W.L. Weller Centennial
  (wheated)
I.W. Harper Gold Medal
Very Special Old Fitzgerald
  (wheated)
Old Charter Proprietor's Reserve

UNFILTERED BOURBON

Booker's

KOSHER BOURBON

Old Williamsburg

STRAIGHT RYE WHISKEYS

Jim Beam Rye
Old Overholt
Pikesville
Wild Turkey Rye

TENNESSEE WHISKEYS

Jack Daniel's
George Dickel
Gentleman Jack

We have chosen not to give "points" to the whiskeys included here for the following reason: Many of the whiskeys are low-priced "around the house" bottlings, and comparing them with bottles that cost, in some cases, five times as much is unfair. Each whiskey is produced for a particular section of the market, and since many brands in different price ranges do not pit themselves against each other, neither have we.

If you desire an "instant reading" for a particular bottling, check the "Overall" category in the tasting notes. There, in a few short sentences, we make our recommendations for using the whiskey. "Around the house" whiskeys are usually fine for everyday consumption; certain bottlings with style and fairly complex palates are pointed out as being good for Manhattans (a complex drink in and of itself), and others are rated as being "suitable for a snifter," denoting that these whiskeys are truly worth savoring for their own intricacies.

Ancient Age Bourbon

DISTILLERY
The Ancient Age Distillery, Frankfort, Kentucky

ABOUT THE BRAND
Ancient Age is available in a variety of bottlings, two of which, the 90° proof and the 10-year-old, are known as Ancient Ancient Age. The 90°-proof bottling also bears a "10 Star" medallion, an in-house rating of high quality. This whiskey also comes with a slogan, although it isn't present on all of the various bottlings: "The Whiskey with Age in its Flavor."

HISTORY
Although Ancient Age didn't hit the market until after Prohibition, and although it was first released as a "bourbon-style" whiskey, it is now a straight bourbon. Its origins go right back to 1849 when Benjamin Harrison Blanton—probably the son of quarry owner Harrison Blanton, the man who provided the stone to build Kentucky's capitol building in Frankfort in 1830—struck a vein and made himself a small fortune in the California Gold Rush.

Benjamin Blanton used his newfound money to buy up most of the business area of downtown Denver, Colorado. A native Kentuckian with strong leanings toward the South, he exchanged these holdings for Confederate Bonds and was commissioned as major in the Confederate Army. After the war, Blanton settled at Rock Hill Farm in Leestown, Kentucky. Soon, he started to make a little whiskey on his property, and the small operation went well. So well, in fact, that four years later, in 1869, the O.F.C. (Old

Fire Copper) Distillery was built on Blanton's land, and business began in earnest. The term Old Fire Copper, by the by, was used in the late 1800s to describe a "sweet-mash" whiskey, as opposed to "sour mash."

In time, Edmund Haynes Taylor Jr., one of the best-known men in nineteenth-century distilling circles and a major force behind the Bottled-in-Bond Act of 1897, entered the picture along with George T. Stagg. They modernized the O.F.C. Distillery in 1873. Details of the next few years are sketchy, but it is known that Taylor owned the plant when it burned down in 1882 and that Stagg bought it (presumably rebuilt) in 1885 and retained Taylor as the plant manager and distiller.

Eventually, the Blanton family returned to the scene. Albert B. Blanton, son of Benjamin Blanton, started work at the distillery as a clerk in 1897, when he was about 16 years old. It was the beginning of a lifelong passion. Three years later, in 1900, the distillery became known as the George T. Stagg Distillery, and in 1912, Blanton was promoted to plant manager.

Although distillation was halted at the Stagg plant during Prohibition, the bottling house continued to operate, bottling whiskey for legal "medicinal" use. During this period in America's whiskey-making history, Blanton was made president of the distillery, but near the end of Prohibition, it was sold to the Schenley Distillers Corporation. There were no fools at Schenley, and the man who put that company on the map, Lewis Rosenstiel, retained the knowledgeable Blanton as manager and distiller. Rosenstiel had been in the spirits business prior to the Noble Experiment and spent the dry years as a whiskey broker, buying whiskey for medicinal use and selling it, along with his own whiskey, through the Schenley Products Company.

The brands of whiskey owned by the Stagg distillery at this time included Old Fire Copper, George T. Stagg and Cream of Kentucky. Ancient Age, a whiskey introduced to the market in 1936, was originally made from "bourbon-style" whiskey produced in Canada, probably because the Stagg distillery needed time to produce and age its own products after Prohibition ended. It wasn't until after World War II that true bourbon made at this distillery was marketed as Ancient Age.

Between 1930 and 1940, the Stagg distillery was modernized and expanded to its present size under the guidance of Colonel Blanton (so called due to his induction into The Honorable Order of Kentucky Colonels, a civic society founded in 1932) and Orville Schupp, an engineer at the plant. It was Schupp who replaced Blanton when he retired in 1953, the year that Schenley, in honor of the Colonel, renamed the distillery The Albert B. Blanton Distillery.

Colonel Blanton died in 1959, one of the few men in the industry to work through Prohibition and carry his nineteenth-century training and knowledge into modern times. Elmer T. Lee, present-day Master Distiller Emeritus at Ancient Age, had the privilege of working with the Colonel for three years before Blanton retired, so we could

COLONEL ALBERT BACON BLANTON

say that he, too, holds some of Blanton's old-time methods of making whiskey.

The Blanton distillery became the Ancient Age Distillery in 1969 and, in 1982, the Ancient Age Distilling Company. That company was purchased in 1992 by Takara Shuzo, a Japanese company, but the physical distillery, along with its physical assets, is owned and operated by the Sazerac Company of New Orleans under the name of the Leestown Company. Takara Shuzo distributes the brand in Japan. Two of Sazerac's brands—Eagle Rare Bourbon and Benchmark Bourbon—are now produced at the distillery.

One last claim to fame for the Ancient Age Distillery deserves mention as a historical event: In 1984, Blanton's, the first-ever "single-barrel bourbon," was introduced to the market. Others—Rock Hill Farms, Elmer T. Lee, Hancock's Reserve and Benchmark XO—would follow.

TASTING NOTES
Ancient Age, 80°
Ancient Ancient Age, 90°
Ancient Age, Bottled in Bond, 100°

Nose: Vanilla, oaky, hints of honey that are stronger in the 100°-proof bottling than the other two.

Mouth: Slim to medium bodies, rather softer on the 100° but sharp and tangy on the other two. Dry, tobacco, spicy, light, fragrant, some honey and, in the 100°, hints of grass. The finish is short, crisp and dry.

Overall: Perfect over plenty of ice on a hot summer day when you are looking for a refreshing sharp whiskey to make you come alive. Since there is no age statement on any of these bottlings, we expected them to be around four years old. There's a chance, however, that the 100° bottling has spent longer in the wood than the other two.

Ancient Ancient Age, 10 years old, 86°

Nose: Caramel, vanilla, oranges, clover.

Mouth: A medium, silky body gives way to soft fruits—oranges sitting in the midday sun—candy apples, vanilla and a faint hint of tobacco. The finish is medium-long, leaving hints of vanilla.

Overall: Ancient Age really comes into its own at 10 years old. It has developed into a bourbon worthy of a fine cigar, but we still prefer it over ice to drinking it from a snifter. If you enjoy a sprightly whiskey, this is one with sophistication.

Baker's Bourbon

DISTILLERY
The Jim Beam Distilleries, Clermont and Boston, Kentucky

ABOUT THE BRAND
This small-batch bourbon, released in 1992 and named for retired Master Distiller Baker Beam, wears a tan and beige label and bears this statement from Baker: "My Bourbon follows our Beam family tradition of putting our best secrets inside the bottle, not here on the label. I've distilled six generations of Bourbon skill into this bottle. That's a lot of good secrets. Please savor its smooth flavor over ice, with a splash of water, or however you take your bourbon." For a complete history of the Beam family, see **Jim Beam Bourbon**, page 110.

TASTING NOTES
Baker's Bourbon, 7 years old, 107°
Nose: Very fruity, yet light—overripe oranges, peaches and maybe a hint of plums with a strong dash of vanilla.

Mouth: Medium body, rather soft, with vanilla, almonds, tobacco and maybe a touch of mint. There's a spiciness here that lingers on the lips. The finish is medium-long, rather dry and velvety smooth.

Overall: Baker's is a good "apéritif" bourbon—try chilling it and serving it neat alongside some farmhouse cheeses. It's also ideal for drinking on ice—add water or club soda if you wish—and Baker's Bourbon makes a wonderful, stylish Manhattan. We recommend, however, that you shy away from adding flavored mixers to this bottling. Why mask the flavor?

Barclay's Bourbon

DISTILLERY
The Barton Distillery, Bardstown, Kentucky

ABOUT THE BRAND
No one at the Barton Distillery knows where this brand name came from or even where the name Barton came from, for that matter. But that's part of the charm of this plant; it's there simply to make bourbon. "Barclay's is a brand name that we bought some years ago," said a spokesperson for the distillery. The Barclay's label bears a crest

proclaiming "Quality, Character, Value" on scrolls that lie atop a couple of horses that hold a shield inscribed with a letter *B*.

TASTING NOTES
Barclay's Bourbon, 80°

Nose: Sweet oakiness, a heavy shot of vanilla and a light hint of fruit (pears?).

Mouth: A light body, rather spicy and with a certain "macho" quality. The finish is medium.

Overall: A good "around the house" bourbon. Drink it on ice, with a splash of water or club soda if you desire, or in highballs and mixed drinks.

Very Old Barton Bourbon

DISTILLERY
The Barton Distillery, Bardstown, Kentucky

ABOUT THE BRAND
Three out of the four bottlings of Very Old Barton are aged for six years—two years longer than most bourbons on the market. The bottled-in-bond bottling (denoting 100° proof and a minimum of four years in the wood) has a gold and white label rather than the sophisticated gold and black labels on the others. All four bear a crest held by two stately lions. Whoever Barton was—and no one at the company is quite sure—we are sure that he or she would approve of the way in which the bourbon is presented. For a complete history of this distillery, see **Tom Moore Bourbon**, page 159.

TASTING NOTES
Very Old Barton, Bottled in Bond, 4 years old, 100°

Nose: Oak, hints of vanilla and a light fruitiness.

Mouth: A medium body, spicy-hot, fairly oaky. The finish is medium-long and hot.

Overall: A decent "around the house" bourbon. Drink it however you like.

Very Old Barton, 6 years old, 80°
Very Old Barton, 6 years old, 86°
Very Old Barton, 6 years old, 90°

Nose: Initially spicy with just a touch of fruit (oranges?).

Mouth: All three bottlings have a light body; the whiskey is rather spicy with hints of fruit and a touch of caramel. Both the fruit and caramel are more evident in the higher-proof bottlings. The finish on all three is fairly short and sharp.

Overall: These are good "around the house" bourbons, a little more complex than most. Drink Very Old Barton however you like. It's good for all highballs and most cocktails.

Jim Beam Bourbon

DISTILLERY

The Jim Beam Distilleries, Clermont and Boston, Kentucky

ABOUT THE BRAND

Nineteen ninety-five marks the 200th anniversary of whiskey-making in the Beam family, and this event is proudly noted on its regular, white-label bottling, which also sports Jim Beam's signature and the legend "none genuine without my signature." The label also mentions, quite commendably, the age of the whiskey, which is four years old. (Any whiskey under four years old must display its age, but apart from these younger whiskeys, the age is usually found only on bottlings of six-year-old-plus whiskey.) Beam's Black Label bourbon is eight years old and is presented with a sophisticated jet-black label that also bears Jim Beam's signature. Beam's Choice, a five-year-old bourbon, features the number "8" on its label and is qualified with the words "Old Number Eight Formula."

HISTORY

Jim Beam Bourbon might just be the best-known bourbon in the world, and Jim's ancestors were famous for their whiskey for a good long time before he was born. Even before the Civil War, the Beams were known in Kentucky as being among the best producers of fine whiskey, and by the late 1800s, one of the family's first brands of whiskey, Old Tub, was being sold nationwide.

The Beam family has probably had more involvement in the bourbon industry than any other family in the nation. Just to confuse everyone, some family members have, over the years, taken their knowledge to other distilleries and become involved with other bourbon families. There's a Beam here, and a Beam there, dotted throughout the 200-year family history of whiskey, sometimes cropping up in unlikely places, but always with a good still and close to a spring that gushes limestone water.

As is often the case with families whose history stretches back so far, some of the earlier events concerning the Beams are recorded only in the tales that have been passed down through the generations. Recordkeeping wasn't very important in the late eighteenth century, when new settlers in Kentucky had to work hard to stay alive. However, much of the Beam family history was documented in *The Nelson County Record* in 1896, probably just over 100 years after a settler named Jacob Beam sold his first bourbon.

Jacob Beam (originally Boehm) was the first of the line to set foot on Kentucky soil. A German immigrant who landed on these shores around 1752, he lived in Maryland and Pennsylvania before heading west to Kentucky in 1785. He started making whiskey shortly after arriving there.

Jacob, as described in the 1896 article, was "a young man of sterling worth and integrity." He sold his first barrel of whiskey in 1795, an act that laid the foundation for a future empire. (The newspaper indicates that the distillery was built in 1788, but according to the Jim Beam Brands Company, it was seven years later that Jacob first sold his whiskey.) Jacob's small distillery grew into a commercial success. His son, David, helped him while learning the business; he married and had two sons who would do very well indeed at the still. These men, John H. and David M., went their separate ways when, in 1860, John H. founded the Early Times Distillery just a few miles from the family plant. It is David M., however, whose story we must follow in order to track down the illustrious Jim Beam.

David M. Beam was born in 1833. When he was about 20 years old, he succeeded his father as owner-distiller at what had become known as the Old Tub Distillery. David had three children: Nannie, "a most popular lady of strong intellect and rare beauty," Park and a certain James Beauregard Beam—known to us as the one and only Jim Beam. Jim was apparently an energetic man, popular in the community, who loved to entertain guests and dabble in a little politicking. When David tired of his travails in 1892, he turned the Old Tub Distillery over to his son Jim and his son-in-law, Albert J. Hart (Nannie's husband), a farmer and trader who had entered the whiskey business in 1889. The turnover gave birth to the Beam & Hart Old Tub Distillery.

And so the Beam dynasty's firm foundations were laid. Jim Beam's son, T. Jeremiah Beam, came to work with his father in 1913, by which time the distillery had extended its brands to include Pebble Ford and Jefferson Club whiskeys; together, they saw the plant close when Prohibition came along in 1920. After Repeal in 1933, the James B. Beam Distilling Company was formed, and once again, Jim and Jeremiah Beam started making their Old Tub Whiskey.

The company changed hands in the 1940s, when Harry Blum, a Chicago liquor merchant, took over operations, and again in 1967, when the company was bought by a company now known as American Brands, Inc. But through all the changes in ownership, the Beams have remained in charge of making their whiskey. Carl Beam (Jim's nephew) and his son Baker—known in his younger days as a ladies' man who enjoyed fast motorbikes—were both master distillers for Beam. Booker Noe (Jim's grandson) is still Master Distiller Emeritus for the company. Booker, however, doesn't seem to be too aware of his "retired" status, and even though he spends much of his time touring the world to promote the Beam's "small-batch" bourbons, when he is in Bardstown, you can find him at the Clermont plant making sure that the whiskey "feels, smells and tastes" like Jim Beam whiskey should.

TASTING NOTES
Jim Beam, 4 years old, 80°

Nose: Oak, slight vanilla, a hint of cinnamon.

Mouth: A medium, soft body, with a touch of vanilla and a slightly sweet spiciness. Even, well balanced. The finish is short, sharp and pleasant.

Overall: This bottling of Jim Beam is probably exactly what the distiller meant it to be—a good all-around bourbon, not too complex, but fine for drinking on ice or with any mixer.

Beam's Choice, 5 years old, 80°

Nose: A light oakiness with a touch of spice but none of the sweet vanilla present in the four-year-old bottling.

Mouth: A medium body with a spicy palate that bears hints of grandmother's attic. The finish is medium.

Overall: This bottling isn't in the same style as the four-year-old Jim Beam; it's a little more complex and quite a bit spicier—fine for drinking over ice and/or adding ginger ale or other mixers.

Beam's Black Label, 8 years old, 90°

Nose: Vanilla, caramel, cinnamon, honey.

Mouth: A big, round, soft body full of oak, rich with vanilla and hints of plums, prunes and maybe raisins. The finish is quite long, very smooth and soothing.

Overall: This eight-year-old is truly worth paying a little extra (than the four-year-old) for. It has lots of complexity and is suitable for sipping neat, on the rocks or with a splash of any mixer. This bottling is also ideal for mixing any cocktails; its sophistication really shines through.

Jim Beam Rye Whiskey

DISTILLERY
The Jim Beam Distilleries, Clermont and Boston, Kentucky

ABOUT THE BRAND
Jim Beam straight rye whiskey was introduced before 1944. The bottle bears a bright yellow label that declares the whiskey to be "The World's Finest Rye," along with other statements such as "Mild and Mellow" and, on the back label, "No Finer Whiskey in all this World." Jim Beam's signature, verifying that this is genuine Beam whiskey, also appears on the front label.

TASTING NOTES
Jim Beam Rye, 80°
Nose: Light floral notes give way to hints of pepper and a certain winey quality. Is there perhaps some aniseed lurking in the background?

Mouth: A slim, delicate body, spicy, flowery and perfume-y. The finish is short and smooth with just a light crispness bursting through at the last minute.

Overall: A good "around the house" bottling. Mix it with ginger ale or lots of club soda for a long, refreshing summertime drink.

Benchmark Bourbon

DISTILLERY
The Ancient Age Distillery, Frankfort, Kentucky

ABOUT THE BRAND
Benchmark was introduced as a Seagram brand of premium bourbon in 1967 and was purchased in 1989 by the Sazerac Company of New Orleans. Sazerac also owns the Ancient Age Distillery, where this bourbon is produced. The regular bottling bears a smart black label, and the back of the bottle is embossed with an eagle, its wings outspread. The Benchmark XO Single Barrel Bourbon (introduced in 1995 and for export only) is the latest single-barrel offering from the Ancient Age Distillery and is presented in a tall, rectangular bottle with a sleek, extra-long neck topped with a cork-finished stopper. Its back label offers an explanation of how single-barrel bourbons are selected, citing a "honey spot" in warehouses where "the conditions for whiskey aging are perfect." The whiskey chosen for this bottling is selected by Master Distiller Gary Gayheart. For

a complete history of this distillery, see **Ancient Age Bourbon**, page 104.

TASTING NOTES
Benchmark Premium Bourbon, 80°

Nose: Strong vanilla.

Mouth: A light body, lots of vanilla, a little sweetish, smooth and pleasant and hints of fruits (oranges?). The finish is medium with a hint of mint.

Overall: A good "around the house" bourbon. Drink it however you wish.

Benchmark XO Single Barrel Bourbon, 94° (for export only)

Nose: Vanilla, mint, clover.

Mouth: Medium-full body, rather spicy—cinnamon, a little vanilla and a touch of mint. Very warming and smooth.

Overall: A good bourbon that might possibly serve as an after-dinner whiskey. We, however, suggest you drink it on ice; feel free to add soda or water, but don't adulterate it with ginger ale or other flavored mixers.

Blanton's Single Barrel Bourbon

DISTILLERY
The Ancient Age Distillery, Frankfort, Kentucky

ABOUT THE BRAND
Blanton's, introduced in 1984, was the first single-barrel bourbon on the market and is considered by many to be the jewel in this distillery's crown. Each squat eight-sided bottle has a decanter-style stopper finished with a metal horse and jockey and bears a label denoting a registered number, the date on which the whiskey was "dumped" (removed from the barrel), the number of the barrel, the warehouse in which it was aged and the number of the rick on which the barrel stood. The label also proclaims, "We believe this is the finest bottle of whiskey ever produced, affording you extra flavor, bouquet and character." The whiskey chosen for this bottling is selected by Master Distiller Emeritus Elmer T. Lee.

HISTORY
Blanton's is named for Albert B. Blanton, the son of Benjamin Blanton, who first made whiskey on the site of the current Ancient Age Distillery in 1865. Albert B. worked at this plant from 1897 until 1953, and upon his retirement, the distillery was renamed the Albert B. Blanton Distillery. In 1969, it became the Ancient Age Distillery.

For a complete history of this plant and the Blanton family, see **Ancient Age Bourbon**, page 104.

TASTING NOTES

Blanton's Single Barrel Bourbon, 93° (bottle no. 173, dumped on 12-19-94 from barrel no. 74, stored in warehouse H on rick no. 25)

Nose: Honey, vanilla, blackberries, "thick," cinnamon.

Mouth: A smooth, round, full body with flavors of oranges, vanilla and spices such as cinnamon, allspice and a hint of cloves. A lingering finish with a touch of butterscotch.

Overall: A great bourbon; one look and you know why they used to call this spirit "red liquor"—it bears a deep, clear, mahogany hue. Sip it from a snifter, make a marvelous Manhattan or simply pour it over ice. Here's a whiskey that you can drink when you really deserve a treat.

Booker's Bourbon

DISTILLERY

The Jim Beam Distilleries, Clermont and Boston, Kentucky

ABOUT THE BRAND

Released in 1989 and the first small-batch bourbon on the market, Booker's Bourbon is named for a truly great distiller, Booker Noe, a sixth-generation Beam family member and grandson of Jim himself. It took some guts and plenty of foresight to bring this whiskey to the general public, and we are sure that it was at Booker's insistence that it is bottled unfiltered and at barrel proof (usually around 126°)—just the way he loves it. By not filtering whiskey, the distiller runs the risk that if the bottle should get too cold, it will acquire a "chill haze." This "cloudiness" is anything but a bad sign, but most distillers prefer to filter their whiskey so they don't get complaints from customers who don't understand why their whiskey turns cloudy on ice or when cold. Indeed, its unfiltered condition should be seen as a plus, since filtering whiskey can remove flavors.

Each bottle of Booker's is sealed with black wax and bears a label, printed from a handwritten original—we can't expect Booker to spend his days writing every single label—that notes the exact proof of the whiskey (it varies a little, barrel to barrel), the lot number from whence it came and the age of the whiskey. Booker notes on the label that Jim Beam liked whiskey that was between six and eight years old, and Booker's Bourbon is always from within that range. Each barrel used for Booker's Bourbon is selected by Booker Noe himself. For a complete history of the Beam family, see **Jim Beam Bourbon**, page 110.

TASTING NOTES

Booker's Bourbon, 6 to 8 years old, barrel proof (bottle sampled from lot C87-B-19, aged seven years, three months, 126.5°)

Nose: Smoldering wood, vanilla, a hint of oranges.

Mouth: Look at the color here; it's a gorgeous shade of walnut—medium amber with flashes of red. Booker's has a big body, is very smooth (even without dilution) and tastes of tobacco, peaches, mysterious attics, a little smoky. The finish is very crisp, long, very warm and full of fine cigars.

Overall: Booker's Bourbon is a great example of a whiskey whose high alcohol content doesn't get in the way of flavor to the slightest degree—probably because it is unfiltered. Booker's can be sipped neat (or with a little water and no ice) in a snifter; it can be savored on ice for hours on end while you reflect on life, or it is a delicious sippin' whiskey when you add ice and lots of water (just the way Booker likes it) and sit on the front porch watching the neighbors stroll by. You may also want to sip it, heavily diluted, with a steak dinner.

Colonel Lee Bourbon

DISTILLERY

The Barton Distillery, Bardstown, Kentucky

ABOUT THE BRAND

We assumed that the name of this whiskey referred to *the* Lee, the legendary Confederate general who is as respected by Northerners as he is loved in the South, but it isn't so—this Colonel Lee is a fictitious character. The orange label with gold and red lettering bears a drawing of a gentleman in a wide-brimmed hat, with a Colonel Sanders-style mustache and beard, standing in front of an antebellum mansion. He might be an imaginary figure, but the whiskey in the bottle is very authentic. For a complete history of the Barton Distillery, see **Tom Moore Bourbon**, page 159.

TASTING NOTES

Colonel Lee, Bottled in Bond, 100°

Nose: Stone fruits (peaches), caramel and vanilla.

Mouth: A medium-light body with a good degree of complexity—oak, vanilla, honey, caramel. The finish is fairly long, and honey seems to linger in the mouth.

Overall: This is an "around the house" bourbon with a lot more style than most in the category. Drink it on ice, add water or club soda, or make any highball or cocktail you desire with this whiskey.

Elijah Craig Bourbon

DISTILLERY

The Heaven Hill Distillery, Bardstown, Kentucky

ABOUT THE BRAND

Here's a whiskey that hasn't been on the market very long but is named for the man who many people credit as the "inventor" of bourbon. Elijah Craig was a Baptist minister, born in Orange County, Virginia, in 1743.

Elijah Craig Bourbon is available in one bottling only—at 12 years old. None of the labels on the bottle make any claim to this whiskey's being tied to the illustrious Elijah Craig, but the back label does make mention of "a special yeast recipe that's been a family secret for generations." The yeast used at the Heaven Hill Distillery was brought there by a member of the Beam family—and few families have as much whiskey knowledge in their blood as do the Beams.

HISTORY

Wine journalist Rod Smith is descended from Elijah's brother, Jeremiah Craig, and although his family's papers say little about Elijah himself, they do shed light on the family as a whole.

The history of the Craig family in the United States started when the then recently widowed Jane Craig (née Taliaferro) arrived sometime between 1704 and 1705 to join her brothers in Virginia. Her son, Taliaferro Craig (known as Toliver), married and became the father of 11 children, Elijah Craig among them.

Taliaferro was a soldier in the Virginia Militia and, according to the family papers, "a defender of Bryan's Station (near Lexington, Kentucky) when it was under attack by the British under Caldwell and by the Indians under the instigation of the renegade Simon Girty (Dirty Girty).

"The Craigs had come to Kentucky because of religious persecution. Three of Taliaferro's sons were Baptist ministers, and their preaching was contrary to that of the Established Church of England in Virginia. The whole family decided to come so that they might live in peace and better the conditions of their children."

And finally, Elijah is mentioned: "Elijah settled at Lebanon, now Georgetown, Kentucky. He was a Baptist minister. He advertised the opening of a school in Kentucky, now Georgetown College, and, together with a Mr. Parker, erected the first paper mill in Kentucky near Georgetown in 1792."

You will note here that there is no mention of Elijah's operating a whiskey still. Maybe Mrs. V.T. Craig, the family chronicler, wasn't too proud of that fact, but Elijah was indeed a whiskey man, and his still was erected on the site of the mill mentioned in the document. According to Richard Collins, author of *The History of Kentucky*, 1874, "the first bourbon whiskey was made in 1789 at Georgetown, at the fulling mill at the Royal Spring." The mill to which he refers is indeed Elijah Craig's, and according to *The Kentucky Encyclopedia*, he made paper, rope and whiskey there.

So how did Elijah Craig become known as the "creator" of bourbon? It's all hypothetical, but most modern-day historians tend to believe that during the later years of the nineteenth century, when temperance societies and prohibitionists were spouting the Bible to further their cause, the pro-whiskey forces of the time jumped at the chance to declare that a Baptist minister had invented bourbon whiskey in the first place. Fact is, bourbon gained its name from Bourbon County—an area in which Craig never lived—and the probability that he aged his whiskey at all, let alone in charred oak barrels, is fairly remote, given the techniques at the time.

All that noted, however, at sometime around 1795, Craig was shipping whiskey down to St. Louis and New Orleans. Although it probably wasn't shipped in charred casks, he *could* have used the term "bourbon" to promote his whiskey (the name was just starting to be used right around that time). But here's the catch: If Craig called his whiskey bourbon because distillers from Bourbon County had popularized the name, then he couldn't have been the first distiller of bourbon whiskey—the men he took the name from must have beaten him to the mark.,

In 1795, Craig, along with over 170 other men, was found guilty of making whiskey without a license. He was fined about $140. After that time, mention of Elijah Craig, whiskey-maker, ceases until he died in 1808. In Craig's obituary, the *Kentucky Gazette* declared, "If virtue consists of being useful to our fellow citizens, perhaps there are few more virtuous men than Mr. Craig."

TASTING NOTES
Elijah Craig, 12 years old, 94°

Nose: Hay, mint, leather, light oranges and vanilla.

Mouth: A medium, velvety body, fruity, caramel, dates, vanilla and a touch of oak. The finish is long, slow, comfortable, warming and snug.

Overall: A great bourbon from Heaven Hill, with the distillery's style—the hint of mint in the nose. It's very sophisticated; sip it from a snifter as you read about Elijah Craig, and know that he would have been proud to have his name on the bottle. Don't be afraid to make a Manhattan with this bottling—it will be very special.

Jack Daniel's Tennessee Sour Mash Whiskey

DISTILLERY

The Jack Daniel Distillery, Lynchburg, Tennessee

ABOUT THE BRAND

Jack Daniel must be the most famous whiskey man on the face of the earth. His Tennessee sour mash is sold around the globe. Sipped by Scots who defy their ancestral spirit, trendy Italians and crusty 80-year-old Tennesseans alike, it's a whiskey for everyone's enjoyment.

Jack Daniel's comes in two bottlings. The familiar black label version is designated "Old Time No. 7 Brand," and the green label, slightly lower in proof, is designated "No. 7 Brand." Both of these bottles boast the seven "highest gold medals" awarded to the whiskey between 1904 and 1981, along with the words, "Whiskey made as our fathers made it for 7 generations" and "The oldest registered distillery in the United States." The distillery's motto, "Y God, we'll do the best we can every day" can't be found on either bottling.

HISTORY

Jack Daniel's life was recorded by *Fortune* magazine in July 1951, *True* magazine in 1954 and by author Ben A. Green in *Jack Daniel's Legacy*, 1967. Specific dates of Daniel's early years differ from one account to the next, although the details are largely the same. The dates, although not all of the details, used in this account are the ones found in Green's book.

Jack Daniel was born to Calaway and Lucinda Daniel in the autumn of 1846. His grandfather, Joseph Daniel, was an Englishman who eloped to the Colonies in the 1770s and, after fighting in the Revolutionary War, moved west to Franklin County, Tennessee. Jack's mother died in the year following his birth, and shortly after his father remarried some five years later, Jack left home to live with neighbors. About two years after that, he moved on again when he went to live with Dan and Mary Jane Call. Why Jack, at such an early age, moved around so much, is not clear, although he first left home, according to most accounts, after he found that he didn't get along with his stepmother.

Dan Call was a farmer-distiller who had inherited land from his family and owned a country store where he sold the whiskey he produced at his farm. It was at the Call farm that Jack is said to have learned the art of distillation from Nearest Green, a slave who served as Call's master distiller. But as well as being a farmer, a distiller and a storekeeper, Dan Call was also a minister, and pressure from his congregation made it hard for him to preach the gospel while selling firewater to the local populace. Around 1860, he sold his still to 14-year-old Jack Daniel, who set up his own business and is said to have made quite a decent living during the Civil War, traveling to neighboring towns to sell his whiskey.

In 1866, after a brief partnership with another distiller, Colonel Hughes, Jack expanded his business when he gained use of land near Lynchburg, then part of Lincoln County, Tennessee, and founded the Jack Daniel Distillery. According to most sources, although excise taxes had been reintroduced in 1862, they weren't enforced until after the Civil War. Thus, by being a stand-up distiller and registering immediately, Jack became owner of the first registered distillery in the country after the Civil War. Whiskey trivia buffs have long argued as to whether or not this statement is true, and no records at the Bureau of Alcohol, Tobacco and Firearms can verify it. However, almost every account ever written about this distillery, including both articles from the 1950s, pays homage to the claim, and the fact remains that the title "Jack Daniel's Number 1 Distillery" has been accepted for so many years that it's either true or it has become so.

LITTLE JACK

AS A FULL-GROWN MAN, Jack Daniel stood no more than five feet five inches tall and weighed about 120 pounds, hence "Little Jack" was commonly used in reference to him. However, Jack Daniel never went unnoticed, since even when performing manual labor, he dressed very well in a knee-length frock coat, a colorful vest, a string tie and a wide-brimmed planter's hat. Sporting a goatee, he was every inch, all 65 of them, the Southern gentleman.

The land on which the distillery stood was known as The Hollow at Cave Spring and boasted its own source of the limestone-filtered water so important in the making of good whiskey. Indeed, Alfred Eaton, the man who is credited with "inventing" the Tennessee whiskey mellowing method known as the Lincoln County Process, is said to have operated a still on the exact same spot where the Jack Daniel Distillery stands and chose the location for the quality of its water supply. Originally, the Lincoln County procedure of filtering new whiskey through vats of sugar-maple charcoal was probably performed to soothe the raw whiskey before aging whiskey became common practice. Jack named his first whiskey "Belle of Lincoln" to pay tribute to the county, but according to the *True* article, "many a grandmother years later shed a tear of nostalgia over Little Jack's having named his whiskey for her."

In the early 1880s, Jack's nephew, Lem Motlow, began working at the distillery. He performed menial tasks for his first year and then worked in the office. Within four years, Motlow had become, for all intents and purposes, the manager of the whole plant. According to legend, Motlow was the man who persuaded Jack Daniel to bottle his whiskey rather than selling it only in jugs or casks. In 1895, Motlow married Clara Reagor, who bore him one son, John Reagor Motlow, who was always referred to as Reagor. Clara died six years later, and in 1904, Motlow married again, this time to Ophelia Evans, who gave him three sons—Robert, Daniel and Clifford; together with their half-brother Reagor, they would become known as the "Shirtsleeve Brothers" when they took control of the company.

By the turn of the century, both the Daniel and the Motlow families had expanded their horizons—Jack Daniel, Lem Motlow and his brother, Frank Motlow, were partners in the Farmer's Bank in Lynchburg. Their primary product, however, was spreading farther afield, and Jack Daniel's whiskey was available in Alabama, Louisiana and Texas. In 1904, the whiskey won a gold medal at the Louisiana Purchase Exhibition, and shortly thereafter, Jack Daniel's Tennessee Sour Mash was being shipped overseas. During the following 11 years, Jack Daniel's was awarded four more gold medals in Europe and has since acquired two more awards, a Star of Excellence in Brussels, 1954, and a Gold Medal with Palm Leaves in Amsterdam, 1981.

The turning point for Jack Daniel was in 1905, when he kicked a safe that refused to open, an act that proved to be his downfall. He injured his toe. Nowadays, an injured toe

LEM MOTLOW

may not sound like much, but in pre-penicillin days, some very small maladies could lead to some very big problems, and in 1909, his toe had to be amputated. Unfortunately, the amputation came too late—after suffering a series of operations over the next couple of years, Jack succumbed to his injury in October 1911.

However, in 1907, Jack had the foresight to make sure his whiskey was in the right hands, and he turned his company over to his cousin Dick Daniel and his nephew Lem Motlow. By the time Jack died, Motlow had become sole proprietor. And he had shown his uncle that he could take care of business.

Lynchburg, the tiny town where the Jack Daniel Distillery stands, is in Moore County, an area that was voted dry in 1909 and remains dry today; you can see a lot of whiskey at the distillery in Lynchburg, and since a new law was passed in 1995, you can actually buy a bottle of Jack Daniel's right there for carrying away. But there are no bars, no saloons and no liquor stores in Lynchburg. The only way you can toss off a shot is from your own hip flask.

The drys moved quickly in Tennessee, and in 1910, state-wide prohibition was declared. Typically, Motlow took charge of the situation in his forward-thinking style; he opened a distillery in St. Louis and carried on making traditional Tennessee whiskey in Missouri. A couple of years later, Motlow opened another distillery in Birmingham, Alabama, and after a fire destroyed the St. Louis plant, he simply built a new one. But disaster for the entire industry was just around the corner in the form of national Prohibition in 1920, when all but a few "medicinal whiskey" distilleries were closed.

When Prohibition ended in 1933, the whiskey industry in Kentucky reawakened; but in Tennessee, producing liquor remained illegal and Motlow had to fight for the right to make Jack Daniel's whiskey. Well, fight he did, and in 1938, he was granted permission to fire up the old stills.

Sadly, a year later, he suffered a stroke that left both his right arm and foot paralyzed; although he had a wheelchair, he took to being carried around by an employee. Motlow died on September 1, 1947, and his sons assumed control of the operation with Reagor at the helm as president of the company. Reagor is said to have received a letter from the Treasury Department that declared Tennessee whiskey was a distinctive product in its own right because of the leaching process peculiar to its distilleries.

By 1956, the Motlow family was doing a very brisk business due, in part, to the fact that many celebrities had publicly proclaimed their love of Jack Daniel's. However, the Motlows were also running into some cash-flow problems. Stock in the company was owned by the Motlow family as a whole, rather than being split among individuals, and if one of them should die, the surviving members of the family faced a very complicated inheritance tax. Coupled with that, the company didn't have enough hard cash to keep up with the excise taxes that had to be paid on the vast amounts of whiskey aging in their warehouses. Luckily for the Motlows, help was at hand in the form of another family-owned company that understood the importance of keeping tradition alive by ensuring that generations of the same family kept running the business.

Brown-Forman, a Louisville-based beverage company operated to this day by the founding Brown family, bought the Jack Daniel Distillery for a reputed $18 million and left the Motlows to run the business. Reagor Motlow became a member of the board of directors at Brown-Forman, and both companies have prospered to this day. There's a lot to be said for not fixing what ain't broke.

OLD TIME NO. 7

THE STORY BEHIND THE "NO. 7" DESIGNATION ON THE Jack Daniel's Tennessee whiskey label is unknown, but several theories have been put forth. One tale goes that sometime around 1887, Jack Daniel took a trip to nearby Tullahoma to see a friend who owned seven stores. There was something about that number that tickled Jack's fancy, and from that time on, Jack Daniel's best whiskey was called "Old Time No. 7." Another story has it that seven barrels of whiskey were once "mislaid," and upon their recovery, the number seven had been chalked on their sides. The retailer who received these barrels forever after asked for "that number seven" whiskey, and the name stuck.

TASTING NOTES

Jack Daniel's No. 7 Brand (green label), 80°

Nose: Sweet, caramel, some light grassy notes.

Mouth: A slim body, with a sooty sort of pale palate and a short, hot finish.

Overall: This bottling isn't available everywhere, but there are fans of this whiskey who drink it neat—from a shot glass, not a snifter. It's not a sophisticated whiskey, nor does it pretend to be, but it's pure Tennessee. Bake a nice fruitcake and saturate it with green-label No. 7. Use it to make a Tennessee bread pudding; macerate some fruits in it. If you want an inexpensive cooking whiskey, this one really does work well in the kitchen. If you want a blast of old-fashioned sour mash, drink it neat.

Jack Daniel's Old Time No. 7 Brand (black label), 86°

Nose: Warm, sweet, caramel, hints of tobacco.

Mouth: A light, almost silky body, and then, there it is: the flavor that makes you yearn for an old mahogany bar with a mule or two tied up outside. This whiskey is as sooty as a chimney sweep; it jumps around, tickling your tongue with the odd burst of a ripe peach and a sprinkling of pepper to boot. The finish is medium-long, leaving a dusty trail of sootiness and a hint of ashes.

Overall: The black-label bottling is great for many an occasion—drink it from a shot glass, drink it on the rocks, add club soda, water or any other mixer if you must, but this is not a whiskey that you want to hide under the skirts of, say, orange juice. True, it mixes well with cola, and if that is your style—go for it.

J.W. DANT

J.W. Dant Bourbon

DISTILLERY

The Heaven Hill Distillery, Bardstown, Kentucky

ABOUT THE BRAND

The label on J.W. Dant Bourbon bears a trademark depicting the top of a whiskey barrel with the letters *D, A, N* and *T* around the circumference in colorful shields. The Dant family name has long been connected to Kentucky bourbon—it has a history that could have faded away if the Heaven Hill Distillery hadn't bought the brand.

HISTORY

The story of J.W. Dant Bourbon starts with Joseph Washington (J.W.) Dant, who in 1836 was "running it on a log" at Dant's Station, Marion County, Kentucky. Running it on a log? That's right, a poplar log. The term comes from an old-time method of making whiskey that involved hollowing out a section of a tree trunk, running a copper pipe through it, and filling the log with fermented mash (distiller's beer). Old distillers would run steam through the pipe to heat the beer and start distillation. The complete process is described on page 37.

J.W. had a few sons, and one of them, Joseph Bernard, went off on his own to found the Cold Spring Distillery and create the Yellowstone brand of whiskey. His brother George Dant, on the other hand, stuck with dear old dad and helped him at his new commercial distillery, built at Dant's Station in 1870. By this time, J.W. must have made enough money to retire his faithful old log. George went on to become president of the J.W. Dant Company, which produced J.W. Dant Bourbon until Prohibition.

During the Noble Experiment, J.W. Dant Bourbon was stored at the Stitzel warehouse in Louisville and sold as medicinal whiskey. After Repeal in 1933, when the big guys in the whiskey business were all scrambling to acquire distilleries and distinctive brand names, the J. W. Dant Distillery changed hands a few times and the brand name eventually found its home at the Heaven Hill Distillery.

TASTING NOTES
J.W. Dant, 100°

Nose: Slightly perfume-y, with hints of vanilla and just a touch of oak.

Mouth: A lean body with some oak, leather and a hint of eucalyptus. The finish is short and rather hot.

Overall: A good, lean "around the house" bourbon. Ideal for mint juleps and mixed drinks, especially whiskey sours.

George Dickel Tennessee Sour Mash Whisky

DISTILLERY

George A. Dickel's Cascade Distillery, Tullahoma, Tennessee

ABOUT THE BRAND

Handsome labels adorn the three Dickel bottlings, all of which bear Mr. Dickel's bearded likeness. Note that Dickel spells "whisky" without the *e* that usually appears in the American spelling of the word (whiskey); the distillery claims that it was either in homage to Scotch whisky (although Dickel was German) or that he just couldn't spell. He could, however, make whiskey. Dickel's No. 8 and No. 12 bottlings include short histories on their labels. Both these bottlings' labels denote the distillery's motto: "There Ain't Nothing Better."

Although neither the No. 8 nor the No. 12 brand bears an age statement (which indicates that they are at least four years old), the distillery says that the average age of these whiskeys is around seven years. The main difference between the two is the proof at which each is bottled.

The George Dickel Special Barrel Reserve was released in 1994, and at 10 years old, it is a very special bottling of Tennessee whiskey.

HISTORY

Dickel makes true Tennessee sour-mash whiskey using the old Lincoln County Process that distinguishes Tennessee whiskeys from all others. Since the late fifties, it has been made on the site where it originated, in a sleepy hollow in Tullahoma, Tennessee.

George Dickel, the man for whom the whiskey is named, was born in Darmstadt, Germany, in 1818, and immigrated to the United States in 1844. Nine years later, Dickel settled in Nashville, Tennessee, and reputedly went into business as a shoemaker. But Dickel was more of a whiskey man than a cobbler. Over a decade later, in 1866, he entered the "rectifying and bottling" business, buying whiskey from distilleries, probably "mingling" them together for consistency and selling the resulting liquor at his retail store. As time went by, however, the whiskey from the nearby Cascade Distillery caught Dickel's attention, and he ended up buying that whiskey exclusively.

By all accounts, George Dickel was a very civic-minded gent, a member of the local fire department, an active Freemason and a generous giver to various charities. He was also determined to make life better for his own family. By 1870, when Dickel was 53 years old, he had married Augusta, a local woman who was some 19 years his junior, and was listed in a local census as owning real estate valued at $4,000, with a personal estate of $5,000. His profession was "retail liquor dealer."

In that same year, the area of Cascade Hollow supported a small, nameless distillery and a sawmill that employed six men. However, by 1880, the community had grown to include another distiller, a miller, two storekeepers, a sawmill owner and five prostitutes.

By 1881, Dickel's brother-in-law, Victor Schwab, was a partner in George A. Dickel & Co., and by 1888, he had gained controlling interest in the Cascade Distillery. That same year, the distillery gave sole bottling and distribution rights to Dickel's company. It was known as Cascade Whisky—"Mellow as Moonlight." But along with good fortune came Dickel's downfall—literally. He fell from a horse that same year, was forced into retirement and died in 1894.

By the turn of the century, local prohibition laws in Tennessee permitted towns of less than 2,000 inhabitants to banish the retailing of liquor. The Cascade Distillery's whiskey, however, was being sold locally, where laws permitted, and by mail order. But younger minds were about to change all that. By this time, Schwab's son George was working for the company, and being a man of the times, he contracted an advertising agency to promote Cascade Whisky at home and abroad. The campaign was so success-ful that in 1904, the Cascade Distillery ex-panded into the largest distillery in Tennessee.

Then prohibition hit. Not the Noble Experiment of 1920, but the statewide pro-hibition that Tennessee approved in 1910. All distilleries had just one year to close their doors. George Dickel's Cascade Whisky moved the operation to Louisville, Kentucky, where, in 1912, production recommenced at A. Ph. Stitzel's distillery. Although Tennessee whiskey wasn't recognized as a differentiated product from bourbon until 1941, Schwab knew that his whiskey had to be filtered through at least 10 feet of sugar-maple char-coal to retain its distinctive Tennessean char-acter. So leaching vats were installed at the Stitzel distillery, and Cascade Whisky re-mained true to its roots until nationwide Pro-hibition (and the laws that led up to it) stopped production in 1919.

A CASCADE CROCK

Repeal came in 1933, and two years later, Cascade Whisky was again being sold by Stitzel, who by that time had joined forces with the Weller family. Six years later, the same whiskey was being made at the George T. Stagg Distillery in Frankfort, Kentucky. However, after World War II, Schenley (who, by this time, owned the rights to the Cas-cade name) hired veteran distiller Ralph Dupps to rebuild the old Cascade Distillery just three-quarters of a mile from its original site in Tullahoma, Tennessee. George Dickel's Tennessee whiskey had come home at last. Dupps used original documents to re-create the old distillery and researched old documents to make sure that the whiskey would be the same one that George Dickel himself loved. However, it was still labeled Cascade Whisky until 1964, when Schenley finally put George Dickel's name on the bottle.

Though the distillery is now owned by United Distillers, if you should ever visit this picturesque spot where the limestone-filtered water flows from Cascade Spring, you will be forgiven for believing that it is still a family-run business. The giant corporate father of the Cascade Distillery has had the good sense to let the Hollow continue its deceptively sleepy lifestyle and allows its total of 32 employees, headed by Distillery Manager and Master Distiller Jennings "David" Backus, to make their Tennessee whiskey at a leisurely pace.

TASTING NOTES
George Dickel Old No. 8 Brand, 80°

Nose: Light toffee, followed quickly by the characteristic Tennessee sootiness.

Mouth: Sleek, somewhat supple body with a crisp refreshing "bite" of apples (it's in all of the Dickel bottlings), underripe pears, quickly followed by a warming spiciness that balances the whiskey well. The finish is medium-long and pleasant.

Overall: Drink this whiskey whenever you feel like a slug of that singular Tennessee whiskey taste. Throw some ice in there and play the tough guy or the town flirt; it's a no-nonsense bottling.

George Dickel No. 12 Superior Brand, 90°

Nose: Honey-apple notes and, again, Tennessee sootiness.

Mouth: The body is just a bit thicker than the No. 8, and the palate bears a touch of mint with hints of tobacco and that signature distillery touch of crisp apples. The finish is medium-long and, again, pleasant.

Overall: Toss it back neat, sip it on the rocks or add a splash of soda. Put some ginger ale or cola in there if that's what you want—the flavors will still shine through. Drink this whiskey in your local neighborhood tavern, or order a shot at the poshest hotel bar in town.

George Dickel Special Barrel Reserve, 10 years old, 86°

Nose: Warm, creamy, vanilla, thick with an "adult" toffee character and a fair crack of Tennessee sootiness.

Mouth: The body is thick, elegant and soft, giving way to a sophisticated spicy-fruity palate (dates, nutmeg, cinnamon), rich with vanilla and, of course, that sweet sootiness that, at 10 years old, has smoothed out into a wonderful "ash-y" note. Once again, the crisp apples are present and let you know exactly which distillery made this whiskey. The finish is long and fine, bouncing around for a very respectable length of time and reminding you that you just tasted something special.

Overall: It's just fine to drink this whiskey on the rocks, and you can add just a touch of water or even club soda, if that is your wont. But you might also savor it in a snifter after dinner.

Eagle Rare Bourbon

DISTILLERY
The Ancient Age Distillery, Frankfort, Kentucky

ABOUT THE BRAND
Both Eagle Rare Bourbon and the Ancient Age Distillery where it is made are owned by the Sazerac Company of New Orleans. Originally, however, the brand was owned by the Seagram Company and reportedly was introduced to the marketplace in the mid-1970s. The squat port-like bottles of Eagle Rare have a patriotic motif, as well they might—the country's national spirit, bourbon, together with a bald eagle and some stars here and there make a fine combination. The 10-year-old bottling comes at 101° proof and wears a dark brown, gold-edged label that almost disappears into the dark whiskey within; the 15-year-old version, available only in the export marketplaces, wears an antiqued, leathery-looking front label and is presented at 107° proof.

TASTING NOTES
Eagle Rare Bourbon, 10 years old, 101°
Nose: Vanilla, oak, caramel, maybe a touch of basil.

Mouth: Medium-full velvety body, very complex; honey, overripe blackberries, tangerines and a hint of smoldering wood. The finish is long, slow and comfy.

Overall: This is an exceptional bourbon—a little port-like in flavor, with a deep tortoiseshell-amber hue. Although it fares well on ice, we hesitate to put this whiskey in anything other than a snifter, where we can savor its distinguished delights while relaxing after dinner. We are amazed that this brand is not marketed more aggressively—it's a fine find.

Eagle Rare Bourbon, 15 years old, 107° (for export only)
Nose: Is it camphor, or maybe eucalyptus? Whatever—it lies beneath layers of berries (raspberries, blueberries) and a hint of honey.

Mouth: A dry velvety mouthfeel with myriad flavors—sweet butter, vanilla, oak, cigar ashes, butterscotch—finishing long, smooth and with a certain oiliness.

Overall: After five extra years of aging, this bourbon seems to be kin to a fine Armagnac or maybe even a Calvados. This is another Eagle Rare bottling that we hesitate to adulterate, even with a cube of ice. Although this bottling is available only on the export market, the Sazerac Company says there is a chance they will release it in the United States. No dates or promises are yet available.

Early Times Bourbon

DISTILLERY

The Early Times Distillery, Louisville, Kentucky

ABOUT THE BRAND

One of the earliest brand names in American whiskey history, Early Times got its start with John H. Beam, the late, great Jim Beam's uncle. The whiskey is currently made by Brown-Forman, and although Early Times Bourbon is currently available only in export markets, Early Times Old Style Kentucky Whisky (no *e*) is still available in the United States. But since this whiskey is partially aged in used barrels, it cannot legally be called a straight bourbon whiskey.

The familiar pale yellow label on the Early Times 80°-proof bottling depicts an artist's rendering of the facade of the original Early Times Distillery near Bardstown, Kentucky, along with the distillery number (354) and the words "Established 1860."

HISTORY

The Early Times Distillery was founded by John H. Beam in 1860, located at that time close to his brother's plant near Bardstown. By 1895, the distillery was producing Early Times and A.G. Nall (presumably named for a member of John Beam's wife's family—her name was Maria Nall) sour mash whiskeys, as well as a sweet-mash variety known as Jack Beam.

In an article published in *The Nelson County Record* in 1896, John Beam, whose home was set on 1,000 acres of "one of the finest blue grass farms in Kentucky," was reported as being a true believer in the "early times" methods of producing whiskey. It went on to say that what he didn't know about distilling just wasn't worth knowing. However, despite John's old-fashioned beliefs, the distillery had heated warehouses—a relatively new concept then.

During the early years of the twentieth century, the Early Times Distillery changed hands a couple of times, and when it closed because of Prohibition in 1920, it was left with whiskey that could be sold only by dealers with a license to market "medicinal" spirits. Luckily, along came Brown-Forman, a company with just such a license and a need to build up stocks for the thousands of sick folk who would have suffered even more without a dram or two of Early Times. Brown-Forman bought the entire stock of Early Times Bourbon, along with the brand name.

By 1953, Early Times had become the top-selling bourbon in the country, and because Brown-Forman strongly believed in "quality whisky at quality prices," it was never offered at discount. Early Times Bourbon remained popular for many years, but in 1983, the company decided to market the brand domestically as Old Style Kentucky Whisky. Early Times is now made by Master Distiller Lincoln Henderson at the Early Times Distillery in Louisville, where Old Forester Bourbon is also produced.

TASTING NOTES
Early Times Bourbon, 80° (for export only)
Early Times Bourbon, 86° (for export only)

Nose: Light and fragrant with more sweet notes (honey, vanilla) coming through in the higher-proof bottling.

Mouth: A medium to full body on both bourbons. The palate is wonderfully old-fashioned, bearing tobacco, leather, wildflowers, oak and the "feel" of an old bar steeped in tradition. The finish is warm and soothing—longer in the higher-proof bottling, but distinctive in both.

Overall: Early Times is a very stylish bourbon. For some reason, the "old-fashioned" quality keeps coming to mind—this could be bourbon as our forefathers drank it; it is full of a sterling character that makes us yearn for a cheroot and a thick pastrami sandwich to complete the experience. Drink Early Times however you please—it's a no-nonsense bourbon that proudly wears a string tie and sits in a plush leather chair.

Ezra Brooks Bourbon

BOTTLER AND MARKETER
The David Sherman Company of St. Louis, Missouri

ABOUT THE BRAND
The bottles of both Ezra Brooks Bourbons are tall, sleek, cork-finished and sophisticated. The label on the 90°-proof bottling of Ezra Brooks tells a tale of a "little distillery in Kentucky" where this bourbon is made and suggests: "Next time you're down our way, stop in and visit us." Don't go looking for this place; it doesn't exist. The company says that the wording was on the label when they bought the brand name, and they just left well enough alone. The distillery that makes Ezra Brooks is a trade secret, but it is located in Kentucky.

HISTORY
Ezra Brooks didn't hit the marketplace until the mid-1950s, when, even though this whiskey is bourbon and not Tennessee sour mash, the brand was created to compete with Jack Daniel's Tennessee whiskey. The Hoffman Distilling Company first introduced the brand, but it eventually fell into the Medley Distillery's portfolio. The Med-

AN ADVERTISEMENT FOR A DEFUNCT WHISKEY BRAND

leys were an important Kentucky whiskey family whose history shouldn't be forgotten.

In 1800, John Medley VI, a descendant of Englishman John Medley, who settled in Maryland in 1634, arrived in Kentucky, set up a still or two near Lebanon and was running a commercial distillery by 1812. The distiller's art was passed down from father to son, and in 1901, George E. Medley bought the Daviess County Distilling Company, a plant opened by Richard Monarch in 1873.

As many progeny are wont to do, George Medley's six sons followed him into the family business, and after Medley's death in 1910, his son Thomas took over the business. The distillery suffered losses the following year when a fire destroyed a bonded warehouse and a bottling building at the distillery, but the Medleys battled on, surviving Prohibition by selling their stock to the American Medicinal Spirits Company.

In 1940, the company was sold to the Fleischmann Distilling Company, but the Medleys weren't out of the picture quite yet. That same year, the Medley brothers bought the Green River Distillery in Owensboro, a plant that had been around since 1889, and fired up the old stills. Things went smoothly, and in the mid-1950s, the family ran into a little luck. Due to popular demand (and probably because the country was made aware of Frank Sinatra's favorite brand of whiskey), the Jack Daniel Distillery was running short of product. Enter a new brand of bourbon—Ezra Brooks, a whiskey introduced by the Hoffman Distilling Company, bought by the Medleys and the brainchild of still someone else.

Ezra Brooks was not an early pioneer in Kentucky, nor was he involved with the Bottled-in-Bond Act of 1897. According to Bob Schecter, a man involved with marketing the brand when it first hit the shelves, this whiskey was the product of the imagination of one Skip Cosman, a Chicago advertising man.

Meanwhile, in 1959, the Owensboro plant was sold, but a couple of the Medleys still ran the distillery. Another duo of Medley brothers built a new distillery on the site of the Old Stanley Distillery in Kentucky in 1960 and ran it until it closed in 1987. Eventually, the Ezra Brooks name landed in the hands of the David Sherman Company of St. Louis, Missouri, which still bottles and markets the whiskey today.

Tasting Notes
Ezra Brooks Kentucky Straight Bourbon, 90°
Nose: Honey, wildflowers, clover.

Mouth: A medium to full body with a rich sweetness of vanilla, honey and a hint of chocolate. The finish is warm and not too long.

Overall: Although this bourbon isn't *very* complex, it makes a great "around the house" bottling. Drink it on ice or with whatever mixer you please.

Old Ezra Rare Old Sippin' Whiskey, 7 years old, 101°
Nose: Butterscotch, leather and mint.

Mouth: A medium body giving way to a sweet richness with vanilla, oak, chocolate and butterscotch. The finish is long and soothing with just a hint of mint.

Overall: This is a very good bourbon. Sip it neat, add ice, water or club soda, or mix it into a fairly sophisticated Manhattan.

Four Roses Bourbon

DISTILLERY

The Four Roses Distillery, Lawrenceburg, Kentucky

ABOUT THE BRAND

You can buy Four Roses blended whiskey in the United States, but much to our regret, all of its straight bourbon is earmarked for export and duty-free stores, where it commands fairly high prices. Rumor has it, though, that a single-barrel bottling might be made available in the United States in 1996.

All four bottlings of Four Roses Bourbon feature the Four Roses emblem, and interestingly enough, two of them tell different stories about how the whiskey got its name. The 80°-proof bottling, with the yellow label, states that the whiskey was named for the four daughters of the Rose family. But the tale on the black-labeled "Fine Old Bourbon" bottling details a story of a "lovely Southern girl" wearing four roses to signify that she accepted a proposal of marriage from a certain Paul Jones—the man who brought the brand to Kentucky in 1888.

FRANKFORT DISTILLERIES

HISTORY

Four Roses was made popular by Paul Jones, who started a whiskey business in Georgia shortly after the Civil War. During the 20 years that followed, he must have moved around, since in 1886, he arrived in Kentucky after already working as a whiskey salesman in Tennessee. Two years later, having acquired the rights to a brand of whiskey owned by the Rose family of Tennessee, the Paul Jones Company introduced Four Roses whiskey to Kentucky.

In 1902, Jones' company was absorbed by Frankfort Distilleries, along with several other whiskey companies that had formed a mini-conglomerate. They were able to make more money by working together than competing with one another. Frankfort Distilleries, then headed by Lawrence Jones, Jr., grandson of the founder, was one of the firms selected to produce medicinal whiskey during Prohibition.

In the mid-1940s, Samuel Bronfman's company, Joseph E. Seagram and Sons, bought Frankfort Distilleries, along with the Four Roses brand name and the Four Roses Distillery, a plant that had been known as the Old Joe Distillery but was originally called the Old Prentice Distillery. It's very confusing, but that's the way many distilleries operated—one company bought the name, another bought the distillery. The same plant had once been owned by J.T.S. Brown and Sons. It is there, in Lawrenceburg, that Four Roses Bourbon is still produced, lovingly tended by Master Distiller Jim Rutledge and Master Distiller Emeritus Ova Haney.

TASTING NOTES
Four Roses Bourbon, 80° (for export only)

Nose: Light and fragrant—mint, lemons, oak.

Mouth: A medium body with a smokiness not generally found in bourbon—it's probably oak, but it seems more complex than the normal oakiness found in American whiskey. There's also a nice balance of sweet honey and gentle spices. The finish is medium, soft and a little hot.

Overall: It's tempting to call this a superlative "around the house" bottling, but this whiskey is more complex than that. Sip it from a shot glass; add ice, water, club soda or ginger ale. This bourbon is well crafted and carefully made.

Four Roses Fine Old Bourbon, 86° (for export only)

Nose: Mint, hay, caramel, cloves.

Mouth: A medium to full body, rather simple, but very well balanced. Honey and caramel play off spices that dance on the tongue. The finish is long and rich.

Overall: A well-crafted bourbon; drink it neat or on ice with a splash of water if you wish. Here's a good whiskey that you can drink every day of the week if you really like yourself.

Four Roses Super Premium Bourbon, 86° (for export only)

Nose: Caramel, honey, cloves.

Mouth: A medium to full body, this bottling is richer in sweet notes than the previous two—there's caramel, oak, honey, vanilla and a hint of chocolate. The finish is long, warm and rich.

Overall: This bourbon can be sipped from a snifter; there's something almost liqueur-like in the body—very gentle and soothing. Two ounces of this whiskey can serve as a great after-dinner potion, or if you pour it over ice, you can sip it all evening and pretend that you deserve a treat like this. Also makes wonderful Manhattans.

Four Roses Single Barrel Reserve, 86° (for export only)

Nose: Caramel and honey with spices darting out from all directions.

Mouth: A huge body, very thick and honeyed. The balance of sweet honey with rich vanilla and a host of delicious spices (cinnamon, nutmeg, a hint of cloves) serve to remind you that this is a whiskey selected for its complexity. The finish is long, warm, gentle and oh, so rich.

Overall: Another great bottling from Four Roses. Worthy of a snifter, great over ice, but we suggest you don't add anything other than a splash of water (which it doesn't really need), unless you want to impress guests with a top-notch Manhattan.

Gentleman Jack Rare Tennessee Whiskey

DISTILLERY

The Jack Daniel Distillery, Lynchburg, Tennessee

ABOUT THE BRAND

Gentleman Jack, the "super-premium" bottling of the Jack Daniel Distillery, is designated "Rare Tennessee Whiskey" in white and gold letters on its jet-black label. Introduced to the marketplace in 1988, it is presented in a handsome, 12-sided bottle modeled after a decanter Jack Daniel himself supposedly designed to commemorate the gold medal his whiskey won at the 1904 St. Louis World's Fair. The label also explains that the whiskey has been "charcoal mellowed twice," the main difference between this and the regular bottling of Jack Daniel's. A small booklet tied to the neck of the Gentleman Jack bottle explains that traditionally, this was the style of whiskey left anonymously on the doorstep of households that were celebrating a special occasion. Legend has it that the bottle would appear with a note signed "The Lynchburg Toasting Society," and we are led to believe that this society was none other than the benevolent Jack Daniel himself.

TASTING NOTES

Gentleman Jack Rare Tennessee Whiskey, 80°

Nose: Sophisticated sooty sweetness with a faint honeyed tone.

Mouth: A thick, maybe even syrupy, body bearing many more fruits than the black-labeled Jack Daniel's (plums, dates), pepper dances around the tongue, but hold on a second—what has happened to the sootiness? We thought that since this whiskey has been through the sugar-maple charcoal filtration vats twice, the sootiness would be increased (we have tasted day-old Jack Daniel's both before and after the leaching process, and the charcoal is definitely the process that adds this dimension to Tennessee whiskey), but no—it's still there. It seems to have grown up a bit—it doesn't yell any-more—now it just sits in a corner, its presence noted, but it no longer needs to be the center of attention. The finish is medium, warm, pleasant and sophisticated.

Overall: Gentleman Jack can be served on the rocks, with a splash of club soda or water, or you can even savor it in a snifter—but not if you're going to put on any airs and graces. This is a sophisticated Tennessee whiskey with no pretensions—it tastes better on the front porch than in a stuffy club.

Hancock's Reserve Single Barrel Bourbon

DISTILLERY
The Ancient Age Distillery, Frankfort, Kentucky

ABOUT THE BRAND
Hancock's Reserve was first released in 1991 and is presented in a squat, decanter-style bottle with a "pleated" base and fine cork-finished wooden stopper. The name Hancock refers to Hancock Taylor, one of the men who surveyed the Leestown area in 1774 and was killed by Native Americans for his trouble. The whiskey chosen for this bottling is selected by Master Distiller Gary Gayheart.

TASTING NOTES
Hancock's Reserve Single Barrel Bourbon, 88.9°

Nose: Initially deep, thick and assertive, but followed by some interesting fragrant tones (wildflowers).

Mouth: A big, soft, thick, round body—honey, vanilla, cigars, caramel, overripe oranges. The finish is very long.

Overall: A contender, along with Blanton's Single Barrel Bourbon and Eagle Rare, for the title of the jewel in this distillery's crown. Hancock's belongs in a snifter; it should be served completely unadulterated. However, having said that, this bourbon also sits very well on ice—but nothing more, please.

ISAAC WOLFE BERNHEIM

I.W. Harper Bourbon

DISTILLERY

The Bernheim Distillery, Louisville, Kentucky

ABOUT THE BRAND

I.W. Harper is known as the "gold medal" bourbon with good reason: It attained gold-medal status in competitions in 1885, 1893, 1900, 1904 and 1915, and you can see all of them on the label of the regular bottling. At one point, the whiskey was advertised as "I.W. Harper—This whiskey was winning gold medals when you were a boy." The I.W. Harper Gold Medal bottling contains 15-year-old bourbon and bears the slogan "It's Always a Pleasure" surrounding a silhouette of a gent carrying a cane and doffing his hat.

HISTORY

The man responsible for bringing us I. W. Harper wasn't called Harper at all; he was Isaac Wolfe Bernheim, born in Schmieheim, Germany, in 1848. Bernheim emigrated to the United States in 1867 and settled in Pennsylvania, where he worked as a peddler, selling haberdashery door to door. Eventually, he saved enough money to buy a horse and wagon.

When his horse died one winter, he sold off all of his stock and trekked westward to Kentucky. During his early days in the Bluegrass State, Bernheim worked as a store clerk and a bookkeeper for a liquor company and eventually started his own whiskey business.

In 1872, Bernheim, his brother Bernard and a silent partner by the name of Eldridge Palmer formed a company called Bernheim Bros. in Paducah, Kentucky. Bernard put his life savings ($1,200) into the business, giving the company assets of $3,200, a little knowledge and a lot of ambition. Since they didn't yet own a distillery, Bernheim Bros. was primarily a wholesale whiskey business. They bought whiskey and sold it via a traveling sales force and by mail order. Although similar companies during this period bought whatever whiskey was cheapest and often adul-

ELDRIDGE PALMER

terated it before offering it to the public at large, those with more foresight selected choice whiskeys and "mingled" (never say the word "blend" to a dealer of straight whiskey) them together to achieve a consistent product. For I. W. Harper Bourbon to have prospered and survived so well, the Bernheims must have taken the latter tack.

Still, though, where did the "Harper" come from? Apparently, Mr. Harper was a friend of Bernheim who bred racehorses in Lexington, and it is just possible that Harper had political connections that Bernheim wished to influence. Is there a better way to win a friend than to name a good bourbon after him? Of course, the other reason that Bernheim didn't want his own name on the bottle was that he possibly thought that a good old Anglo-Saxon name would be better received in his adopted country. Still, he used his own initials along with his friend's surname.

Bernheim was a savvy businessman. In 1875, he observed that whiskey would look much better in glass bottles so that buyers could see its clarity—most whiskey was sold in ceramic jugs and wooden casks. In 1879, he wisely registered a trademark for I.W. Harper Bourbon; six years after that, the whiskey won a gold medal at the 1885 New Orleans Exposition.

In 1888, the Bernheim company moved to Louisville, where the brothers bought shares in the Pleasure Ridge Distillery and maintained headquarters on Main Street. Their whiskey won another gold medal at the 1893 Chicago World's Fair, and by 1895, they were selling their whiskey "from Maine to Texas and New York to California."

The following year, a fire at the Pleasure Ridge Distillery destroyed a warehouse full of I.W. Harper whiskey. Turning a blind eye and a deaf ear to Bernheim's pleas, the government still wanted the company to pay $1 million in taxes on the whiskey—even though it had gone up in flames. During the 18 months of litigation that ensued before Uncle Sam canceled the debt, the Bernheim brothers kept busy building their very own distillery in Louisville. When it went into production in the spring of 1897, I.W. Harper was finally being made by the Bernheims.

Prohibition, from 1920 to 1933, saw I.W. Harper being sold as a medicinal whiskey, but after Repeal, the brand was bought by Chicago whiskey brokers Leo Gerngross and Emil Schwarzhaupt. Luckily, neither of them wanted their names on a bottle of whiskey, so I.W. Harper returned to the liquor store shelves.

Isaac Wolfe Bernheim died in California in 1945, after seeing his whiskey change hands yet again when Schenley Distilleries bought the brand in 1937. Schenley was bought by United Distillers in 1987, but I.W. Harper is still going strong. It is now made by Master Distiller Ed Foote at the brand-new Bernheim Distillery in Louisville.

TASTING NOTES
I.W. Harper, 86°

Nose: Clean, fresh, flowery, developing into fruit (peaches?).

Mouth: A medium-full body with a glorious balance of fruit and spices (pepper, cinnamon, peaches). The finish is long, warm and soothing.

Overall: If this is your "around the house" bourbon, you are treating yourself well. Drink it on ice, with a splash or a healthy pour of water. Distinctive in mixed drinks, and makes a very good Manhattan.

I.W. Harper, 101°

Nose: Spicy with hints of leather and some interesting high notes (citrus?).

Mouth: A medium-full body with a good balance between sweet vanilla and a hint of cream playing off some fruity, berry-like notes. The finish is long and rather hot.

Overall: This bottling strikes us as a perfect bourbon to sip from a shot glass, although it holds up very well on ice. The whiskey is also great to mix with ginger ale.

I.W. Harper, 12 years old, 86°

Nose: Sweet honey and warm spices (nutmeg?).

Mouth: A medium body with a palate that follows the nose but is more complex—honey, vanilla, caramel, nutmeg, leather and just a hint of fruit. The finish is surprisingly short but wonderfully spicy.

Overall: If you sip this bottling from a snifter, add a few drops of water. This is a perfect bourbon to pour over ice and spend the evening doing something you enjoy. Don't adulterate this whiskey with anything other than water, and don't waste a drop of it.

I.W. Harper Gold Medal, 15 years old, 80°

Nose: Honey, vanilla, oak, leather.

Mouth: A medium-full body, leaning more toward full. The palate is beautifully balanced with honey, vanilla and a hint of wildflowers playing off hints of leather, oak and light spices. The finish is medium and refreshingly crisp and light.

Overall: Here's a bourbon worthy of a snifter but actually preferable over plenty of ice. Don't adulterate this whiskey with even a splash of water—it has been bottled at a perfect proof.

I.W. Harper President's Reserve, 86° (for export only)

Nose: A big fruitiness gives way to a host of spices (cinnamon, nutmeg, cloves).

Mouth: A medium-full body with a palate that reverses its nose—spices come first and give way to fruits (dates, raisins) and a hint of both oak and leather.

Overall: Why, oh, why is this bottling reserved for export? The whole line of I.W. Harper displays great balance and sophistication, and this particular bottling deserves a place alongside the 12-year-old. Sip it from a snifter, or pour it over ice.

Basil Hayden's Bourbon

DISTILLERY

The Jim Beam Distilleries, Clermont and Boston, Kentucky

ABOUT THE BRAND

First introduced in 1992, this small-batch bourbon comes in a very smart bottle. Reportedly modeled after an early-twentieth-century design, it bears a metallic band around its "waist" and a bib-style label that relates a short story about Basil Hayden. Hayden was, in fact, one of Kentucky's earliest whiskey distillers, and you have probably heard about him before—he was the one and only "Old Grand-Dad." For a complete history of Basil Hayden, see **Old Grand-Dad Bourbon**, page 174.

TASTING NOTES
Basil Hayden's Bourbon, 8 years old, 80°

Nose: White pepper, very faint lemon zest, vanilla and a touch of mint.

Mouth: A medium-light body, but the rye shines through in the form of pepper, nutmeg and high lemon notes playing off undertones of honey and plums. The finish is medium-long, sophisticated and spicy—this is where you actually taste the rye.

Overall: This is an uncomplicated bourbon with a very definite style—the high rye content, familiar in Beam's Old Grand-Dad bottlings, gives us a spicy whiskey, ideal for "on-the-rocks" sipping or even chilled as an apéritif. It's a shame to add much more than water to Basil Hayden's, and at 80°, water is unnecessary; but if you love tall drinks, the spiciness of this bourbon makes it ideal to mix with ginger ale.

Heaven Hill Bourbon

DISTILLERY
The Heaven Hill Distillery, Bardstown, Kentucky

ABOUT THE BRAND
"Time Tempered" is the legend printed on the Heaven Hill "Old Style Bourbon" labels, and indeed, this whiskey is available in three different ages—10 years old, 6 years old and the regular bottling, which is a minimum of 4 years old.

Heaven Hill Bourbon was created by the Shapira brothers when they opened the Heaven Hill Distillery in 1935. The plant also produces Evan Williams, J.T.S. Brown, Henry McKenna, Mattingly & Moore and Elijah Craig bourbons and owes its name to William Heavenhill, who, in the nineteenth century, owned and operated a farm on the site. Heavenhill was a rough-looking character, and his dark eyes look down today from an old photograph on the distillery's wall. For one reason or another, his surname was split into two parts when the distillery was founded—Heavenhill became Heaven Hill.

HISTORY
This distillery wasn't founded, like some other notable distilleries, when Kentucky was but a wilderness that Daniel Boone had recently explored; it came into being when a group of businessmen raised enough cash to build it—and to keep up with all the new regulations that followed Prohibition. However, the truth is that the entire bourbon business was more or less reinvented after Repeal. The founders of the Heaven Hill Distillery were, in many ways, off on the same footing as everyone else in 1935.

Max Shapira, Executive Vice President of the company, explained that when his

WILLIAM HEAVENHILL

father Ed and uncles David, Gary, George and Moses invested in the company, they "didn't know a barrel from a box." But when there was a financial problem with other investors (who did know the whiskey business), they had no choice but to take control, dig in their heels and learn. Sometimes it's the best way.

The first order of business for this fledgling company was to produce quality bourbon. Although whiskey can be made in a matter of a few days, it must age for years before it can be sold. Meanwhile, figurative stacks of cash are sitting in the clean Kentucky air and taking their own good time to develop into salable stock. Well, the Shapiras had enough money to get the business off the ground, but it wasn't long before they decided to put a two-year-old bourbon, Bourbon Falls, onto the market. Luckily, it sold well enough to keep the business going until the rest of the stock matured to at least four years old, the age at which most bourbons are bottled.

Heaven Hill Bourbon hit the marketplace in the early 1940s and became the distillery's signature bourbon. About a decade later, the Shapiras made a wise move: they hired Earl Beam, nephew of Jim Beam, to be their distiller. It's said that Earl brought Jim Beam's yeast strain with him, but whiskeys made at the Jim Beam distilleries are of an entirely different style from those made at Heaven Hill.

In 1957, the Shapiras decided to name a whiskey for the pioneer Kentucky distiller Evan Williams. It was the beginning of a trend for Heaven Hill; though the distillery dated only to 1935, dozens of famous distillers from the past could be honored by naming a whiskey after them. Heaven Hill now owns the names J.T.S. Brown, Henry McKenna and Mattingly & Moore and has created a brand named for the famed Elijah Craig. The distillery also makes Pikesville rye whiskey, which can be hard to come by unless you live in Maryland, where it is still available.

The Beams remain the distillers at Heaven Hill, and to this day, the business is owned and operated by Shapira family members. Parker Beam, Earl's son, and Craig Beam, Parker's son, are in charge of making the whiskey, and they still quote Earl when they talk about their products. Unfortunately, one of Earl's traditions is no longer carried on at Heaven Hill, but we don't think it has affected the whiskey. Once a week, Earl and an assistant would spend the day growing yeast in their dona room, and the two of them took turns in preparing huge "fry-ups" for lunch. It was their treat for keeping the yeast strain alive.

TASTING NOTES
Heaven Hill, 80°

Nose: Light, flowery, with a hint of vanilla.

Mouth: Light body with an uncomplicated palate, a little hot and bearing an oaky quality. The finish is medium and rather hot.

Overall: This is a decent bottling of an "around the house" bourbon. Drink it on ice with a liberal splash of water, add any mixer, or make whiskey sours—but not Manhattans.

Heaven Hill, 6 years old, 90°

Nose: Light, sweet, a little perfume-y, hints of vanilla.

Mouth: A medium body, fairly rich and sweet, a touch of honey, some leather, a little hot in the mouth. The finish is medium and sweeter than the 80°-proof bottling.

Overall: A good "around the house" bottling. At six years old, Heaven Hill is ready for drinking on ice or with just a splash of water or club soda, and still good for making mixed drinks.

Heaven Hill, 10 years old, 86°

Nose: Oaky, hints of both honey and vanilla.

Mouth: A medium to big body, very soft in the mouth. The honey and vanilla come on strong with some subtle notes of chocolate and maybe prunes. The finish is warming and long in the throat but somewhat short in the mouth.

Overall: Ten years in the wood has matured this bourbon well. This isn't a "snifter" whiskey, but it makes a very good Manhattan and is enjoyable on ice, or with a splash of water or club soda.

A.H. Hirsch Bourbon

DISTILLERY

Michter's Distillery, near Shaefferstown, Pennsylvania (now closed)

MERCHANTS

Cork n Bottle, Covington, Kentucky

ABOUT THE BRAND

Sample these whiskeys while you can—they are very special products. The A.H. Hirsch bourbons were produced in 1974 at Michter's Distillery, Pennsylvania, which closed its doors in the late 1980s. They are the only bourbons of their type available today; both of the bottlings had their second distillations in a pot still, rather than in a doubler or a thumper. A pot still is a beautiful apparatus: Usually made from copper, it looks somewhat like a plump onion sprouting a sleek, long neck from its top. Using a pot still is slower, more work-intensive and therefore more expensive than other methods, and unlike other stills, the pot variety must be cleaned out after each distillation. All of the extra bother is worth it, however, since the pot-still whiskey is often more flavorful than that produced by any other method.

Both of the Hirsch bourbons are individual, big, rich, complex whiskeys, but since they have been aged for 16 and 20 years—considerably longer than most bottlings—and details of the entire production process are not available, it's hard to point directly to the still as the sole reason for their complexities. The whiskeys are named for Adolf Hirsch, a former Executive Vice President at Schenley, who bought some of the whiskey that remained when Michter's Distillery closed. About 5,000 barrels of whiskey are still aging at the plant.

In 1990, Hirsch's whiskey was bought by the Hue family of Kentucky, who put it into bottles bearing very fancy labels. Some of it was bottled immediately, but much of it was transferred into stainless-steel tanks where the aging process would be halted—

the whiskey was already 16 years old, and the Hues weren't sure whether it would age well for much longer. However, some remained in barrels and was bottled at 20 years old.

HISTORY

The Michter's Distillery of Pennsylvania has a fascinating history that dates back to the mid-eighteenth century, when Kentucky was still a twinkle in Daniel Boone's eye. Although whiskey is no longer made there, the distillery building has been designated a National Historic Landmark and can't be torn down; perhaps someone will come along in the not-too-distant future and reestablish Pennsylvania's whiskey-making traditions.

According to the National Register of Historic Places, whiskey production on the site of Michter's (once known as Bomberger's) began in 1753, when John and Michael Shenk, both Swiss Mennonite farmers, built a distillery to complement their farm and gristmill. Around 30 years later, when Michael's son-in-law, Rudolf Meyer, decided to focus on making whiskey instead of working his farm, it became one of the first commercial whiskey distilleries in the country.

When Meyer died, the distillery fell into the hands of his granddaughter, Elizabeth Shenk Kratzer, and her husband, John Kratzer, who ran the distillery from the late 1820s until 1860. Then, in 1861, the plant was sold to Abe Bomberger, another relative by marriage, and he gave the distillery its original name. The distillery was owned and operated by the Bomberger family, who made rye whiskey, until Prohibition.

During Prohibition, the plant was sold to a farmer, Ephrim Sechrist, and there is speculation that he may have fired up the old stills from time to time to keep the local population happy. Louis Forman, who had worked in the whiskey business since 1929, took over the distillery in 1942, left in order to do national service ("against my will," as he puts it) the following year and returned to the plant in 1950.

Forman, now 86 years old and still involved with the industry as a consultant, is not the sort to do anything by halves. When he came across some records from Abe Bomberger's time, he started to research the history of the distillery and the methods used to make the whiskey.

Forman then installed a pot still at the plant and hired, as master distiller, Charles Everett Beam, a direct descendant of Jacob Beam, the eighteenth-century distiller whose family gave us Jim Beam Bourbon. According to Mr. Forman, Charles Everett Beam was recognized as a man who really knew his craft; so when these men put their heads together and decided to make whiskey, they believed they could make the best whiskey in the land. Forman maintains that Beam had never been allowed to make the kind of whiskey that he wanted to, simply because it was too expensive. But this was a small operation that wanted to make good whiskey—costs be damned.

Michter's Pot-Still Whiskey first hit the market in 1956. The distillery itself became known as Michter's in 1975 and closed its doors in the late 1980s after making the only post-Prohibition pot-still bourbon in America.

PRODUCTION TECHNIQUES

Although, as noted, Michter's is now closed, details of its production methods were as follows: Michter's was a sour-mash whiskey that used a sour-wine yeast strain which was propagated in a yeast mash containing hops. It was aged in "medium-charred" barrels in a single-story unheated warehouse and was chill-filtered before bottling.

TASTING NOTES

A.H. Hirsch Reserve Pot Stilled Sour Mash Straight Bourbon, 16 years old, 91.6°

Nose: Sweet sandalwood, leather, pine, mint.

Mouth: A very big body, thick and rich with an elegant, almost syrupy sweetness bearing vanilla, oranges and a hint of mint. The finish is long, warm and soothing.

Overall: This whiskey is a true after-dinner drink, but it could even be served as dessert itself. Serve it in a snifter—don't add even a drop of water—and savor it for its complexity and sophistication.

A.H. Hirsch Pot Stilled Sour Mash Straight Bourbon, 20 years old, 91.6°

Nose: Oak, vanilla, mint and caramel.

Mouth: A huge body, rich and thick, and now some caramel and oak come into play with the vanilla along with a host of spices and a hint of mint that peppers the tongue in a long, long dance. The finish is very long and almost port-like.

Overall: As with the 16-year-old bottling, we suggest that the only way to serve this superlative bourbon is neat. Light up that cigar, rest your feet on a huge Old English sheepdog and dream of your spectacular future. Among our handwritten notes was: "Like a melted ice-cream parfait made from rich vanilla ice cream with a hint of crème de menthe."

J.T.S. Brown Bourbon

DISTILLERY

The Heaven Hill Distillery, Bardstown, Kentucky

ABOUT THE BRAND

J T.S. Brown Bourbon was first made by a member of the same family that created Old Forester; it is now made at the Heaven Hill Distillery, a plant that has kept more than one brand name alive when it was in danger of extinction.

The label of the J.T.S. Brown bottle includes photographs of John Thompson Street

OLD PRENTICE DISTILLERY

Brown and two of his sons, with the legend "Kentucky's Finest," and the date "1855." That particular date was the year that Henry McKenna, whose namesake bourbon is also produced at the Heaven Hill Distillery, first fired up his stills. Its appearance on this bottling is an error; when the Heaven Hill Distillery bought the J.T.S. Brown brand name, the wrong date was already on the label.

HISTORY

J.T.S. Brown Bourbon has been tied to various distilleries throughout the years, and those distilleries have operated under various names at different times—even going so far as to exchange names with one another. The history that follows, therefore, is an account of the historical facts as they can be pieced together.

In 1870, John Thompson Street Brown Jr., his half-brother, George Garvin Brown, and a cousin, John Barret, formed a company in Louisville called J.T.S. Brown and Brother. Their product was called Old Forester, the first whiskey to be sold only in sealed bottles. J.T.S.'s partnership with his brother didn't last more than five years, and present-day Brown family members believe that the parting of the ways might have arisen from George's belief that top-quality whiskey would make more money in the long run, whereas J.T.S. might have wanted to sell some less expensive whiskey to make a few bucks while the firm was finding its feet. It's pure conjecture, but there could be some truth in it.

At this point in the story, J.T.S. seems to disappear for a few years. The next time we hear about him, aside from vague references to his "operating his own plant," is in the early years of the twentieth century, when a company called J.T.S. Brown & Sons built the Old Prentice Distillery in Anderson County. In 1910, Creel Brown, one of J.T.S.'s sons, built a new "Old Prentice" Distillery just across the way from the original plant.

The Old Prentice Distillery was closed down during Prohibition, but J.T.S. Brown & Sons purchased the defunct Early Times Distillery in 1923. The name "Early Times," however, was bought by Brown-Forman, the very company that had grown from the initial partnership of J.T.S. and George Garvin Brown in 1870.

In the 1950s, J.T.S. Brown & Sons bought another distillery in Lawrenceburg, which, although it was sold shortly afterwards, remained in existence and operated under the "J.T.S. Brown & Sons" name until the late 1970s. The brand name eventually ended up at the Heaven Hill Distillery, where it is made to this day.

TASTING NOTES
J.T.S. Brown, 80°

Nose: Light, oaky, a touch of perfume and hints of vanilla.

Mouth: A lean, "masculine" body with hints of oak, leather and a touch of mint or eucalyptus. The finish is short and warm.

Overall: This is a good "around the house" bourbon, and the lighter notes make it ideal for mint juleps. It's also good for drinking with a splash of water or club soda or in mixed drinks and whiskey sours.

Kentucky Gentleman Bourbon

DISTILLERY
The Barton Distillery, Bardstown, Kentucky

ABOUT THE BRAND
The label of most bottlings of Kentucky Gentleman Bourbon features a picture of a goateed gent with a stiff white collar, black tie and stovepipe hat, but there isn't a soul who can identify him. For a complete history of the Barton Distillery, see **Tom Moore Bourbon**, page 159.

TASTING NOTES
Kentucky Gentleman, 80°
Kentucky Gentleman, Bottled in Bond, 100°
Nose: Spicy, oaky, hints of clover.

Mouth: Both bottlings have a medium-light body, just a touch heavier in the bottled-in-bond bourbon. The palate is light and dry with some new-mown grass/straw notes and a slight fruitiness—again, more evident in the 100° bottling, where hints of caramel, vanilla and clover also lurk. The finish on both is medium.

Overall: A decent "around the house" bourbon. Drink it however you wish.

Kentucky Gentleman, 6 years old, 86°
Nose: Sweetish, some caramel and a touch of tobacco.

Mouth: A medium, soft body, more complex than the other two bottlings, with a soft spiciness, some vanilla and a hint of tobacco. The finish is short and a little hot.

Overall: Once again, this is a good "around the house" bourbon, perfect for highballs, cocktails and even a Manhattan.

Kentucky Tavern Bourbon Whiskey

DISTILLERY
The Bernheim Distillery, Louisville, Kentucky

ABOUT THE BRAND
According to the label, Kentucky Tavern is "The Aristocrat of Bourbons." The brand was introduced around the turn of the century and was made as a blended whiskey by the Glenmore Distillery. When it was acquired by United Distillers in 1991, the com-

pany decided to use its own wheated bourbon recipe to make straight, not blended, whiskey. The label still sports the red and gold crest of the Glenmore Distillery, and although it is made at the Bernheim plant in Louisville, this particular bourbon is aged in the countryside in warehouses owned by the company in Owensboro, Kentucky.

TASTING NOTES
Kentucky Tavern, 80°
Kentucky Tavern, Bottled in Bond, 100°

Nose: Honey, oak and a slight spiciness.

Mouth: A medium body with a rather dry palate, bearing light notes of leather and citrus balanced with just a little fruitiness (plums?). The 100°-proof bourbon is a little richer than the 80°-proof bottling, bearing a more honeyed palate. The finish is medium-long and warm.

Overall: This is a good "around the house" bottling with a touch of style. Drink it however you wish. It makes a rather good Manhattan.

Knob Creek Bourbon

DISTILLERY
The Jim Beam Distilleries, Clermont and Boston, Kentucky

ABOUT THE BRAND
Knob Creek small-batch bourbon, introduced in 1992, is named for the site of one of Abraham Lincoln's childhood homes—Knob Creek, Kentucky. The area is no more than a 30-minute drive south of Bardstown, and there stands a replica of the remarkably tiny one-room log cabin where the Lincoln family lived during some of Abe's early years.

We love the flask-type bottle in which Knob Creek is presented. The label is adorned with an upside-down clipping from a newspaper titled *The Knob Creek News* and dated October 23, 1935, over which is printed (the right way up) the name of the bourbon, age, proof and the legend: "Hand-bottled in limited quantities for superior taste and smoothness." Another label, this one of brown paper and "slapped" on the side of the bottle, reads: "Deep in Kentucky, tiny Knob Creek spills and rifles down through the hills. Like the Bourbon bearing its name, there's not much of Knob Creek but what there is rewards your finding it." The cork-finished stopper is sealed with a thick coat of black wax.

TASTING NOTES
Knob Creek, 9 years old, 100°

Nose: Toasted almonds, vanilla, honey, dark fruits (blackberries, blueberries).

Mouth: A big, smooth body, with deep, dark fruits (prunes, dates) and some candied apples, vanilla and caramelized oranges. The finish is long, spicy, warming and smooth.

Overall: Knob Creek is first-rate bourbon. It stands up to ice very well, but forget about adding water, club soda or anything else to this whiskey: At 100° proof, Knob Creek is as close to perfection as any bourbon on the market. You can also drink Knob Creek from a snifter—just warm it with the palm of your hand, and that's the only help it will ever need.

Elmer T. Lee Single Barrel Bourbon

DISTILLERY
The Ancient Age Distillery, Frankfort, Kentucky

ABOUT THE BRAND

This single-barrel bourbon is named for the Master Distiller Emeritus at the Ancient Age Distillery and comes complete with his likeness and some biographical notes: "Not a man alive knows more about bourbon than E.T. Lee. A native Kentuckian, Lee was born and raised in the heart of bourbon country. And he's had a hand in producing some of the finest Bourbons ever bottled. But this one's got his name on it. 'I wanted to create a Single Barrel Bourbon for real Bourbon folk,' says Lee. 'One that tastes best out on the front porch . . . All 90 proof of it.'" Also on the label are some historical notes about whiskey production in the Frankfort area, but one fact not noted on the bottle is that Lee actually worked with famed distiller Albert B. Blanton. For a complete history of the Ancient Age Distillery, and the Blanton family, see **Ancient Age Bourbon**, page 104. The whiskey chosen for this bottling is, of course, selected by Master Distiller Emeritus Elmer T. Lee. It was first released in 1992.

TASTING NOTES
Elmer T. Lee Single Barrel Bourbon, 90°

Nose: Sweet, oaky (plums?).

Mouth: A big, soft body, rather hot but pleasingly round. Much heavier flavors than the nose suggests—definite plums, with dates and a touch of raisin. An adamant bourbon—it gets heavier as it goes and elongates in the mouth. A long, dry finish.

Overall: A sexy, complex bourbon—somewhat like Elmer himself. Drink it over ice, savor it in a snifter, or make an elegant Manhattan.

Maker's Mark Bourbon

DISTILLERY

The Maker's Mark Distillery, Loretto, Kentucky

ABOUT THE BRAND

Maker's Mark, a wheated whiskey, is the most popular bourbon in Kentucky, where it is known on a first-name basis as "Maker's." This distillery is now owned by Hiram Walker & Sons, Inc., but luckily, production remains in the hands of Bill Samuels Jr., president of Maker's Mark—head of the family that started the brand and one of the most colorful characters in the bourbon business.

Most bourbon drinkers could look at a silhouette of a bottle of Maker's Mark and name it on the spot. The long-necked, square-based shape is distinctive, as is the red wax that seals the cap. Each bottle is hand-dipped; even the labels are handmade—printed on an old press at the distillery and cut by a manually operated machine. The label bears the family logo, designed by Bill Samuels Sr.: the *S* stands for Samuels, the star denotes the Star Hill Farm distillery site, and the *IV* was supposed to denote the number of generations of Samuels who have made whiskey in Kentucky. Therein lies a tale: "That's my father's dyslexia at work," Bill Samuels Jr. jokes. "He started measuring with my great-great-grandfather, who was the first distiller in our family to register with the Secretary of State—he had no idea that a few generations before him had been whiskey men." Bill researched the family tree and found that he was actually the seventh generation of whiskey distillers in the family. The logo, however, was already established by that time. The label on the regular bottling of Maker's also extends an invitation to visit the distillery—it's a National Historic Landmark that's well worth seeing.

The V.I.P. Maker's Mark contains the same bourbon as the regular bottling, but the packaging is very special: When you buy this whiskey, the retailer will make arrangements for a special label to be printed bearing the name of the person of your choice—or you can use the order form that comes in the box. The design of the sleek but simple eight-faceted bottles was inspired by a late-nineteenth-century bourbon bottle that resides in the Oscar Getz Museum of Whiskey History in Bardstown. After being filled, each bottle has its neck dipped in gold sealing wax, and the front is emblazoned with a hand-stamped rendition of the Maker's medallion.

HISTORY

The history of the Samuels family in Kentucky dates to the spring of 1780, when Robert Samuels, a young officer in the Pennsylvania militia, moved to Kentucky to farm and make whiskey. Since Kentucky, at that time, didn't yet require distillers to register as such, no records exist to prove that Robert actually operated a still on his farm. However, he was registered as a distiller in Pennsylvania in 1779 and 1780, so chances are excellent that he fired up the old stills when he came to Kentucky. Records also show that Robert was an expert at valuing distillation equipment for estates, so it's fairly certain that he knew his business well.

William Samuels, Robert's son, was most certainly a whiskey man, but it was his son, Taylor William Samuels, who established the family's first commercial distillery in Deatsville, in 1844. Fifty-two years later, in *The Nelson County Record*, T.W. Samuels was recognized as being "in the business longer than any man who ever made whiskey within the confines of old Nelson [County]." By that time, Samuels' whiskey was being sold throughout the country, and his warehouses had a capacity of a whopping 14,000 barrels. This man was also Nelson County's largest landowner and served four terms as its High Sheriff.

Taylor's son, William Isaac Samuels, was named superintendent of the distillery in 1866 and also held various titles and posts in Nelson County; he was president of the Nelson County Agricultural and Fair Organization and president of the Bardstown and Shepherdsville Turnpike Company, and in 1895, he was elected president of the Kentucky Swine Breeders Association. The distillery passed into the hands of Leslie Samuels when his father (William Isaac) died in 1898, and he ran the business right up until Prohibition began in 1920.

When Prohibition ended in 1933, Leslie Samuels reorganized the company, built a new plant in Deatsville and reopened the T.W. Samuels Distillery. The business passed on to his son, T. William Samuels, who ran it until he retired in 1943 and sold the distillery. But after so many generations of Samuels in the whiskey business, bourbon must have been in T. William Samuels' blood. He reentered the business just 10 years later when he bought a small distillery in Loretto. This plant had been established in 1805 by Charles Burks and was operated by his grandson in the late nineteenth and early twentieth centuries. Although it had been in operation at various times and under various ownerships since 1937, the place was pretty ramshackle and in need of far more than a coat of paint. T. William Samuels wasn't in the habit of doing anything by halves. He lovingly restored every square inch, and he did it with so much attention to historical detail that the distillery became a National Historic Landmark.

T. William named the plant the Star Hill Distillery after his family farm in Bardstown, and he began producing Maker's Mark Bourbon. The bourbon got its name when T. William's wife, Margie Samuels, a collector of pewter, noted that every piece in her collection bore the hallmark of its maker. It signified to her that whoever made something they were proud of put their "maker's mark" on the product. Margie was also responsible for the bottles' necks being hand-dipped in wax; apparently, Margie was an avid collector of more than just pewter, and her accumulation of old Cognac bottles inspired the signature red wax on Maker's Mark Bourbon.

When T. William Samuels reentered the business, he brought with him the strain of yeast he had used back at the old distillery, along with some definite, if individual, ideas about how bourbon should be made. He consulted Pappy Van Winkle at the Stitzel-Weller Distillery, and to this day, Bill Samuels Jr. gives Pappy credit for helping his father arrive at the distinctive recipe (one of the handful of bourbons that uses wheat instead of rye grain) that is now used by Maker's Mark.

Maker's Mark Distillery still has a "Quart House," a small building where whiskey from the distillery was sold at retail, a toll house and two bonded warehouses that date to the nineteenth century. The old Burks family residence, another building that was restored by the Samuels family, looks down on the distillery from a small hill across the way. The entire operation is situated in an idyllic setting in Kentucky's Marion County. Although Hiram Walker & Sons bought the business in 1981, operations are still very much under the control of Bill Samuels Jr., who joined the company in 1967 and became its president in 1975.

TASTING NOTES
Maker's Mark, 90°

Nose: Honey, raisins, dates, butter and a piquant high note to balance the experience.

Mouth: A huge, soft body full of honey, vanilla, butterscotch, oak, dark berries and a hint of leather. The finish is long, warm and soothing. Among our handwritten notes appeared the phrase "well manicured."

Overall: One sip of this bourbon tells you what all the fuss is about and why Maker's Mark has developed a cult following over the years. All of the time and money that this distillery puts into rotating its stock pays off with a whiskey that shows a true maturity. Drink Maker's however you wish—it is at home in a snifter, comfortable on ice and perfect for lush Manhattans. If this is your "around the house" bourbon, your neighbors should be very impressed.

Maker's Mark Limited Edition, 101°

Nose: Honey, raisins, butter and a hint of dark spices.

Mouth: A huge round body, similar to the 90°-proof bottling but a little spicier, with hints of cinnamon and nutmeg to balance out the oak, honey, butterscotch and vanilla. The finish is long and warm.

Overall: Another well-crafted whiskey from Maker's. Once again, the maturity shines through in the form of a perfectly balanced bourbon that's rich, lush and sophisticated. Drink this bottling however you wish—in a snifter, on ice or in a very stylish Manhattan. Try adding a couple of drops of hot water to this bourbon and serving it after dinner—it's an old Samuels family "trick."

Maker's Mark Select, 95° (for export only)

Nose: Vanilla, honey, dates and butter—just a hint of leather.

Mouth: A huge round body, and whereas the nose shows sweeter notes than the previous two bottlings, the palate reverses and shows itself to be spicier with hints of mint (or is it eucalyptus?) to balance out an underlying fruitiness. The finish is long and warm, again showing a hint of mint.

Overall: It's a shame that this whiskey is available only for the export market, since it seems to show another side of Maker's Mark's craftsmanship. We believe that this whiskey is a little older than the previous two bottlings, and although no bottlings of Maker's bear an age statement, reliable, independent sources tell us that all of the bottlings contain whiskey that's five to six years old. This one seems older still. If you purchase this bottling when traveling overseas, reserve it for a snifter or for making the most marvelous mint juleps.

Mattingly & Moore Bourbon

DISTILLERY

The Heaven Hill Distillery, Bardstown, Kentucky

ABOUT THE BRAND

"Mild and Mellow" is the legend inscribed on the Mattingly & Moore label, along with a scroll bearing the initials *M & M* and "1876," the year that the original Mattingly & Moore Distillery opened its doors.

HISTORY

Here's a bourbon whose origins go back to 1876, when Tom Moore, a 21-year-old Louisville native who worked at the Willet, Franke, and Company Distillery in Nelson County joined with co-worker Ben Mattingly to buy the plant. The distillery was renamed the Mattingly & Moore Distillery, and their main brand of whiskey was called Belle of Nelson.

Just when Mattingly & Moore Bourbon first hit the market is a little unclear. We know that the distillery made Tom Moore Bourbon in 1879 but can't find reference to the company's signature brand until 1896, by which time both Mattingly and Moore had left the distillery. However, a good guess would be that the brand became available shortly after Mattingly and Moore bought the plant in 1876. Moore went on to establish the Tom Moore Distillery (1889) in Bardstown, which, after Prohibition, became the Barton Distillery.

Sometime between 1881 and 1886, John Simms and R.H. Edelen entered the business with Moore. Edelen had been an Internal Revenue gauger, the person who made sure that all of the whiskey was accounted for and all of the taxes paid. By 1896, the plant was offering Simms and Edelen whiskeys (both rye and bourbon) and Mattingly & Moore handmade sour mash. All three brands were available in every state of the Union and also in Canada and Mexico.

In 1902, the Frankfort Distilling Company was formed. It was a collection of small distilleries that joined forces for economic reasons—such companies were quite common at the time. The company bought the Mattingly & Moore name during Prohibition, when it was producing whiskey for "medicinal" purposes, and reorganized right after Repeal as Frankfort Distilleries, Inc. A few years later, the brand was bought by the Seagram company, and eventually, the brand name was purchased by the Heaven Hill Distillery, where it is currently produced.

TASTING NOTES
Mattingly & Moore, 80°

Nose: Sweet, with hints of caramel, vanilla, oak and nutmeg.

Mouth: The body is soft and comfortable with some menthol notes, a touch of caramel, leather and honey. The finish is medium and warm.

Overall: The mintiness of this bourbon is consistent with the distillery's style, but this particular bottling seems to bear a sophistication all its own. This is a very good "around the house" bourbon. Drink it on ice, with a splash of water or club soda, in a mint julep or even in a Manhattan.

Henry McKenna Bourbon

DISTILLERY
The Heaven Hill Distillery, Bardstown, Kentucky

ABOUT THE BRAND
The bottle in which Henry McKenna Bourbon is presented bears the words "Kentucky's Finest Table Whiskey Since 1855," referring to the date on which Henry McKenna first fired up his still.

HISTORY
The brand name, Henry McKenna, was purchased by the Heaven Hill Distillery in the early 1980s, and the whiskey is being made there to this day. The whiskey itself, however, dates to the mid-1800s, when Henry McKenna turned his hand to the still. McKenna arrived on these shores from County Derry, Ireland, in the late 1830s, when

he was in his late teens. By 1855, after marrying Elizabeth Goodwin some eight years previous, he had become a miller in the town of Fairfield, Nelson County, and decided to use up some of his excess grain by making "the creature" (an Irish term for whiskey). McKenna set up a still under an old shed and unknowingly laid the foundation for a booming whiskey business. At that time, though, he couldn't produce more than a barrel of whiskey a day.

McKenna soon abandoned his grain mill in favor of distilling. His first whiskey was apparently made from wheat, not corn, and it is said that he didn't switch to using corn as his predominant grain until two years later. As was common at that time, McKenna's children followed him to the still; his eldest son, Daniel, reputedly entered the business when he was no more than 8 years old. Another son, James, also worked at the distillery some years later.

Around 1858, a fellow Derryman, Patrick Sweeney, became McKenna's distiller. Described in the late 1890s as "the celebrated distiller, known throughout the country," Sweeney had settled in Philadelphia when he was just 12 years old and arrived in Nelson County in the late 1850s.

In 1880, business was so good for the McKennas that James was sent to Louisville to open an office in a building known as the Old Blue House. McKenna's whiskey was about to become very popular, and just two years later, the company had to move to larger premises. In 1883, McKenna built a new brick distillery to replace the old shed at his Fairfield location.

By 1896, H. McKenna Old Line, Hand Made, Sour Mash Whisky was being sold nationwide, although Henry had passed away in 1893. We hope that before he died, he heard the words of Dudley S. Reynolds, M.D., who was quoted as saying, in 1886, that Henry McKenna's whiskey was the purest and best he had ever seen. According to *The Nelson County Record*, 1896, the McKenna Distillery was the only one in Kentucky that refused to sell its whiskey until it had been aged for a minimum of three years.

McKenna's whiskey went from strength to strength, gaining in popularity and sales right through the early years of the twentieth century. Daniel McKenna died in 1917, just before war regulations (World War I) and the upcoming Prohibition closed the distillery. However, the stock from the plant was bought by and stored at the Stitzel Distillery in Louisville, and the brand name was kept alive by the Stitzel sales force, which distributed "medicinal whiskey" during Prohibition.

In 1934, James and Stafford McKenna, who by then were 79 and 73 years old respectively, opened up the old distillery with Coleman Bixler, the pre-Prohibition distiller who had been taught the ways of the still by Patrick Sweeney himself. James sold his shares to Stafford in 1940 and died that same year. Meanwhile, distiller Bixler, one of the few people outside of the McKenna family to own stock in the business, had passed his job along to his son-in-law, Sam Simpson. Simpson was probably trained by Bixler, who was trained by Sweeney, who had been taught to make McKenna whiskey by Henry McKenna himself; it's not at all farfetched to conclude that in 1940, the McKenna Distillery in Fairfield was probably making whiskey that was at least very similar to the whiskey Henry McKenna made back in 1855. Unfortunately, the whiskey was about to change.

In 1941, Stafford McKenna sold the distillery to the Seagram company, but according to our sources, the sale did not include the bourbon recipe—the whiskey died that year. Sam Simpson went on to become Master Distiller for the Barton Distillery in 1943. The McKenna Distillery was laid to rest in 1976 when the Seagram company sold it to various parties and it was dismantled. The McKenna brand name survives solely due to the Heaven Hill Distillery.

TASTING NOTES
Henry McKenna, 80°

Nose: Light and oaky with a light vegetal note and hints of vanilla.

Mouth: A medium-light body with some oaky notes, a touch of leather and hints of mint. The finish is medium and warm.

Overall: Ideal for mint juleps, a good "around the house" bottling and also good for mixed drinks and whiskey sours.

Tom Moore Bourbon

DISTILLERY
The Barton Distillery, Bardstown, Kentucky

ABOUT THE BRAND
Tom Moore Bourbon has been around since 1879, when the brand was created by the "Moore" of Mattingly & Moore fame. Some of the water used to make Tom Moore Bourbon comes from the same spring that Moore himself used. The gold-edged beige label on Tom Moore Bourbon bears a dandy crest depicting two horses, the initials *T.M.* and the words "Since 1879."

HISTORY
Tom Moore was working in the whiskey business in 1876, when he and Ben Mattingly, a co-worker, bought out the Nelson County plant known as the Willet, Franke and Company Distillery and renamed it the Mattingly & Moore Distillery. Their best-known whiskey was Belle of Nelson, but by 1879, Tom Moore Bourbon had hit the marketplace.

Sometime around 1881, Mattingly left the business and Moore took on John Simms as a silent partner and R. H. Edelen, a former Internal Revenue gauger, as a working partner. Eight years later, Moore struck out on his own, establishing the Tom Moore Distillery near Bardstown. He was about 36 years old at the time, had been educated for two years at St. Mary's College, Kentucky, and had 15 years of experience in the whiskey business. Moore was also a good businessman, and by 1911, his distillery's worth was estimated at $150,000 to $174,000.

Moore operated his distillery right up until Prohibition was forced down the throats of thirsty Americans and the plant closed. In 1934, after Repeal, a man named Harry Teur bought the distillery, completely modernized it and renamed it the Barton Distillery. (Teur probably worked with Moore for a short time, but Moore died around 1934.) We know that the modernization was undertaken for efficiency, but we aren't quite sure where he got the name Barton.

In 1944, Oscar Getz, a whiskey man of great renown, and his brother-in-law, Lester Abelson, bought the Barton Distillery. Not only did Getz and Abelson make Tom Moore Bourbon, they introduced Kentucky Gentleman Bourbon. In 1957, after the distillery filled its one-millionth barrel of whiskey, the Barton Museum of Whiskey History was opened at the distillery, and that same year, Getz was elected "Man of the Year" by the American liquor industry.

The museum, now called the Oscar Getz Museum of Whiskey History, was eventually moved to its present site in Spalding Hall, Bardstown. You can wander its halls peering at ancient stills, well-preserved documents and whiskey bottles the likes of which you've never seen before. It is run by Flaget Nally and Mary Hite, two very knowledgeable whiskey authorities. In 1978, Getz published *Whiskey—An American Pictorial History*, a book that lovingly details the story of whiskey in America and includes numerous photographs to illustrate the facts.

TASTING NOTES
Tom Moore, 80°

Nose: Good balance of light floral tones and sweetish vanilla.

Mouth: A light body that develops into a very definite style boasting fruits (dates, plums), a hint of oak and a touch of honey. The finish is medium and leaves a hint of honey on the tongue.

Overall: This is a very good, individualistic "around the house" bourbon. Drink it on ice, add water or club soda, or make any highball or cocktail you desire. Makes a good Manhattan.

Tom Moore, Bottled in Bond, 100°

Nose: Sweet, some burnt sugar and vanilla.

Mouth: A lightish body full of spices (cinnamon, nutmeg) some clover, a very pleasant "grassiness," and is there a hint of lilac here? The finish is medium and, once again, leaves honey on the tongue.

Overall: The 80° bottling is a good bourbon, but this is the one we really recommend. A very stylish "around the house" bourbon. Drink it on ice, with water or club soda and in all highballs and cocktails.

Old Charter Bourbon

DISTILLERY

The Bernheim Distillery, Louisville, Kentucky

ABOUT THE BRAND

Old Charter is available with a distinctive yellow label on its 8-year-old and 10-year-old bourbons, at 12 years old in "The Classic 90" bottling that bears a handsome dark green label and as Old Charter Proprietor's Reserve, 13 years old, in a distinctive flask-shaped bottle with a sophisticated gray label with white and gold lettering.

All of these labels feature a tree, which represents Connecticut's Charter Oak, and "1874," which, according to the distillery, was the date that Old Charter was first made available to the public *under that name*. The 8-year-old Old Charter label includes a clock face to signify that time is an important ingredient in producing good whiskey and dates to around 1950 when then owner Schenley declared that Old Charter was "the whiskey that didn't watch the clock."

HISTORY

Adam and Ben Chapeze, the men who first created this whiskey, were descended from Frenchman Henri Chapiers, a surgeon under Lafayette in the Revolutionary War. Adam and Ben's maternal grandfather, Peter Shepherd, was a farmer-distiller who was granted a piece of land near Long Lick Creek, Kentucky, and established Long Lick Creek Farm—a business where corn was probably grown and a certain amount of whiskey was made.

By 1867, having established their own distillery in Chapeze Station, Kentucky, the brothers had to think of a name for their whiskey. Seven long years later, they decided on Old Charter, possibly to immortalize the charter that granted land to their mother's family in 1782, or more probably, since the brothers were descended from soldier stock, the brand was named after the Charter Oak in Hartford, Connecticut, where the Governor's Charter was hidden from King James' soldiers when they tried to seize it in 1687.

The brand changed hands a couple of times between 1867 and the mid-1890s, but the whiskey and the distillery ended up being owned by Wright and Taylor, a company that owned other whiskeys, such as Kentucky Taylor, Pride of Louisville, Cane Springs and Old Logan. After expanding the Old Charter Distillery in 1896, they offered their first bottles of Old Charter Bourbon, Bottled in Bond, in 1900. Six years later, after adding Old Charter Rye whiskey to their line, Wright and Taylor started selling the brand in California and as far north as Nome, Alaska.

"Ask Any Colonel"

OLD CHARTER
Straight Kentucky
WHISKEY

WRIGHT & TAYLOR
Kentucky's Famous Distillers

OLD CHARTER

When Prohibition hit the country in 1920, all Old Charter stock was stored at the Stitzel distillery's warehouse, and 13 years later, when the Noble Experiment was drawing to a close, the brand and stock were purchased by the Bernheim Distillery. Bernheim, however, was sold to Schenley in 1937, the same year that Chapeze Station was renamed Limestone Springs, and today, Old Charter Bourbon (the rye whiskey no longer exists) is still produced at the Bernheim plant, which has been owned by United Distillers since its acquisition of Schenley in 1987.

TASTING NOTES
Old Charter, 8 years old, 80°

Nose: Dry, peppery, perfume-y followed by hints of honey and vanilla.

Mouth: Medium to full body, entering the palate with a rich, thick dryness that, as in the nose, develops quickly into a full bourbon sweetness with caramel, honey and vanilla balanced with hints of leather and spices. The finish is warm, soft and long.

Overall: A distinguished bourbon. This bottling should be served straight up with a splash of water, on ice with water or club soda or in a Manhattan. If you add flavored mixers, the results will be wonderful, but it's a shame to mask the lighter notes that give this bourbon its marvelous balance.

Old Charter, 10 years old, 86°

Nose: Dry and peppery with an "ashy" note, followed by a rich sweetness (honey and vanilla).

Mouth: A huge body, similar to the 8-year-old bottling but a little richer—the caramel, honey and vanilla still present, the leather gone and replaced by cinnamon and nutmeg. Great balance. The finish is long, slow and comfortable.

Overall: The extra two years in the wood turned this bourbon into a true, smooth, sippin' whiskey. Sip it from a snifter or a shot glass, add ice if that is your wont, but nothing more than a splash of water should be used to dilute this sophisticated bourbon.

Old Charter, The Classic 90, 12 years old, 90°

Nose: The now familiar dryness (pepper, ashes) once again develops into rich sweet notes of honey and vanilla.

Mouth: At 12 years old, the balance in this bottling is starting to change its direction—now the spices are much more intense, and the whiskey has developed a lean but powerful structure. The sweet honey vanilla notes are joined by a hint of oranges. The finish is in accordance—long and spicy.

Overall: Worthy of a snifter, but great on ice with as much water as you care to add. The spiciness also makes it perfect to marry with ginger ale, although you may hesitate to adulterate this whiskey with anything but water or ice.

Old Charter Proprietor's Reserve, 13 years old, 90°

Nose: Dry, peppery, sweet and honeyed—all at once.

Mouth: The body is big, thick and very rich; the bourbon is buttery—coating the whole mouth. Honey notes are evident, along with oranges, syrupy vanilla, cloves and old leather. All these sweet-spicy notes mingle together, giving this bottling a stunning complexity. The finish is long, warm and sophisticated.

Overall: There is something about this bottling which suggests that the whiskey is not merely one year older than the previous Old Charter—this is likely coming from casks that were very carefully selected for the particularly complex way in which their contents developed and matured. Proprietor's Reserve should be served in a handsome snifter, add just a drop of water if you please, settle into your favorite chair, smoke a fine cigar and pamper yourself all evening. Among our handwritten notes was the phrase: "like a fine old silken tapestry."

MARK TWAIN VISITS THE OLD CROW DISTILLERY

The famous humorist considered Old Crow the aristocrat of bourbons
and went to see for himself how it was made.

OLD CROW

Kentucky Straight Bourbon Whiskey

Old Crow is still produced on the same site near Frankfort, Ky.
where James Crow built his first small distillery. Through generations past, Old Crow's superior Kentucky quality has won
for it the high praise and public recognition of some of America's most celebrated men. Have *you* tried Old Crow recently?

A TRULY GREAT NAME

Among America's Great Whiskies

BOTTLED IN BOND · UNDER SUPERVISION OF U.S. GOVERNMENT

100 PROOF · NATIONAL DISTILLERS PRODUCTS CORPORATION, NEW YORK

EARLY ADVERTISEMENT FOR OLD CROW

Old Crow Bourbon

DISTILLERY

The Jim Beam Distilleries, Clermont and Boston, Kentucky

ABOUT THE BRAND

There's a crow on the label of Old Crow Bourbon, and its beak holds a few ears of corn, but if you look closely at the background, you'll see a couple of old whiskey men with a barrel of sour mash. Although it probably isn't an exact likeness of the man, one of them represents Dr. James Crow. The words "The Original Sour Mash" appear on this label, too, along with "1835," which refers to the year that James Crow "invented the sour mash method." Although we can't find documentation to verify that exact year, we do know that he started using his sour mash method somewhere around this time— maybe even earlier. Old Crow is a whiskey of true historical importance: It is the whiskey that set the standards for bourbon *as we now know it* in America.

HISTORY

Dr. James Crow was the first of his kind—a Scottish chemist and physician who turned his skills to the making of whiskey. Crow arrived on these shores around 1820, made his way to Kentucky some three years later and was hired as a distiller. Reportedly, the first man to notice his worth was either Colonel Willis Field or Zachariah Henry, both of whom owned distilleries in Woodford County. Whichever of these men was the first to realize that a chemist made a good whiskey man was wise indeed.

Crow used strange tools to make his whiskey. These days, his implements—or more modern versions of them—are commonplace in every distillery. He dipped litmus paper into the mash tub and the fermenter to test the acidity of the product before it was distilled. He was probably the first to use a saccharimeter to measure sugar levels at various stages of production. And he used a thermometer to measure the temperature of the mash tubs, fermenters and stills. His goal was to figure out exactly what factors were pertinent to the making of fine whiskey and to determine which factors could go awry and result in sheer rotgut. Most important, Crow was the man who perfected the sour-mash method, wherein a portion of the used mash from one distillation is added to the next batch of cooked grains that are ready for fermentation.

Distillers might have used sour mash before Crow came along, but we cannot locate a single reference to its use. As far as we can ascertain, Crow was the first man to make sour-mash whiskey, and perhaps even more important, he was the first to know *why* his whiskey was smoother and better. Crow developed specific formulas that extended a mashbill recipe into an entire process. Furthermore, Crow insisted on aging his whiskey, and there is good reason to believe that since his whiskey was known as "red liquor" as early as 1849, Crow aged his product in charred oak barrels. The result? Considering that he used over 75 percent corn in his whiskey, Crow probably was the first to make what we would recognize today as bourbon.

Crow's reputation was good; according to Charles Cowdery, publisher of *The Bourbon Country Reader*, a very informative newsletter, he ended up as distiller, shortly before 1840, at the Old Oscar Pepper Distillery. The whiskey made at the plant was bottled as Old Pepper and as Old Crow, and both brands became immensely popular. In fact, whiskey from the Old Oscar Pepper Distillery was heralded as "the best" by such major figures as Ulysses S. Grant and Henry Clay.

Crow died in 1856, having made a name for his whiskey and also for himself—as a learned man who liked to recite the poems of Robbie Burns. Like that of Burns, Crow's work took on a life all its own after his death. The new distiller, William Mitchell, had worked with Crow and therefore knew exactly how to reproduce his whiskey, a skill that he passed on to his successor, Van Johnson.

The distillery itself, meanwhile, was purchased by a company owned in part by E.H. Taylor, the man responsible for Old Taylor Bourbon and a dominant force behind the Bottled-in-Bond Act of 1897. We should be thankful that such a responsible soul took control of and retained the formula for Old Crow. Around 1872, a new facility, named the Old Crow Distillery, was built down the road from the Pepper plant, and Old Crow was made there until Prohibition and again after Repeal.

When the distillery was refurbished in the 1960s, Crow's formula somehow was changed. There followed a public uproar, but the new recipe continued to be used right up until the distillery closed in 1987, when National Distillers, who had become owners of the brand around 1947, was purchased by the Jim Beam Brands Company. Beam still produces and markets Old Crow Bourbon, and according to Jerry Summers, assistant manager and, for our purposes, distiller at Jim Beam's Clermont plant, Old Crow Bourbon is made with a massive amount of backset, a practice the good Dr. Crow would no doubt applaud.

TASTING NOTES
Old Crow, 4 years old, 80°

Nose: Tobacco, a faint aroma of oranges and a slight but pleasant mustiness.

Mouth: A medium-light body with lots of high notes (lemons, allspice, new-mown grass) mixed in with teasing hints of fruit, barely there but playing nicely off the spice. The finish is short, sharp and simple.

Overall: A whiskey to which the term "old-fashioned" seems to apply. This is a great apéritif bourbon; serve it on the rocks as soon as your guests arrive. Mix it with water, club soda or ginger ale, but just a splash should do the trick.

BOTTLING OLD JUDGE AT THE OLD FITZGERALD DISTILLERY AROUND 1905

Old Fitzgerald Bourbon

DISTILLERY

The Bernheim Distillery, Louisville, Kentucky

ABOUT THE BRAND

Old Fitzgerald is a wheated bourbon. The labels on the regular and bottled-in-bond products feature a picture of a still that looks very much like the copper doubler at the Stitzel-Weller Distillery (now closed), but it is actually a rendering of the doubler from the John E. Fitzgerald Distillery, which closed its doors when Prohibition began. The label also bears the mottos "Old Fashioned But Still in Style" and "One out of Many" on splendid gold shields.

The label on Old Fitzgerald's "1849" bottle, however, has a bit of a story attached to it. That date has nothing whatsoever to do with Old Fitzgerald's history; it refers to prominent whiskey man W.L. Weller's entry into the whiskey business. At some point, someone (not the current owners of the brand—a company with tremendous archives and a deep commitment to historical facts) transferred the date to an Old Fitzgerald bottle. And there it has stayed—incorrect but, at this point, traditional.

HISTORY

Old Fitzgerald was one of the first whiskeys marketed as an upscale "private label" brand. In the late 1800s, you wouldn't have been able to get your hands on Old Fitzgerald unless you were a member of a posh private club or a passenger on a steamship. In 1870, when John E. Fitzgerald built his first distillery in Frankfort, Kentucky, and made his "John E. Fitzgerald" whiskey, he chose to sell it exclusively to those types of establishments. These days, Old Fitzgerald is made at the Bernheim Distillery in Louisville, where it is one of the few whiskeys that uses wheat instead of rye in its mashbill.

It wasn't until 1889 that this whiskey actually became known as Old Fitzgerald, although the trademark had been registered some five years previously. The brand was sold, around the turn of the century, to S.C. Herbst, a Milwaukeean who also owned the Benson Creek and Old Judge whiskeys. In 1904, Herbst returned triumphant from Europe where he had set up agencies to market Old Fitzgerald in England, France, Italy and Germany; by 1906, he was listed as a distiller with offices in Chicago, New York, London, Paris, Berlin and Genoa. Herbst owned the John E. Fitzgerald Distillery and the Old Judge Distillery, and both whiskeys were made in pot stills (a relatively slow and inefficient way of producing very flavorful whiskey) until at least 1913—placing them among the last whiskeys of that type to be made in America.

During Prohibition, the Old Fitzgerald brand was snapped up by colorful, old-time whiskey man Pappy Van Winkle (see **W.L. Weller Bourbon**, page 191) at the Stitzel-Weller Distillery, and it became a signature brand for the company. Indeed, when the distillery was purchased by Somerset Imports in 1972, they changed its name to the Old Fitzgerald Distillery. That didn't last long, however; the name was changed back to Stitzel-Weller in 1991.

TASTING NOTES
Old Fitzgerald Bourbon, 80°
Old Fitzgerald, Bottled in Bond, 100°

Nose: Light and aromatic with hints of citrus and a nice balance of butterscotch and vanilla. A hint of fruitiness (berries) is present in the 100°-proof bottling.

Mouth: A medium body with a lean, assertive palate—tobacco, leather and a nice balance of butterscotch and vanilla. The 100°-proof bottling bears a hint of oak. The finish is medium-long and very gentle.

Overall: Old Fitzgerald is very stylish, with a lean yet robust masculine character that makes it perfect in a shot glass, over plenty of ice, in a Manhattan or even with ginger ale. Drink these bottlings however you wish—if you keep either one for "everyday" use, guests will appreciate your good taste.

Old Fitzgerald 1849 Bourbon, 8 years old, 90°

Nose: Rich and almost "oily," with oak, leather, butterscotch and just a hint of mint.

Mouth: A big soft body, very mellow and sophisticated. The palate has developed more fruit than the previous two bottlings, but the masculine notes of tobacco and leather are still present. The finish is soft, long and soothing.

Overall: A great bourbon. Drink it from a shot glass, pour it over ice and add a splash of water or club soda if you must—but no flavored mixers, please. It would be a shame to mask this wonderfully balanced, sophisticated whiskey unless you wish to make a very earthy Manhattan.

Very Special Old Fitzgerald, 12 years old, 90°

Nose: Rich and fruity with lots of berries and a hint of leather.

Mouth: A huge body, soft and honeyed, a touch of vanilla, some butterscotch, lots of deep, dark fruits and still the whiskey's high notes shine through with the now familiar balance of leather and tobacco. The finish is very long, very warm and very soothing.

Overall: This is a bourbon worthy of a snifter and a fine cigar. The balance in this bottling is as perfect as any we tasted—it's a whiskey that shows off the whiskey-maker's craft. You might want to drink this whiskey on ice, but we suggest you don't adulterate it with anything more than the tiniest splash of water.

Old Forester Bourbon

DISTILLERY

The Early Times Distillery, Louisville, Kentucky

ABOUT THE BRAND

Old Forester was the first bourbon to be sold exclusively in sealed bottles so that customers would know exactly what they were buying. The man responsible for this act and for giving Old Forester to the world was George Garvin Brown, a nineteenth-century pioneer of quality bourbon whose family still runs the business. The label on the Old Forester bottle is a classic; it reads: "This whisky is distilled by us only, and we are responsible for its richness and fine quality. Its elegant flavor is solely due to original fineness developed with care. *There is nothing better in the market.*" These words are followed by George Garvin Brown's signature.

HISTORY

The tale of George Garvin Brown, his forebears and descendants is lovingly detailed in *Nothing Better In The Market* by John Ed Pearce. It's a saga worthy of a miniseries that takes the reader through the Brown family history from early eighteenth-century Scotland, when the first Browns immigrated to America, through the hard work and persistence of generation after generation of Browns and up to the twentieth-century culmination of their efforts in the form of Brown-Forman, an international beverage company dealing in wines and spirits.

James Brown left Scotland for a new life in the New World in the mid-eighteenth century. One of his sons had occasion to dally with Daniel Boone and was killed by Native Americans in 1782. Another son, however, William Brown, moved to Kentucky in 1792; George Garvin Brown was his grandson.

George Garvin Brown was born in 1846 to John Thompson Street Brown and his second wife, Mary Garvin, who were farmers near the town of Munfordville, Kentucky. He was educated in Louisville (although he quit high school during his senior year) and, in 1865, found work at a wholesale drug company, Henry Chambers & Co. During his days at this company, a Louisville doctor by the name of Holloway complained to George about the quality of the whiskey that was available for treating his patients. At this time, whiskey was the best anesthetic on the market, and it was also prescribed by doctors as, more or less, a cure or treatment for a host of ailments. The quality problem lay in the way the medicinal whiskey was sold: Most whiskey was dispensed from the cask, and doctors had to rely on the druggist to furnish them with the highest-quality whiskey. They were at the mercy of the retailers.

In 1870, George became a partner with his half-brother, John Thompson Street Brown, in J.T.S. Brown & Brother "distillers and dealers in whisky." George got to thinking that he could probably make a killing if he offered top-quality bourbon in sealed bottles so that customers knew exactly what was inside. The company bought straight bourbons from reputable distillers (Atherton and Mellwood and J.B. Mattingly among them), mingled them together for consistency, bottled the resultant whiskey, and called the best of their bottlings Old Forrester (the original brand name was spelled with two *r*'s).

The company saw big changes during its first five years: George Forman joined the company as a salesman and later assumed its bookkeeping duties; George Garvin Brown's old boss, Henry Chambers, bought into the firm, and the Brown brothers had a parting of the ways. Although there are no details of the quarrel, it is assumed that J.T.S. wanted to make an easier buck than George did and didn't like the idea of using only top-quality products.

The company wasn't without its share of disasters. In 1887, the collapse of the Giant Tobacco Company, in which George had invested heavily, left him deeply in debt.

SEALED BOTTLES GUARANTEED OLD FORESTER'S AUTHENTICITY

In response—and here's an insight into his character—George liquidated his assets and paid off, not all, but as much of his debt as he possibly could. He was left with no legal liabilities whatsoever, and on top of that, all of his creditors were satisfied—nobody left the deal feeling any animosity toward Mr. Brown. Luckily, and because he was a well-respected man, a group of his good friends loaned George enough money to keep his company afloat, and all was well. But that's not where this particular episode ends. Some 24 years later, George repaid the remainder of the old debts, regardless of the fact that they had been wiped off the tally sheets and forgiven by his creditors.

The company changed its name a few times over its first two decades: After being named Chambers and Brown in 1873, it became Brown-Thompson and Company in 1881, when Chambers retired and sold part of his stock to James Thompson (George Forman was a junior partner). When Thompson went off to found his own empire in 1890, he sold his stock to his partners, and the company finally assumed the name Brown-Forman. Forman died in 1901, and George Garvin Brown bought up his shares, along with permission to keep using the name.

Two of George's sons, Robinson and Owsley Brown, were important in the company's future: Robinson Brown (who, at less than a year old, developed a high fever that required Aunt Ann, a maid, to bathe him in the cooling alcohol of Old Forester for six full days until the fever broke) didn't play an active part in the company until 1934, right after Prohibition, when he became treasurer of Brown-Forman; his son, Robinson Jr., was made director of sales in 1957 and went on to become one of the best-loved chairmen the company has ever had. Owsley Brown, the elder son, followed his father as president of the company and would impact the whiskey business as a whole.

One of the secrets of Brown-Forman's success lay in the family's ability to turn a bad situation into a good one, and in this respect, it was George himself, followed by Owsley, who led the way. There are many examples of their wile: George was a major opponent of the Prohibition movement and, in 1894, was elected president of The Wine and Spirits Association, a group formed to counter the dreaded drys. In 1910, he published *The Holy Bible Repudiates Prohibition*, a book that detailed passages from the Bible that seem to encourage the use of strong drink. But George wasn't simply using the "word of the Lord" to safeguard his business; he was a deeply religious man who was appalled that the drys would use the Bible to substantiate their philosophy that good Christians should abstain from the evils of drink.

Owsley Brown II, present chairman and CEO of Brown-Forman, said that if George Garvin Brown were alive today, "I think he would be most proud of the citizens of the United States for having seen the wisdom to once again enjoy a drink and not feel guilty about it. He was always deeply hurt by the use of religious arguments against the moderate and proper use of alcoholic beverages. He felt that that was extremely inappropriate."

George's son, the original Owsley, after selling a great deal of whiskey in Europe during the first year of Prohibition, took advantage of a section of a loophole in the law that permitted whiskey to be made, stored and dispensed as medicine if prescribed by a licensed physician. It was also during Prohibition and Owsley's presidency that the company bought the entire stock of the Early Times Distillery, along with the brand name, to ensure that Brown-Forman would have enough aged product to meet medicinal demands.

On a more personal note, Owsley wasn't a 24-hours-a-day businessman. His grandson Owsley Brown II remembers wonderful days spent fishing with his grandfather: "He was a real 'people' person and really enjoyed sitting around in the evening with a group of people, chatting and sipping his Old Forester," he recalls.

Owsley's sons, W.L. Lyons Brown and George Garvin Brown II, joined the company in 1933; Lyons became president in 1945, and George (known as Garvin) succeeded him in 1951. The major contributions of these two brothers was their combined grasp of modern mass-marketing techniques coupled with their knowledge of what had made the company great in the first place.

GEORGE GARVIN BROWN

During World War II, when whiskey production was stopped so that all grain could go to feeding cattle and humans, Brown-Forman converted its distilleries so that it could produce the industrial alcohol needed for the war effort. But the company also took full advantage of federal "distillation holidays" (a few days during World War II when whiskey distillation was allowed in order to replenish stocks for aging) in 1944 to make as much whiskey as possible to ensure that Brown-Forman had mature supplies of its whiskey that would be ready for drinking when the war ended.

Today, Brown-Forman Beverages Worldwide is headed by Owsley Brown II and other family members, such as W.L. Lyons Brown Jr., Owsley B. Frazier, W.L. Lyons III, J. McCauley "Mac" Brown, Robinson S. Brown III and Campbell Brown. Their Old Forester Bourbon is made at the company's Early Times Distillery in Louisville.

TASTING NOTES
Old Forester, 86°
Old Forester, Bottled in Bond, 100°

Nose: Sweet and spicy all at once, some maple, vanilla and leather.

Mouth: A medium to full body, slightly bigger in the higher-proof bottling. The palate agrees with the nose, but it develops so nicely in the mouth—starting out velvety with sweet vanilla, caramel, just a little butterscotch and a hint of oranges that slowly turn into a rich spiciness which can only be termed old-time sophistication. The finish is long but crisp with a deliciously sharp kick of spicy rye.

Overall: Where was Old Forester when we were savoring all the new boutique bourbons? Quietly sitting in a corner waiting to be rediscovered for all the complexities that made it famous in the late nineteenth century. This whiskey should be in every bourbon lover's liquor cabinet to remind us all how Kentucky whiskey used to taste in the days when big flavors were a must. Sip it neat, on ice or with whatever mixer you desire—Old Forester's style will shine through any drink. It also makes an absolutely wonderful Manhattan.

Old Grand-Dad Bourbon

DISTILLERY
The Jim Beam Distilleries, Clermont and Boston, Kentucky

ABOUT THE BRAND
Though many whiskeys have changed drastically over the years—as one distillery or another sells its brand names to another company that changes its recipe or style—Old Grand-Dad Bourbon is *not* one of those whiskeys. When the Jim Beam Brands Company took over the brand in the 1980s, it kept the original formula, which is high in rye grain, and simply moved production to its own plant just down the road from where Old Grand-Dad was first produced in 1882. The familiar orange label on the bottle depicts a bust of Basil Hayden, the man we all know as Old Grand-Dad.

HISTORY
In 1785, Basil Hayden established a Catholic enclave in what would become Marion County, Kentucky. Basil proceeded to make whiskey, and sometime before 1820, his son, Lewis Hayden, took over his father's whiskey business. Lewis was succeeded by his son, Raymond B. Hayden, in the 1840s. Raymond, whose mother, Polly, was a member of the Dant whiskey-making family, would be the man who took the family business into a full-scale commercial production when, in 1882, he built the R.B.

Hayden and Company Distillery at Hobb's Station in Nelson County. Raymond's partner, F.L. Ferriell, whose father and grandfather were both whiskey men, had fought with Union troops in the Civil War and had become a Federal Revenue Agent for a few years before entering the whiskey business.

It was whiskey from the distillery built by Hayden and Ferriell that was first known as Old Grand-Dad. Sometime in 1885, R.B. Hayden died without heirs, and his stock was sold to P.S. Barber, a wealthy furrier and stock breeder. In 1899, the Barber Ferriell & Company Distillery was sold to the Wathen family.

The Wathens had been a whiskey family since their ancestor, Henry Hudson Wathen, fired up his still in about 1787. By the time the family bought the Old Grand-Dad distillery, its company had grown enormously and become part of the Kentucky Distilleries and Warehouse Company, a consolidation of many distillers. When Prohibition started in 1920, the original Old Grand-Dad Distillery was closed, and production of the Hayden family whiskey was later resumed at another Wathen plant.

During Prohibition, R.E. Wathen formed the American Medicinal Spirits Company (AMSC), yet another conglomerate of distilleries and warehouses that was created to comply with new federal laws demanding that warehouses containing "whiskey for medicinal use" be concentrated in just a few locations. It was a move, no doubt, intended to make it easier for the feds to keep an eye on where the whiskey was going.

After Repeal, Old Grand-Dad went through a series of owners: AMSC was taken over by the National Distillers Products Company (NDPC), which, in 1940, bought a Frankfort distillery that it renamed the Old Grand-Dad Distillery, and in 1987, the Jim Beam Brands Company bought NDPC.

TASTING NOTES
Old Grand-Dad, 86°

Nose: Raisins, rye, honey and clover.

Mouth: A medium body, slightly smoky, with lots of oak, some fruits (prunes, dates) and a touch of vanilla that plays nicely against some spicy notes (tobacco, cloves). The finish is long, gutsy and sharp.

Overall: A grand bottling. It has a spicy style all its own, perfect for drinking however you wish—on the rocks, with water or club soda or in cocktails.

Old Grand-Dad Bottled in Bond, 100°

Nose: Honey, oak, leather and spices.

Mouth: A medium-full body, with a good balance of oak, leather, tobacco, cinnamon and cloves. The finish is long and warm.

Overall: This bottling follows in the footsteps of its lower-proof sibling but doesn't seem quite as complex. Drink it however you wish; it's a no-nonsense, old-style, delicious bourbon.

Old Grand-Dad 114 Barrel Proof, 114°

Nose: Vanilla, tobacco, honey, wildflowers.

Mouth: A big, soft body, and look at the color—it's "red liquor." Very smooth, an immediate tummy warmer, lots of oak, vanilla, raisins, cloves and, oh, so spicy. The finish is long, deep, rich and intense—it leaves a wonderful tingling on your tongue.

Overall: If you are a fan of Old Grand-Dad, this is a prize bottling. If you never really liked Old Grand-Dad's style, we recommend you give this one a try. It's worthy of a snifter (add a little water if you like), will last a whole evening on ice and is ideal for a night in front of a roaring fire, watching the stars shine down onto glistening snow.

Old Overholt Rye Whiskey

DISTILLERY

The Jim Beam Distilleries, Clermont and Boston, Kentucky

ABOUT THE BRAND

Old Overholt wears a label that depicts its originator, Abraham Overholt, framed with spikes of rye grain and the legend "Reg. In U.S. Pat. Off." The words "Since 1810" and Overholt's signature also appear on the label.

HISTORY

Although it is no longer made in Pennsylvania, Old Overholt is a fine example of the style of whiskey that used to be known as Monongahela rye whiskey. Old Overholt, one of just four true rye whiskeys left on the market, was first made in western Pennsylvania by farmer-distiller Abraham Overholt around 1810. His son Jacob and cousin Henry apparently took up the business and ran it until, by 1860, they had established a respectable-size distillery in Broad Ford, Pennsylvania.

An amusing story involving this company and some rather prominent people was detailed in *Fortune* magazine's November 1933 article about the National Distillers Products Company:

"The Overholt distillery was founded around 1812 and remained in the Overholt family until the 1890's. One of the Overholts who owned it was the mother of

Henry Clay Frick. When she died her share descended to her son and that son, an acquisitive one, soon owned the whole distillery.

"In that same part of Pennsylvania, just east of Pittsburgh, Andrew W. Mellon's father once made whiskey on his farm. And so Andrew Mellon was born with a knowledge of the still. In one of the many deals between Frick and Mellon a third interest in the Overholt distillery went to Mellon. When Frick died in 1919 Mr. Mellon got another third as trustee. Mr. Mellon, becoming Secretary of the Treasury, turned his interest over to the Union Trust Co. (which he controlled), thereby easing his conscience but not satisfying the Anti-Saloon League or the drys and Democrats in the Senate. Thereafter for four years Overholt was a white elephant that kept lumbering around under Mr. Mellon's window in the Treasury Department."

The article goes on to tell of the troubles that Mellon encountered while trying to rid himself of the "white elephant." One businessman who had acquired a considerable stock of Old Overholt prior to Prohibition sold it as medicinal whiskey, but some of it found its way onto the black market. "It was all very embarrassing for Mr. Mellon, one of whose jobs was that of chief prohibition agent," says the article, and it continues, saying that Mellon's agents authorized a man named John F. Pell "to sell the stock, which was then about two million gallons, to some foreign buyer, to be put to some non-beverage use."

The deal, unfortunately for Mellon, was discovered by the press:

"Out came newspapers with headlines screaming: 'SECRET MELLON WHISKEY DEAL BARED.' Mr. Mellon called Mr. Pell, said that he would go through with the deal if Mr. Pell could swear the whiskey would stay in England. Honest Mr. Pell knew perfectly well it would be back in the U.S. in a month. Mr. Pell got paid his expenses and the whiskey remained on Mellon's hands until 1925 when David Schulte put down $4,500,000 in cash and took it over, the distillery with it."

Two years later, Schulte sold the whiskey to Lewis Rosenstiel of the Schenley Distillers Corporation, although by that time, the two million gallons of whiskey "through evaporation and otherwise" had shrunk by half.

Although Schenley had bought the whiskey, it was the National Distillers Products Company that bought the Old Overholt brand name and distillery during Prohibition. National was acquired by the Jim Beam Brands Company in 1987, and Old Overholt is currently being produced in both of Beam's Kentucky distilleries.

TASTING NOTES
Old Overholt Rye, 4 years old, 80°

Nose: Light spices and pepper mixed with a slight fruitiness.

Mouth: A big, full body with a great balance of delicate rye qualities (spring flowers and light spices)playing off some deep dark fruits. The finish is crisp and clean, with a burst of sweetness.

Overall: This is a good example of a straight rye whiskey. Well crafted, well balanced and very flavorful. Sip it from a shot glass, drink it on ice, and definitely try this one with ginger ale—they were made for each other.

Old Taylor Bourbon

DISTILLERY
The Jim Beam Distilleries, Clermont and Boston, Kentucky

ABOUT THE BRAND
This old-style whiskey label is a favorite because it honors one of the great men in whiskey history, Colonel Edmund Haynes Taylor Jr. The label bears his signature, an actual photograph of the man and the words "since 1868." The Castle Distillery, "erected in 1887," is also depicted on the label. The 1868 date is somewhat confusing, although Taylor was most likely in the whiskey business at that time. The Castle Distillery, however, was built by Taylor in 1887, and that year also marked Old Taylor Bourbon's marketplace debut.

HISTORY
Colonel Edmund Haynes Taylor Jr. came from an influential family; his father, E.H. Taylor Sr., was involved in a pre-Civil War community group that organized the Bank of Kentucky and the Frankfort public school system and he was also related to President Zachary Taylor.

E.H. Taylor Jr. was born in 1832 and became a banker in Versailles, Kentucky, before taking up the whiskey business. Around 1869, he might have been involved with the original building of the O.F.C. (Old Fire Copper) Distillery, later to become known as the Ancient Age Distillery. What is certain is that four years later, in 1873, Colonel Taylor modernized that plant, and by 1882, he owned it. George T. Stagg worked for him at that point, and Stagg went on to buy the distillery in 1885. The company, however, was still known as the E.H. Taylor Jr. Company, and Taylor held the position of manager and master distiller.

In 1887, Taylor built a distillery in Woodford County, and the whiskey bearing his name, Old Taylor, was first made available to the public. Soon after that, Taylor began consorting with political types in order to safeguard the good name of straight whiskey. Around this time, many whiskeys were sold that were no more than cheap fabrications of true bourbon, and they were being marketed as the real thing. Whiskey dealers bought bulk whiskey, adulterated it with flavorless neutral grain spirits and flavored it with all sorts of "non-whiskey" products, such as sherry, tea and cloves. They then sold the product as bourbon, sometimes under deceptive names that made buyers believe that they were getting the good stuff. Indeed, the practice had been going on for many years, and Taylor and some of the other reputable whiskey men had grown sick and tired of it. Less than two-tenths of 1 percent of the nation's bourbon was actually straight whiskey in 1896; the rest had been married to inferior spirits and flavored.

During his crusade for governmental control of fine Kentucky bourbon, Taylor wrote some eloquent words on the subject. He accused the whiskey traders of "pouring into the lap of the trade streams liquid spirit having as its chief characteristic a reputation for quantity instead of quality." He went on to say, "The ancient bourbon flavor has departed, and the stomach groans under the dominion of the new ruler."

Not being the sort merely to shout when he was outraged, Taylor found an ally in John G. Carlisle, Secretary of the Treasury under Grover Cleveland, and together with other reputable distillers, they successfully argued for what would become the Bottled-in-Bond Act of 1897. With this bill, buyers were guaranteed that whiskey carrying the government's bottled-in-bond stamp (which bears Carlisle's likeness) was straight whiskey, aged for four years and bottled at 100° proof.

By 1911, Taylor's firm, E.H. Taylor Jr. and Sons, was worth one million dollars. During Prohibition, it was absorbed by the American Medicinal Spirits Company, a conglomerate that became part of the National Distillers Products Company in 1936. Finally, in 1987, National Distillers was bought by the Jim Beam Brands Company, and it is at its distilleries in Clermont and Boston, Kentucky, that Old Taylor is being made today.

Taylor died in 1922 at the age of 90. He had effectively helped bring nineteenth-century bourbon into the twentieth century and saved one of the nation's treasures from being buried under a sea of imitation whiskey. His name should not be forgotten.

TASTING NOTES
Old Taylor, 6 years old, 86°

Nose: Spicy-sweet, rich, tobacco and vanilla.

Mouth: A medium to big body with a nice point/counterpoint in its spiciness (cinnamon, nutmeg, tobacco) and underlying sweetness (caramel, vanilla). The finish is medium-long with a burst of rye dryness.

Overall: Old Taylor tastes old-fashioned, and it's a style that makes you yearn for a pre-Prohibition free-lunch table and a good panatela. Sip it on ice, add a touch of water if you wish or make a stylish Manhattan. Good with ginger ale—but just a splash should do it.

Old Williamsburg Bourbon

OWNER
The Royal Wine Corporation, Brooklyn, New York

ABOUT THE BRAND AND HISTORY

Old Williamsburg, introduced in 1994, is the only kosher bourbon we know of. Although the name might conjure images of the old colonial town, the whiskey was in fact named for the Williamsburg section of Brooklyn, New York. Jay Buchsbaum, vice president of marketing for the Royal Wine Corporation, filled us in on its origins and its peculiarities.

During the late nineteenth century, Williamsburg, Brooklyn, was home to many breweries, and hence it was the district where brewery owners built architecturally elaborate mansions. According to Buchsbaum, the brewers' liquor of choice was bourbon.

Unless you look closely at the neck label on Old Williamsburg, you won't realize that it's a kosher product. But hidden away on the back of this label is a stamp that bears Hebraic lettering. Buchsbaum translated: The stamp asserts that the bourbon has been "certified by a body known as Hisachdus Harabonim," and the bourbon in the bottle can be consumed in any kosher household.

The difficulty of producing a kosher liquor lies in the fact that some kosher products are known as "non-Passover" items, designated *chametz sheover olov al pesech*, and these products lose their kosher status during Passover. Since bourbon must be aged for a minimum of two years (and therefore two Passovers), this designation must be avoided. Although it seems nearly impossible, they've done it. Certain procedures are followed, rules and regulations are adhered to, and Old Williamsburg Bourbon is certified kosher for use at any time.

TASTING NOTES
Old Williamsburg No. 20, Kentucky Straight Bourbon, 36 months old, 101°

Nose: Oaky, a little vegetal and just a hint of prunes.

Mouth: A medium body with a spicy palate—some leather and a little grain-y. The finish is short with a touch of eucalyptus.

Overall: An "around the house" bottling. If only it were left in the wood a little longer—it's so close to becoming a lean, masculine bourbon with a sense of style. Sources tell us that Old Williamsburg will very soon be available as an older bourbon. Look for a bottling without an age statement (denoting a minimum of four-year-old whiskey) or anything that tells you it was aged for longer than 36 months.

James E. Pepper Bourbon

DISTILLERY

The Bernheim Distillery, Louisville, Kentucky

ABOUT THE BRAND

James E. Pepper Bourbon is available only to the export market, so you may have to leave the country to get your hands on a bottle. Bourbon lovers are lucky that the brand has been kept alive, since the Peppers were one of the most important whiskey families in American history.

The label on James E. Pepper is just marvelous—it bears the legend "Old 1776" and the slogan "Born with the Republic." The label also lays claim to this whiskey's being "Kentucky's First Bourbon," and although technically that fact may be disputable, the company has good grounds on which to stake such a claim.

HISTORY

The tale of the Pepper family begins at the birth of the nation in 1776, when Elijah Pepper settled at Old Pepper Springs in Kentucky County, Virginia. By 1780, Pepper had established himself as a farmer-distiller who traded his whiskey with neighbors and the folk who were passing through Versailles (west of Lexington, about equidistant from Frankfort and Lawrenceburg), the site of his distillery. In 1794, the year in which the Whiskey Rebellion came to a head in western Pennsylvania, he was one of the few Kentucky distillers with enough dollars to pay the excise tax that Washington was demanding. Indeed, other farmer-distillers of the time are said to have quit their stills and taken their grain to Elijah, who would transform it into whiskey.

Elijah died in the early 1830s and was succeeded by his son, Oscar, who built the Old Oscar Pepper Distillery in 1838. Oscar hired James Crow as his distiller—the wisest move he ever made. Crow was a physician and chemist who applied his skills to the art of distillation, and the results reputedly were magnificent. Together, these men produced the first Old Crow Bourbon and Pepper's brand, which was marketed as Old 1776—Born with the Republic.

After Crow perfected his formula, business was brisk. In fact, although Crow died in 1856, Old Crow became one of if not *the* most popular whiskeys of the Civil War era.

AN EARLY JAMES E. PEPPER ADVERTISEMENT

When Oscar Pepper went to meet his maker in 1867, his son James E. took over the distillery and sold the Old Crow label to a company owned partially by E.H. Taylor, a man who would later help establish the Bottled-in-Bond Act of 1897 and a major figure in shaping the modern whiskey industry.

As head of the Old Oscar Pepper Distillery, James E. Pepper is said to have indulged himself somewhat. Legend has it that he took the Old-Fashioned cocktail, said to have been his favorite drink at Louisville's Pendennis Club (where it was first concocted), and introduced it to New York when he moved there in 1870.

In 1878, Pepper sold the family business to James Graham and Leopold Labrot, and the distillery became the Labrot and Graham Distillery, which was sold to Brown-Forman in 1940. The Pepper family was out of the business—but not for very long. Just one year after selling out, Pepper took George Starkweather as his partner, and they built the James E. Pepper Distillery with a $25,000 investment. Subsequently, they purchased the small Henry Clay Distillery and produced James E. Pepper and Henry Clay bourbons. It is said that Henry Clay, the famed U.S. senator who would "rather be right than be president," was fond of Oscar Pepper's whiskey and was thus immortalized by Oscar's son on a whiskey bottle.

In 1890, when much whiskey was being adulterated by disreputable whiskey brokers or so-called rectifiers, Pepper applied for a license to bottle his whiskey at the distillery. He was so upset with the people who were marketing inferior products under deceptive names that one year later, he announced in *The Wine and Spirit Bulletin* that he had patented his label and trademark and that any other whiskey bearing the name "Pepper" was not true Pepper whiskey.

Pepper died in 1906, and by 1911, the company with capital valued at over $250,000 had been purchased by investors from Chicago. The new owners seem to have been of a like mind to the Peppers, so they plowed some of the profits back into the business and practically rebuilt the distillery. In 1912, they included the slogan "Born with the Republic" in an advertisement for James E. Pepper whiskey. In *The Social History of Bourbon*, Gerald Carson tells the story of a soldier who returned from World War I in 1918 to find that the distilling industry had been halted in the United States by the Lever Food and Fuel Act and that national Prohibition was likely to occur in the very near future. Dismayed, the soldier suggested that future signs should read "Born with the Republic—Died with Democracy." Prohibition *was* around the corner, and in 1919, the company shipped 30,000 cases and 4,000 barrels of Pepper's whiskey to Germany.

The brand and the distillery were purchased by Schenley after Prohibition ended, but the James E. Pepper Bourbon was discontinued in the 1960s. It was revived by United Distillers (who bought Schenley in 1987) in recent years, but for the export market only.

TASTING NOTES
James E. Pepper, 80° (for export only)

Nose: Honey followed by a light fruitiness.

Mouth: A light body, not too complex, hints of leather and oak. The finish is short and spicy.

Overall: A decent "around the house" bottling. Drink it any way you wish.

Pikesville Supreme Rye Whiskey

DISTILLERY

The Heaven Hill Distillery, Bardstown, Kentucky

ABOUT THE BRAND

Very little information is available about the origins of this straight rye whiskey, except for the fact that it is named for the community of Pikesville in Baltimore County, Maryland. Whatever its history and origins, Pikesville Supreme is one of only four straight ryes currently being produced in the United States—and all four now are made in Kentucky. The back label on Pikesville Supreme reads, "The Aristocrat of Straight Whiskies Pikesville was distilled under an old Maryland formula and stored in selected charred white oak casks in modern warehouses to age and mellow." This bottling can be hard to find outside of Maryland.

TASTING NOTES
Pikesville Supreme, 80°

Nose: Clean and simple with a hint of mint.

Mouth: A light body with hints of perfume and a spiciness that tickles the tongue. The finish is short and crisp with a touch of mint.

Overall: A light style of rye, perfect for mixing with lots of ginger ale.

Rebel Yell Bourbon

DISTILLERY

The Bernheim Distillery, Louisville, Kentucky

ABOUT THE BRAND

Rebel Yell, a wheated bourbon that has acquired a cult following all its own, is a whiskey created in 1936 to "personify the South." The antique-style label declares that this whiskey is "Especially for the Deep South" and also bears the date "1849." This date actually applies to the W.L. Weller brand of bourbon, which is made at the same distillery, and the label on Rebel Yell states that the same recipe is used for both of them. Aside from the wording, the label shows a line drawing of a Rebel soldier, sword in hand, galloping off to fight.

HISTORY

Alex Farnsley, one of the owners of the Stitzel-Weller distillery, had a nephew, Charlie P. Farnsley, who was a well-loved politician but had nothing to do with the business side of whiskey. Mayor of Louisville from 1948 until 1953, Charlie Farnsley was once described as being the most remarkable leader in Louisville's history. According to *The Kentucky Encyclopedia,* he was a disciple of Thomas Jefferson's philosophies as well as those of Confucius, and he held weekly meetings so that he could personally listen to complaints from citizens. He worked for the general good, instituting a fund to support the arts, paving streets and building parks. Though he was thought to be somewhat eccentric—rarely seen without his signature black string tie—he also was recognized as an astute politician who understood that all aspects of life, cultural through big business, were dependent on one another. In addition to serving in the Kentucky House of Representatives and in the U.S. Congress, Farnsley wanted to create a bourbon specifically for the people of the Deep South. And Uncle Alex did it.

REBEL YELL

The original Rebel Yell was produced on a limited basis with distribution solely in the South. The brand was discontinued for a while, but it was reintroduced in 1961 to commemorate the centennial of the Civil War. Rebel Yell has become so popular that the company finally allowed it to be sold to Yankees in 1984.

TASTING NOTES
Rebel Yell, 90°

Nose: Honey, butter and raisins.

Mouth: A big, round body with a palate that directly follows the nose—honey, butter and just hint of dark fruit (plums, raisins). The finish is long, warm and interesting in that a touch of spiciness, not present in the palate, seems to come into play.

Overall: This is a good bourbon with a very definite style. Drink it from a shot glass or maybe even a snifter, but best over ice with no water, no club soda—nothing. Rebel Yell is well balanced and shouldn't be tampered with unless you wish to make a very good Manhattan.

Rock Hill Farms Single Barrel Bourbon

DISTILLERY
The Ancient Age Distillery, Frankfort, Kentucky

ABOUT THE BRAND
Rock Hill Farms Single Barrel Bourbon, introduced in 1990, is named for the farm, previously owned by the Blanton family, that stood on the site of the Ancient Age Distillery. The whiskey is presented in a decanter-style square bottle with a handsome, cork-finished glass stopper and wears a brass necklace that proclaims its name. The clear bottle is decorated with gold-painted silhouettes of horses set in scenes in and around Rock Hill Farms. This whiskey is the only bottled-in-bond offering in the distillery's line of five single-barrel bourbons, denoting that it is at least four years old and is bottled at exactly 100° proof. The whiskey in the bottle is chosen by Master Distiller Gary Gayheart.

TASTING NOTES
Rock Hill Farms Single Barrel Bourbon, Bottled in Bond, 100°
Nose: Cinnamon, honey, vanilla, charcoal.

Mouth: A soft, full body with tobacco, caramel, tangerine and a hint of mint and cloves. A medium finish that leaves a pleasant spiciness in the throat.

Overall: A great bourbon to serve neat or on ice. Add water or soda if you will, but don't mask this one with flavored mixers; its "leanness" needs to shine through.

Ten High Bourbon

DISTILLERY
The Barton Distillery, Bardstown, Kentucky

ABOUT THE BRAND
Ten High is a familiar brand to bar-goers; it is often the bourbon that is poured from the "well" when you don't specify a brand name. The label features a distinctive line drawing of a country gent with glass in hand, his foot on a barrel of whiskey and a dog by his side. The words "EST'D 1879" appear on this label, and this date refers to the year that Tom Moore, the distiller who established the Barton Distillery, first marketed his namesake bourbon.

TASTING NOTES
Ten High, 80°

Nose: Cinnamon, vanilla.

Mouth: A medium-light body with hints of caramel, vanilla and oak.

Overall: A good "around the house" bourbon with a little complexity all its own. This whiskey is fine on ice and ideal for all mixed drinks—even a Manhattan.

Van Winkle Bourbon

BOTTLER AND PRODUCER

J.P. Van Winkle and Son, Louisville, Kentucky

ABOUT THE BRAND

The president of this company, Julian Van Winkle III is the grandson of Julian "Pappy" Van Winkle, one of the whiskey industry's most colorful men. Julian has been in the whiskey business since 1977, when he joined his father, Julian Van Winkle Jr., to help market Van Winkle's signature wheated bourbons.

The family name fits very well with the age of these whiskeys—the 10-year-old bottling depicts Rip Van Winkle sleeping atop a tree stump with the words "Asleep Many Years in the Wood" inscribed beneath. The label on the 20-year-old "Family

OLD RIP VAN WINKLE PREDATES PROHIBITION

Reserve" bottling features a picture of Pappy himself, with a back-of-bottle label showing Pappy playing golf with his faithful caddy, a dog pulling a small golf cart, by his side. On the 12-year-old "Van Winkle Special Reserve" bottling, a stylish, plain label proclaims the whiskey came from "Lot B."

HISTORY

The first whiskey to include the Van Winkle name was Old Rip Van Winkle, a fine bourbon that was introduced just prior to Prohibition. The label was reintroduced by Julian Van Winkle Jr. in 1972. Van Winkle Bourbon is still made according to standards set by Pappy, who preferred to drink wheated bourbon that was at least 10 years old. For more history on Pappy Van Winkle, see **W.L. Weller Bourbon**, page 191.

TASTING NOTES

Old Rip Van Winkle Kentucky Straight Bourbon, 10 summers old, 107°

Nose: Cinnamon, nutmeg, followed by vanilla and rich fruits (raisins, prunes).

Mouth: A big body with an interesting palate that starts out in grandmother's attic (a pleasant mustiness), develops a rich fruitiness and then pulls some spices out of its hat—very complex. The finish is long, warm and spicier than expected.

Overall: A "snifter" bourbon, worthy of a fine cigar. However, you can also drink this whiskey on ice or make a very special Manhattan. No flavored mixers, please.

**Van Winkle Special Reserve Kentucky Straight Bourbon,
12 years old, Lot "B," 90.4°**

Nose: Caramel, vanilla, berries.

Mouth: A big body with a palate somehow reminiscent of Oloroso sherry. The bourbon coats the entire mouth and is somewhat more lean and masculine than its 10-year-old brother, with hints of tobacco here and there. The finish is long, warm and spicy.

Overall: Another "snifter" bourbon from Van Winkle, but feel free to add ice or make a great Manhattan. This is a bottling that cries out for a plush leather chair and a good historical novel.

Pappy Van Winkle Family Reserve Kentucky Straight Bourbon, 20 years old, 90.4°

Nose: Very fruity (raisins, dates, blackberries) and a piquant high note lingering in the background.

Mouth: A huge body, thick, rich and chewy, with a sophisticated palate, again with some sherryish qualities along with butter, vanilla and just a hint of fruit.

Overall: Snifter only, please. Even though we are tempted to tell you to make a Manhattan from this bottling, we can't bear to think of adulterating it in any way.

Virginia Gentleman Bourbon

DISTILLERY

The A. Smith Bowman Distillery, Fredericksburg, Virginia

ABOUT THE BRAND

Here's the only bourbon on the market from Virginia. The label on Virginia Gentleman depicts three Colonial gents in an idyllic scene in front of an antebellum mansion and bears the words "VIRGINIA WHISKEY" boldly. Underneath this designation, however, you will find the qualifier: "Straight Bourbon Whiskey."

Virginia Gentleman was first made by a gentleman farmer-distiller who supplemented his farm income by building a distillery, using the wood from the trees on his land to make barrels and feeding his cattle with the by-products from the whiskey-making. It's not a unique story until you discover that A. Smith Bowman wasn't an eighteenth-century pioneer but a man who made a lot of money running a motor coach company in Indianapolis and bought himself a farm in Virginia in 1927. He is a wonderful twentieth-century example of the farmer-distillers of yore.

HISTORY

A. Smith Bowman Sr. had been in the distillation business before Prohibition, and in 1927, when he bought his 7,000-acre farm (3,000 acres were forested with oak trees), then known as Sunset Hills, his first crops were corn, rye and barley—everything needed to make bourbon. When Prohibition ended in 1933, Bowman decided to build a distillery and start making whiskey.

Production at the distillery began in 1935, and two years later, a two-year-old bottling of Virginia Gentleman hit the market. In 1939, a four-year-old bottling was introduced. The whiskey's name was decided by Bowman's younger son E. DeLong Bowman, who admired William Byrd II, "the first gentleman of Virginia" and founder of Richmond.

Virginia Gentleman soon gathered a cult following, especially in nearby Washington, D.C., where many politicians still swear it's the best whiskey in the land. Indeed, the company boasts that Virginia Gentleman was shipped to England during World War II for General Douglas MacArthur, that the product is stocked on board the Presidential yacht *Sequoia* and that some of its whiskey is privately labeled "Gentlemen of the Press" for the National Press Club.

A. Smith Bowman Sr. died in 1952 and was succeeded by his sons, A. Smith Bowman Jr. as chairman and E. DeLong Bowman as president. In 1960, much of the family's land was sold so the town of Reston could be established there, but the Bowmans retained the distillery site and the surrounding 30 acres of land.

Over the years, some very interesting people have been involved with this company: Robert E. Lee IV (his sister Mary married A. Smith Bowman Jr.) became head of sales in 1970; John "Jay" Buchanan Adams Jr. joined the family when he married DeLong Bowman's daughter and took charge of production in 1971; and in the 1980s, Al Durante joined the company to help with marketing. These people are exactly who you are thinking they might be: Present chairman Lee is the great-grandson of General Robert E. Lee; President and CEO of the company Adams is related (albeit distantly) to three U.S. presidents—Adams, Jefferson and Buchanan—and Durante is a nephew of the almighty Jimmy "Schnozzle" Durante.

In 1988, Jay Adams moved the distillery to Fredericksburg, on the banks of the Rappahannock River. The A. Smith Bowman Distillery now produces other liquors—gin, vodka, rum, blended whiskey and the like—and makes its distinctive bourbon from low wines (the result of the first distillation) that are made at another distillery according to Bowman's specific requirements. The high wines (second distillation), however, are distilled, aged and bottled at A. Smith Bowman Distillery in Virginia.

TASTING NOTES
Virginia Gentleman Bourbon ("Virginia Whiskey"), 80°

Nose: Floral with honey notes and a slight hint of mint.

Mouth: A medium body, very round and smooth, oak, caramel, honey and light spices. The finish is medium, very warm and very soothing.

Overall: This is a fine, delicate bourbon. Sip it neat from a snifter, add ice if you wish—but not too much—or make a magnificent toddy with a liberal spoonful of honey and one or two cloves.

Walker's DeLuxe Bourbon

PRODUCER
Hiram Walker & Sons, Inc., Detroit, Michigan

ABOUT THE BRAND
The label on Walker's DeLuxe bears the likeness of Hiram Walker himself, along with the date when this Canadian whiskey man started out—1858. The back label, just as it did when it premiered in the forties, describes the whiskey as "light." Although the producer of this whiskey is based in Michigan and Canada, the bourbon is made in Kentucky by an independent distillery.

HISTORY

Walker's DeLuxe Bourbon was introduced in the 1940s, when it was marketed as a six-year-old straight bourbon whiskey at 90.4° proof. Around this same time, the company suggested that its salespeople should make this pledge for greater sales:

"Because I believe that every time a bourbon drinker tries Walker's DeLuxe he will become a steady customer of the brand, I hereby pledge to myself and my company the following: (1) That I will impress every account with the prestige of Walker's DeLuxe (2) Get over to my accounts the excitement and soundness of our advertising and display programs (3) Set as my goal a constantly increasing percentage of bourbon sales in each account (4) Work energetically to open new accounts where Walker's DeLuxe will become the favored premium brand. As a result of this I expect to increase substantially my weekly earnings."

Another missive to salespeople suggested they use "ten dollar words" such as elegant, exquisite, excellent, magnificent, marvelous, superb, splendid and wonderful to describe this whiskey.

TASTING NOTES
Walker's DeLuxe Straight Bourbon, 80°
Nose: A light fruit-spiciness with just a hint of caramel.
Mouth: Light body with a hint of caramel. The finish is short and rather hot.
Overall: This is, as the label promises, a light bourbon. Ideal for mixing with ginger ale, but a little too light to drink with water or club soda. Make mixed drinks and summertime cocktails (whiskey sours) with this bottling, but not Manhattans.

W.L. Weller Bourbon

DISTILLERY
The Bernheim Distillery, Louisville, Kentucky

ABOUT THE BRAND
W.L. Weller, one of the few wheated bourbons in the marketplace, has ties to some of the most illustrious names in bourbon history: Weller himself, who was a major figure in Kentucky distilling circles; the Stitzel brothers, distillers of great renown; and Pappy Van Winkle, a very colorful character indeed.

The Old Weller Antique bottling wears one of our favorite labels—complete with a line drawing of the whiskey's creator, W.L. Weller, a sketch of a shady glen that represents the Stitzel-Weller Distillery where this whiskey once was made and the marvelous legend "7 Summers Old." The whole thing looks as though it has been stored in an attic since 1849 and conjures thoughts of whiskey-makers of bygone years.

W.L. Weller Special Reserve comes with a smart, stark-white label and the words: "From the moment of distillation until this whiskey was bottled it remained in the custody of the distiller." W.L. Weller Centennial is presented in a sleek flask-shaped vessel with a handsome maroon and gold label.

HISTORY

Daniel Weller, the first of the "Whiskey Wellers," floated into Kentucky on a flatboat in 1794. The Whiskey Rebellion in Pennsylvania was quelled by Washington's troops that same year, and 32-year-old Weller, like many others, headed west, presumably in search of inexpensive land.

By 1800, Daniel Weller had built and opened a distillery near Bardstown. Eight years after his death in 1807, his son Samuel returned from service in the War of 1812, bought himself some stills and barrels and became a distiller in his own right.

William LaRue Weller was born around 1825 and fought with the Louisville Brigade in the Mexican War. But not long after that, he formed a whiskey company called William LaRue Weller & Brother with his sibling, Charles D. The company started trading in whiskey in 1849, using as its slogan "Honest Whiskey at an Honest Price."

W.L. Weller had two sons, William and George, and a much younger brother, John H., who he raised as a son after their parents were killed by typhus. All three fought with the Confederate Orphan Brigade during the Civil War, and John was wounded in the Battle of Chickamauga. (Although Kentucky was officially neutral during the Civil War, sympathies among whiskey men generally lay with the South.) In 1862, Charles Weller, W.L.'s brother and partner, was murdered in Tennessee by two gunmen who killed him and stole his cash.

By 1876, the company name had been changed to W.L. Weller and Son (George), and four years later, its whiskey was being sold as far west as Harold's Club, in Reno, Nevada. Business continued to be good, and in 1893, Julian "Pappy" Van Winkle joined the company as a salesman. According to Harry Harris Kroll, author of *Bluegrass, Belles, and Bourbon—A Pictorial History of Whiskey in Kentucky*, Pappy had been born in Danville, Kentucky, in 1874, the same year that the Women's Christian Temperance Union was formed in Ohio. He grew up, by all reports, to be a very outgoing fellow who could tell tales until sunup but also had the patience to listen to what other people had to say. Traveling for two months at a time by railroad and horse and buggy, he was said to have been so good at his job that he actually sold whiskey to moonshiners, who would mix it with their white lightning to add a little flavor and color.

In 1908, Pappy and another salesman, Alex T. Farnsley, gained controlling interest in the company. W.L. Weller had retired from the business in 1896, signing it over to his sons, John and George; he died just three years later from asthma and complications to his heart.

Around the turn of the century, the Weller company started doing business with Frederick and Philip Stitzel, renowned Louisville distillers since 1872. Indeed, in 1879 Frederick Stitzel had invented and patented the system of barrel "ricking" (the tiers of wooden beams on which the barrels rest). After losing its first distillery to fire in 1883 and rebuilding it on the same site, the Stitzel company contracted to sell whiskey to W.L. Weller around 1903. This was a clever move for all concerned: Weller was known as a major marketer, and the Stitzel brothers' whiskey had won a "Certificate of Distinction" in 1900 at the Centennial Exposition in Paris.

In 1912, a contract between the Weller company and the Stitzels effectively leased the Stitzels' distillery to Weller, making it possible for the Weller company to be listed as a distiller instead of a trader. By that time, the two companies were marketing W.L. Weller, Cabin Still, Mammoth Cave and Mondamin whiskeys.

In 1920, Prohibition put an end to legal drinking—almost. The A. Ph. Stitzel Distillery, as it was then known, was one of six distilleries licensed to produce medicinal whiskey. Together with the Weller company (known as W.L. Weller and Sons by this time), they bought whiskey from other, less fortunate distilleries and stored it in their licensed warehouses. By the end of Prohibition, the Stitzel and Weller companies decided to merge, and Stitzel-Weller was born. Their distillery opened in Shively on Derby Day 1935.

The Stitzel-Weller Distillery was closed in 1992 by its present owners, United Distillers, but the brands associated with it are still being produced just down the road at the company's Bernheim Distillery. They receive much love, care and attention from Master Distiller Ed Foote.

TASTING NOTES
Weller Special Reserve, 7 years old, 90°
Nose: Honey, a slight hint of berries, caramel and light spices.

Mouth: A medium body, rather rich with honey, a wonderful tingling spiciness, hints of raisins and lots of butterscotch. The finish is long, warm and full of butterscotch.

Overall: Here's a great sippin' whiskey. Drink it on ice, add a splash of water or club soda, or try chilling it and serving this bourbon as an apéritif. Makes a very heady Manhattan.

Old Weller Antique, 7 summers old, 107°
Nose: Sweet, honey, floral, oak, vanilla.

Mouth: A big, round body, very rich; honey and raisins are evident along with good doses of both oak and vanilla and a crisp spiciness that balances the palate nicely. The finish is long and warm.

Overall: Worthy of a snifter; great over ice with a splash of water, in a top-notch Manhattan or diluted heavily to sip alongside a good steak dinner. The oakiness in the Antique bottling is deep and rich, making this a fine bourbon to sip while smoking a good cigar.

W.L. Weller Centennial, 10 years old, 100°

Nose: Sweet vanilla, honey and deep, dark fruits (raisins, plums, dates).

Mouth: A huge, soft, round body with a palate that shows what three extra years in the wood can do to a bourbon that was already very good at age seven. This bottling is much fruitier than the previous two—full of berries and raisins and a full hit of vanilla, and then there's some butterscotch that rounds out the experience. The finish is long, warm, soft and mellow.

Overall: After stating that the Antique bottling is worthy of a snifter, it's hard to describe just how special this bourbon truly is—sip it from your most treasured Murano glass or your oldest Waterford thistle. The Weller Centennial is ideal for special occasions or no occasion at all—just don't rush this rich experience.

Wild Turkey Bourbon

DISTILLERY

The Wild Turkey Distillery, Lawrenceburg, Kentucky

ABOUT THE BRAND

Wild Turkey Bourbon, one of the best-known brands on the shelves, was named during a turkey shoot by the men who first sampled it in the 1940s. Though it didn't appear as a brand name until 1942, the lineage of the bourbon and the company that owns the brand stretches right back to the mid-nineteenth century. The labels on all of the Wild Turkey bottles are fairly simple; each one bears a likeness of this awkward-looking fowl. But no matter how ungainly this bird may appear, it is, just like the bourbon in the bottle, a true native of the U.S.A.

HISTORY

Wild Turkey's history has three components: the Ripy family, Austin Nichols and the whiskey itself.

THE RIPYS

According to a June 1906 edition of *The Anderson County News*, in 1869, Thomas B. Ripy (T.B.) and his partner W.H. McBrayer bought Distillery Number 12 in Tyrone, Kentucky, close to Lawrenceburg. Ripy was of Irish descent, his father having named the town of Tyrone after his home county. T.B. soon was renowned as a master of his art, and his whiskey gained recognition far and wide. He wasn't, however, yet satisfied with his surroundings. Having bought out his partner after just one year, he proceeded to extend the premises, and then moved to a new location altogether. By 1880, the company had reportedly moved to larger accommodations a full five times.

In 1885, T.B. Ripy bought the Old Joe Distillery, which he sold one year later to Captain Wiley Searcy. By 1892, Ripy owned the Old Hickory Spring Distillery in Anderson County. Though his distillery was absorbed by the Kentucky Distilleries and Warehouse Company around the turn of the century, Ripy still played an active role in the business. At that time, when taxes had to be paid before the whiskey was properly aged, Ripy had the bright idea to ship his whiskey to Germany for aging. The concept was that he could age his whiskey for as long as he pleased without paying taxes on it until he shipped it back to the United States to bottle and sell. Ripy must have been a stickler for good aged bourbon.

By 1905, Ripy had been laid to rest, and his four sons bought the D.L. Moore Distillery, also in Anderson County. According to *The Anderson County News*, the brothers were "new to the manufacture of this important commodity" but had "had much experience under their able father." Things went well for the boys, and in 1911, they bought one of their father's old places, the Old Joe Distillery. In 1934, after Repeal, the Ripy brothers started afresh at the D.L. Moore site. Soon after opening, though, the old place's ownership changed hands several times, although one or two of the Ripys continued his involvement with the distillery in one capacity or another. When Jimmy Russell, the present Master Distiller for Wild Turkey, first went to work there in 1954, the distillery manager was Ernest W. Ripy Jr., and it was he, along with Master Distiller Bill Hughes, who taught Jimmy the fine art of making whiskey.

AUSTIN NICHOLS

In 1855, Friend P. Fitts made himself a fortune in the California Gold Rush and started a food importing and distributing company in New York. The company prospered, and with Repeal, the company's president, Thomas McCarthy, set his sights on expanding into the wine and liquor business. The company was called Austin, Nichols & Company, Inc.

Though it imported some beverages, Austin Nichols began domestic production of its own line of liqueurs, gin and blended and straight whiskeys. In the early 1940s, McCarthy took a bottle of one of the company's straight bourbons to an annual wild-turkey hunting trip. His guests were three men who were his regular bridge partners. They tasted the bourbon and were greatly impressed, so impressed, in fact, that Mc-Carthy named the bourbon Wild Turkey in homage of their yearly hunt for one of America's indigenous birds. The brand was introduced in 1942.

THE WHISKEY

In 1970, when Austin, Nichols bought the distillery that had been built by the Ripy brothers, it found none other than Ripy's protégé Jimmy Russell tending the stills. Luckily for us, Russell remained at the plant, where he is still abiding by the most important rule his predecessor taught him: Don't change anything.

TASTING NOTES
Wild Turkey, 80°

Nose: Deep, thick, straightforward bouquet with hints of oranges, honey and vanilla.

Mouth: Big body, uncomplicated, slightly hot palate with notes of cinnamon, oranges and rye bread. The finish is very warm, toasty and long, with cinnamon notes that tickle the throat.

Overall: This is an unpretentious, well-crafted bourbon with excellent character. Ideal on the rocks in a smoky barroom and perfect for those who enjoy bourbon with club soda or even ginger ale.

Wild Turkey Old Number 8 Brand, 101°

Nose: Light notes of white pepper, nutmeg, tangerine and tobacco.

Mouth: Big body—the tangerine becomes heavy with deep orange flavors, honey, spices (nutmeg and cinnamon) and hints of vanilla; very soothing. The finish is not as long as the 80° bottling, but very warm and soothing, with honey-orange notes at the back of the throat.

Overall: A sophisticated bourbon; the craftsmanship of the distiller shines through. Perfect on the rocks, ideal for cocktails, with big enough flavors built in to stand tall in the glass with any mixer.

Wild Turkey, 12 years old, 101°

Nose: The first aroma that comes to mind here is of a deep, rich, ruby port. Also hints of dates and, with a splash of water, some lighter notes of spring flowers and new-mown hay.

Mouth: A huge, round body with a deep, rich palate incorporating notes of dark fruits (blueberries, blackberries) and hints of maple syrup and oranges. A long finish, with distinct notes of bitter almonds. The bourbon is almost syrupy and is very long in the throat.

Overall: Here is a bourbon worthy of a snifter and a long after-dinner discussion that could right all the wrongs of the world. However, it's excellent in a very sophisticated, very big-flavored gutsy Manhattan.

Wild Turkey Rare Breed, Barrel Proof (usually 109.5° to 112°) (bottle sampled was from batch W-T-02-94, 109.6°)

Nose: Full of spring flowers, with a touch of black pepper and almonds.

Mouth: A medium to full body with a remarkably smooth palate, considering its high alcohol content. Extremely assertive, with hints of light oranges and mint and tones of sweet tobacco that remind you of your grandfather's pipe bowl. Finish is very long, warm and nutty, lingers in the mouth with hints of hot peppers and well-toasted whole wheat bread.

Overall: Here is a style of bourbon that will appeal to bourbon lovers and to anyone new to the category. Its somewhat lighter, complex body displays a handcrafted whiskey with layers and layers of flavor. This bourbon sits well on its own in a snifter (add water if you wish) but is perfect on the rocks where it will remain flavorful throughout several rubbers of bridge, a long evening of reading a Civil War history or a relaxing evening chatting with friends.

Wild Turkey Kentucky Spirit, Single Barrel Bourbon, 101° (sample bottled on 9-29-94 from barrel No. 04 stored in warehouse C on rick No. 41)

Nose: Walnuts, tobacco, mint and cloves are all evident here.

Mouth: A huge body with complex layering of almonds, honey, blackberries and leather. The finish is almost aristocratic—long, dark, lingering and crying out for a fine cigar.

Overall: Don't add water, don't add ice, don't add anything—this bourbon is strictly for savoring after dinner. Ideally, it should be served in dark green rooms with leather and mahogany furniture and a fire if the weather is chilly—sip it as you admire the hunting scenes on the wall.

Wild Turkey Straight Rye Whiskey

DISTILLERY
The Wild Turkey Distillery, Lawrenceburg, Kentucky

ABOUT THE BRAND
A hunter green label makes this bottling of straight rye jump out from its Wild Turkey Bourbon brethren, and again, Master Distiller Jimmy Russell's favorite proof—101°—comes back into play. The back label reads: "A straight whiskey distilled from 100% selected grains stored in charred oak barrels, and matured into a whole-bodied, smooth and mellow whiskey." Wild Turkey Straight Rye Whiskey was first introduced in the 1940s.

TASTING NOTES
Wild Turkey Straight Rye Whiskey, 101°
Nose: Spicy, raw with "masculine" notes of cloves, old leather and some lighter citrus tones (lemons).

Mouth: A big body, the palate is sharp and almost perfume-y; quite hot in the mouth, with hints of dried cherries, honey and an almost oaty tone. The finish is quite short, with a burst of gentle heat in its rich, deep flavor.

Overall: This is an outstanding example of rye whiskey—robust, yet with a certain delicacy and raring to go. A shot of this whiskey could seal any deal, it can sit on ice for a long time and still the flavors will shine through, and it makes a wonderful medium for ginger ale, ginger beer or any other mixer.

Evan Williams Bourbon

DISTILLERY
The Heaven Hill Distillery, Bardstown, Kentucky

ABOUT THE BRAND
In 1957, a *Life* magazine advertisement for Old Grand-Dad, Old Crow, Old Taylor, Sunny Brook and Hill and Hill whiskeys included the name of a distiller in large print at the top of the page. The name was Evan Williams, whiskey pioneer. It gave the Shapira brothers, founders of the Heaven Hill Distillery, food for thought. In the 1960s, the distillery introduced Evan Williams Bourbon to the marketplace, and it hasn't looked back since.

Evan Williams Bourbon comes in three bottlings: the regular bottling, which is a minimum of four years old; a seven-year-old; and a very special bottling, the first vintage-dated bourbon we know of since bottles bearing the dates of distillation and bottling appeared back in the 1930s. Evan Williams Single-Barrel Vintage Bourbon is presented in an elegant bottle with a cork-finished stopper and a sophisticated black-wax seal. It bears the legend "Put in Oak in the Autumn of 1986," and each bottle also carries the number of the barrel in which it was aged. It is possible that Heaven Hill will release more vintage bottlings, although it doesn't necessarily follow that it will put one on the market every year. At this time, the 1986 vintage is the only such bottling from this distillery.

HISTORY

According to *The Kentucky Centenary* by Reuben T. Durret, 1893, Evan Williams was a distiller who settled in Louisville in 1783. In fact, though Durret claimed that Williams was the very first distiller in the region, it has since been discovered that others preceded him. Distiller William Calk had brought his stills from Virginia in 1775—when Kentucky was still Fincastle County, Virginia—and settled in the new town of Boonesborough. Others—John Ritchie, Wattie Boone and Elijah Pepper—were distilling in Kentucky shortly before Williams came along; however, Williams operated Kentucky's earliest recorded commercial distillery in 1783. The story of Williams' distillery is recorded in *A Memorial History of Louisville*, edited by J. Stoddard Johnston, 1896. This book asserts that Williams, in addition to owning a distillery on the corner of Fifth and Water Streets, was also a member of the Board of Trustees of Louisville. When he was first appointed to this prestigious group, Williams innocently brought along a bottle of his whiskey to share with his fellow trustees; he was completely unaware of the censure—or fine—that such an act could incur.

The first time Williams did this, the board was duly grateful, and the whiskey was shared among the group. At the next meeting, however, sat a man who had been absent from Williams's first display of generosity, and he didn't see any fun in drinking whiskey while considering the city's future. The man, Wil Johnson, happened to be the clerk for the board, a stuffy sort who was accustomed to imported wines and liquors. He objected strongly to the donation and suggested that Williams be expelled from the meeting. In response, Williams accused him of having "the perverted taste of an aristocrat," and apparently Johnson's objections were overruled. It's said that Williams left the meeting with an empty bottle.

Records also show that Williams was distilling without a license until 1788, when he was "found out" and indicted by a grand jury. He dutifully paid the fee and continued making his whiskey in Louisville until the neighbors complained in 1802. At that point, his business was declared a nuisance and closed. So Evan Williams had enjoyed at least 19 years in the whiskey business, although it is entirely possible that he just moved his stills to another location and resumed distilling. The next incident involving this pioneer, as far as we know, was when his name appeared in that fateful issue of *Life* magazine in 1957.

TASTING NOTES
Evan Williams, 80°

Nose: Oaky with a light perfume-y note and hints of vanilla.

Mouth: A light body with some oak, leather and a vegetal note that turns sweetish in the mouth. The finish is short and warm.

Overall: There's something about the light notes in this bottling that make this bourbon ideal for mint juleps. Also good for mixed drinks and whiskey sours.

Evan Williams, 7 years old, 90°

Nose: Light and minty, some vanilla.

Mouth: At seven years old, this whiskey has grown up well. The body is medium to light, and the palate bears some leather, tobacco, vanilla and hints of caramel. The finish is medium to long, and oh, so warm and soothing.

Overall: Here's an "around the house" bottling that's a lot more sophisticated than expected. Drink it on ice, with a splash of water or club soda, or make above-average cocktails and mixed drinks with this bourbon.

Evan Williams Single Barrel Vintage, 9 years old
(distilled in Fall 1986, bottled in Fall 1995), 86.6°

Nose: Light, flowery, some eucalyptus and light oats.

Mouth: The body is almost syrupy, and the palate holds some pine notes and hints of wildflowers. The finish is medium.

Overall: This vintage bottling is very stylized and bears little resemblance to the two other bourbons that carry the Evan Williams name. A great bourbon with which to make mint juleps, good for drinking on ice or with a splash of water or club soda and very good with ginger ale. If you drink this whiskey neat, do it on a balmy summer evening, rather than a deep winter's night—it's a sprightly bourbon that heightens your senses rather than making you feel snug and cozy.

Yellowstone Bourbon

BOTTLER & MARKETER

The David Sherman Company of St. Louis, Missouri

ABOUT THE BRAND

Here's a bourbon with a terrific label—a photograph of Old Faithful gushing clouds of steam into the sky and the legend "Tradition of Excellence." Yellowstone does, indeed, have a tradition of excellence and a long history that involves one of the great whiskey-making families in Kentucky—the Dants.

HISTORY

Yellowstone Bourbon was a product first made by Joseph Bernard (J.B.) Dant, son of Joseph Washington (J.W.) Dant, the man who gave the world J.W. Dant Bourbon. J.W. started making whiskey in Kentucky in 1836, and he passed on his knowledge to his sons.

J.B. Dant, however, decided that he could make some serious money from the whiskey business—but only if he went about it in a businesslike manner. Accordingly, in 1865, he went to Gethsemane, Kentucky—not too far from his father's place—and built the Cold Spring Distillery. Some sources say that J.B. had developed the formula for Yellowstone back in 1854, some 12 years before opening his own plant. But once he got going, Dant moved swiftly. As soon as the distillery was up and running, he contracted with a Louisville company to market his wares to the post-Civil War public. In 1872, Charles Townsend, one of Dant's salesmen, returned from a trip out West where he had visited the newly opened Yellowstone National Park. He had the idea that if the name Yellowstone were put on a bottle of good whiskey, chances were good that the folks out West would buy it, and since the park was receiving publicity, the name would stick in everybody's mind. The thought found its way to J.B.'s ears, and Yellowstone whiskey was born. Though the date of its initial offering can't be ascertained, the whiskey was on the market by 1886.

Still, J.B. wasn't content; next, he set his sights on the company that distributed his whiskey—Taylor and Williams. Having fared so well with his Yellowstone brand, he took over that operation at the turn of the century and, 12 years later, built the Taylor and Williams Distillery in Gethsemane.

During Prohibition, Dant's Yellowstone Bourbon was bottled for medicinal purposes, and with Repeal, Taylor and Williams built the Yellowstone Distillery in Louisville. Both the plant and the brand name were sold to Glenmore in 1944, and the brand went on to become what was said to be the biggest-selling bourbon in Ken-

THE LOADING DOCK AT THE TAYLOR AND WILLIAMS DISTILLERY CIRCA 1900

tucky in the 1960s. Glenmore became part of United Distillers in 1991, and in 1993, the Yellowstone brand name was sold to The David Sherman Company.

TASTING NOTES

Yellowstone Kentucky Straight Bourbon, 90°

Nose: Vanilla, honey, oranges, caramel, "scorched custard" and a hint of spices and mint.

Mouth: A medium body with a touch of sweet caramel and hints of heavy fruits (prunes?). The finish is short, with a touch of eucalyptus.

Overall: This is a good "around the house" bourbon. Drink it on ice, with water, club soda or flavored mixers. The sweetness also makes this whiskey good for Manhattans.

CHAPTER FOUR

A WHISKEY PRIMER

GOOD STRAIGHT AMERICAN WHISKEY CAN FIT INTO ANY situation. It's as comfortable in a Manhattan or as snug and warm in an Old-Fashioned as it is completely unabashed all alone in a shot glass or a fishbowl snifter. For some, bourbons and Tennessee whiskeys personify the South. They can sit side by side in old rockers on the front porch and watch the day go by. But these whiskeys— along with their cousin rye—can switch hats at any given moment. They can be smooth and sophisticated, complex and deep, soulful and reflective, brash and bold, up-front and serious or even kind and gentle. American whiskey can blend into the company of a throng of thugs or a swarm of sophisticates. It has dog-eat-dog attitude when need be and eloquent manners when protocol is required. There's only one persona that American whiskey never adopts—it is never, ever shy and retiring.

American whiskey—whether it's rye, Tennessee or bourbon—is the product of a combination of grains and water that are cooked together until they form a soft mash. Yeast is added, along with a portion of mash from a previous distillation, and it is this addition that makes the whiskey "sour mash." Fermentation then begins, producing alcohol by breaking down the sugars from the grains. At this point, the mixture needs to be distilled: heated with steam until the alcohol vaporizes and separates from the water and solids. The vapors are collected and condensed, and then the liquid is distilled a second time to purify the alcohol further and increase its strength. The end product is the colorless, clear liquid that we call raw or new spirit. It is put into brand-new oak barrels that have been charred on the inside and then is stored, usually for at least four years. During this aging period, the liquid takes on color, flavor and character from the charred wood. When the whiskey is deemed ready, it is filtered and bottled.

The Words of Whiskey—Working Definitions

LIKE ANY TOPIC, THE VOCABULARY THAT SURROUNDS WHISKEY RANGES FROM accessible to arcane. Becoming familiar with a few of the terms and the specific meanings they have in the whiskey industry makes understanding whiskey easier. Be warned, however; these are casual, "working" definitions and are not technically complete.

Backset: Also **Sour mash** and **Setback**. The thin, watery part of a previously distilled batch of whiskey mash that is added—or "set back"—into the next batch.

Barrels: Full-size (53-gallon) closed wooden casks that are constructed by hand from oak. Their interiors are charred over open flames, and the barrels are then used to age whiskey.

Beer: Also **Distiller's beer**. The fermented mixture of water, grains and yeast that is distilled into whiskey. It is a thick, yeasty, porridge-like mash that has fermented enough to create an alcohol content of about 9 percent. At this point, it is ready to be distilled. This "beer" resembles soupy corn-bread batter.

Beer still: Also **Continuous still**. A giant apparatus in which the main component is a very tall (sometimes several stories high) chimneylike metal column. Stills separate the alcohol from the water in the distiller's beer by vaporizing the alcohol content. The spirit produced by the continuous still is known in American whiskey-making as "low wines."

Charcoal mellowing: The filtration process that Tennessee whiskey goes through before aging. The whiskey passes through a vat filled with a minimum of 10 feet of sugar-maple charcoal in a procedure that takes between a week and 10 days. Also known as "mellowing," "leaching" or the "Lincoln County Process."

Charring: The process of setting fire to the inside of a new oak whiskey barrel for a brief time in order to blacken its interior surface.

Continuous still: See **Beer still**. The apparatus used to process the distiller's beer and concentrate the alcohol; in American whiskey-making, continuous stills are used to accomplish the first of two distillations.

Distillation: Purifying the liquid part of a mixture by a series of evaporation and condensation processes.

Distiller's beer: See **Beer**. The thick, fermented porridge of cooked grains, water and yeast that will be distilled in the continuous still.

Doubler: The name of one of the types of still that is used to accomplish the second distillation of American whiskey; it effectively removes impurities and concentrates the alcohol even further. "Low wines" go in; "high wines" come out. (See **Thumper** for the other type.)

Fermenter: A giant—12-to-25-foot wide and 10-to-20-foot deep—wooden or metal (usually steel) tub in which the mash of cooked grains and water meets the yeast. They mingle, the yeast begins to act on sugars in the grain, and fermentation occurs over a few days, producing alcohol within the mash and turning it into distiller's beer.

High wines: The name of the distilled spirit after it has passed through a doubler or thumper for its second distillation. Sometimes called "doublings."

Low wines: In American whiskey-making, the name of the spirit after it has passed through the beer or continuous still for its first distillation. Sometimes called "singlings."

Malt: Malted grain; in American whiskey-making the grain is almost always barley.

Malted barley: Barley that has been steeped in water, warmed slightly until partially germinated and then heated or roasted (kilned) to stop any further germination. Malted barley (or any malted grain) contains enzymes not present in unmalted grains that will convert starches into the fermentable sugars on which yeast feeds.

> ## WHY BOOZE?
>
> **E.** G. BOOZ, A PHILADELPHIA distiller, issued his Old Cabin Whiskey in a bottle shaped like a log cabin in 1840, and some say it was his name that became a slang term for alcohol, but it's doubtful. The Egyptians brewed a beer they called *boozah* some 3,000 years ago, and there was a word in middle English, *bousen*, that meant, basically, "to drink with gusto."

Mash: The mixture of cooked grains and water before the yeast is added to start fermentation. Mush would also be an appropriate term. Cooking the mixture of grains reduces the starches to fermentable sugars.

Mash tub: A large metal tub in which the grains are combined with water and cooked to soften them and to break down the starch into simple sugars before the resulting "mash" is transferred to the fermenter.

Mashbill: The grain recipe used to make a specific whiskey. For example: 70% corn, 20% rye and 10% malted barley.

Proof: The scale, measured in degrees, used to denote alcohol content; in the United States, 200° is equal to 100% alcohol, and therefore 80° would equal 40% alcohol.

Small grains: Refers to any and all grains, other than corn, that are used in an American whiskey recipe.

Sour mash: Think of sour mash as "whiskey DNA," just as the sourdough starter used in bread-making is "sourdough DNA." Sour mash is a measure of the liquid called backset that is a by-product of the first distillation of a previous batch of whiskey. It is "set back" into a subsequent batch of mash, along with some fresh yeast, to help get fermentation going on its own particular "genetic" or "family" path. Using a sour-mash mixture in a new batch of whiskey is one of the ways in which distillers keep their products consistent, allowing the identity and qualities of the "mother mash" to be reborn in the new batch.

Spent beer: The mixture of liquids and solids that are the by-products of the first distillation; the alcohol has escaped as vapor, and the wet, sludgy mush of spent beer is piped out of the bottom of the still. The spent beer is strained to produce two valuable components: The liquid backset, or sour mash, that will be used in the next batch, and the grain solids that will be dried and sold as cattle feed.

Sweet mash: Mash that is fermented using fresh yeast only, without the addition or help of any backset from a previous distillation. Most breads could be called sweet-mash breads in that they use fresh yeast; sourdough breads could be thought of as sour-mash breads in that they rely on a lactic yeast or "soured" starter. No straight American whiskeys currently being produced use the sweet-mash method.

Thumper: The name of one of the types of still that is used to accomplish the second distillation of American whiskey; it effectively removes impurities and concentrates the alcohol even further. "Low wines" go in; "high wines" come out. Thumpers differ from doublers in that the low wines enter a thumper as vapors that are bubbled through water, causing the still to make a thumping sound; a doubler makes no distinctive noise, since the low wines enter in condensed liquid form.

Whiskey: A spirituous liquor distilled from grains; its near relative, brandy, is distilled from fruits. Originally, whiskey was the product of areas that had cold or cool climates—places where grains would grow but most fruits didn't fare well. Of course, whiskey can be made anywhere, as long as you have all of the necessary ingredients.

WHISKEY OR WHISKY?

THE BASIC RULE IS: THE SCOTS and the Canadians spell the word W-H-I-S-K-Y, whereas Americans and the Irish tend to add an *e*, making it W-H-I-S-K-E-Y. But as with all rules, there are exceptions. Federal regulations governing whiskey, for instance, don't spell the word with the *e* even though they are home-grown directives. And neither do George Dickel, Maker's Mark, Old Forester or Early Times use that *e* when labeling their bottles—though they all are American whiskeys.

BOURBON—THE OFFICIAL WORD

On January 7, 1964, the eighty-eighth Congress of the United States of America passed a "Concurrent Resolution" declaring that bourbon whiskey "is a distinctive product of the United States and is unlike other types of alcoholic beverages, whether foreign or domestic; and whereas to be entitled to the designation 'Bourbon whiskey' the product must conform to the highest standards . . . and whereas Bourbon whiskey has achieved recognition and acceptance throughout the world as a distinctive product of the United States . . . it is the sense of Congress that the recognition of Bourbon whiskey as a distinctive product of the United States be brought to the attention of the appropriate agencies."

Yeast: Cells of fungi that, under certain conditions, cause fermentation by secreting an enzyme that converts simple sugars into ethanol (alcohol) and carbon dioxide. In bread-making, it is the carbon dioxide that is most useful to the process, since it is trapped within the dough and results in leavening. In whiskey-making, the objective is to harvest the alcohol produced by the fermentation reaction.

Yeast mash: A porridge of cooked grains in which yeast is "grown" to provide enough yeast for the entire mash in the fermenter.

The Ingredients Needed for Making Whiskey

Three ingredients—the water, the grains and the yeast—are key to whiskey-making; without them, you just can't do it.

THE WATER

The water in the areas where most American whiskey is produced—Kentucky and Tennessee—is perfectly suited for whiskey-making. Much of it is spring water that is naturally filtered through the limestone shelf that underlies Kentucky's Bluegrass Region and Pennyroyal Plateau and Tennessee's Highland Rim. The water is free of iron and rich in minerals, especially magnesium and calcium—some of the sweetest water in the world. Each distillery gets its water from its own source, sometimes a nearby spring or a spring-fed lake and, in one instance, the Kentucky River (don't worry—it's thoroughly filtered). The Louisville distilleries use city water to make their whiskey, but the water, rich in calcium and magnesium (both of which are assets in whiskey-making), is filtered to remove any undesirable fluorides, flavors or odors.

THE GRAINS

American whiskeys depend on a mixture of three out of four grains for their manufacture: corn, barley and either rye or wheat. Since all of these crops are plentiful within our borders, the supply is sure. Bourbons and Tennessee whiskeys use corn in the largest proportion; rye whiskey is primarily made from rye grain. A very basic recipe for bourbon would consist of 70 percent corn, 20 percent rye or wheat (but not both) and 10 percent malted barley. Generally speaking, a high percentage of small grains will yield a more flavorful whiskey. One unchanging factor for all whiskeys is the use of malted barley (although any malted grain would suffice). The germination and kilning process it goes through are essential, since they produce diastase, an enzyme that aids in breaking down starches into simple sugars the yeast can work on.

THE YEAST

Yeast is a living organism that feeds on fermentable (simple) sugars, such as glucose and fructose, and changes them into beverage alcohol and carbon dioxide. Along the way, the reaction produces some heat and tiny amounts of flavor-enhancing impurities known as congeners. The strain of yeast used by each distillery is its lifeblood, since each yeast strain is individual and produces its own amount of alcohol and different predominant flavors. If a distillery lost its particular strain of yeast, its whiskey would never taste quite the same again. To prevent such a disaster, most distilleries stash a cache of yeast somewhere away from the distillery.

Distilleries can use specific strains of commercially produced yeast developed especially for whiskey-making, or they can grow their own. This homegrown variety, called "jug yeast," requires patience and care on the part of the distiller, though the ones who do it swear by the fruits of their labors. Jug yeast is a particular strain of yeast that is carefully propagated at the distillery, usually in a medium of malted barley and rye. The distiller literally starts this yeast in small "jugs" and then transfers the yeast to larger vessels known as dona (pronounced DOE-nuh or DOE-nee) tubs, where the yeast feeds on the rich cooked grains in the yeast mash and multiplies until there is enough to ferment an entire batch of cooked grains. Growing yeast in a dona tub is a very old-fashioned practice and represents another way that a distiller can make his whiskey different from the others.

Whiskeys made from dona-tub yeasts can be further individualized when hops are added to the process or the yeast mash is "soured." Most of the distillers who use hops aren't quite sure why they are doing it—it's an old Kentucky custom that has been passed down through generation after generation of whiskey families. The significance was lost, but the practice continued nonetheless. Presumably, the procedure began as a way of preserving the yeast, just as hops were first added to beer for their preservative qualities. However, the hops do add flavors to the product and are responsible for the nuances of certain whiskeys. A distiller who doesn't use hops once experimented by adding some to his dona tub to see what kind of difference it would make. He says that it totally altered his whiskey, adding flavors and aromas that weren't usually present.

Another style of dona-tub propagation produces what's called sour yeast mash—not to be confused with sour mash. Making a sour yeast mash involves adding lactic bacteria to the yeast mash and allowing them to increase the acidity and "sour" the yeast mash. During this process, the lactic bacteria add their own nuances to the yeast mash; if the souring agents are not added, the yeast is known as a "sweet yeast mash."

Definitions of the Types of Whiskeys

Straight whiskey IS A DISTILLED GRAIN SPIRIT MADE FROM AT LEAST 51 PERCENT of one single type of grain and any mixture of other grains. It must be distilled to no more than 160° proof, must enter charred new oak barrels at no higher than 125° proof, must be aged for at least two years, and bottled at a minimum of 80° proof. No neutral grain spirits (characterless spirits distilled out at very high proofs) or any other substances can be included or added.

The term "mingling" is used by whiskey-makers to describe the process in which a number of barrels of straight whiskey are mingled together in order to achieve a consistent style. Usually, whiskeys aged in the high temperatures at the top of tall warehouses are mingled with whiskeys aged on the center and bottom floors. The term is used so that the word "blending" doesn't confuse people into thinking that blended whiskey is being produced. *Blended whiskey* is straight whiskey that has been blended with neutral grain spirits, often with the addition of coloring and flavor enhancers. There are many fine blended whiskeys on the marketplace—they should not be dismissed out of hand.

Specific types of whiskey have strict legal definitions. To avoid whiskey confusion, it pays to know the differences among them.

SOUR-MASH WHISKEY

All sour-mash whiskeys use a measure of backset to bring continuity of style to subsequent batches of fermentable mash. *Every* straight bourbon, rye and Tennessee whiskey being made at present is made by the sour-mash method. Regulations used to require a minimum of 25 percent of the total mash be made up of backset in order for a whiskey to use the words "sour mash" on the label. Although that rule no longer applies, most distilleries still use upwards of 20 percent.

As well as assuring the continuity of style, adding backset is the way in which distillers control the pH level in the mash, providing the yeast with an ideal medium in which to produce alcohol and the all-important congeners that develop into bold flavors as the whiskey ages.

Because the addition of backset also helps the yeast produce more alcohol, more whiskey can be made from each batch. Now, that may be important to the distillers, and it certainly influences the price we pay for our shot of whiskey, but finances aside, the sour-mash method is good because it brings additional flavor to the whiskey. Since a little of each batch is used for the next, we are, in most cases, looking at an ongoing style of whiskey (and strain of yeast) that dates to when Prohibition ended in 1933.

HOW TO TELL A WHISKEY'S PROOF

To roughly determine the proof of a bottle of whiskey, shake the bottle. If large bubbles appear on the surface, the whiskey is probably over 100° proof, if smaller bubbles appear and disappear quickly, the whiskey has a lower proof.

STRAIGHT BOURBON

Federal law requires that:

• Bourbon must contain at least 51 percent corn in the grain recipe, or mashbill. The other grains used are malted barley and either rye or wheat, although this is not stipulated by law. Most bourbon mashbills contain considerably more than 51 percent corn.

• The spirit must finish its second distillation at no more than 160° proof (80 percent alcohol).

• The spirit must be aged, at no more than 125° proof, for a minimum of two years in charred new oak barrels.

• If the whiskey is aged for less than four years, the age of the whiskey must be stated on the label.

• No coloring or flavoring may be added to straight bourbon whiskey.

• Straight bourbon must be bottled at a minimum of 80° proof.

STRAIGHT TENNESSEE WHISKEY

Tennessee whiskey must conform to the same regulations as bourbon, and although corn need not be the predominant grain, it always is. However, before it is aged, Tennessee whiskey is filtered through huge vats that contain at least 10 feet of sugar-maple charcoal, in a procedure known as the Lincoln County Process. The Tennessee distilleries often refer to it as "charcoal mellowing" or "leaching," but basically, it's a filtration method that adds certain distinctive qualities while removing unwanted flavors or components. Bourbons and rye whiskeys are filtered *after* they have aged, as are Tennessee whiskeys, but this filtration is largely cosmetic and very quick. It doesn't contribute the sooty flavors of the long and leisurely leaching process that Tennessee whiskey-makers employ *before* their whiskey sees the inside of a barrel.

STRAIGHT RYE WHISKEY

Straight rye whiskey must conform to the same standards as straight bourbon, with the exception that the predominant grain must be rye, not corn. Most rye whiskey mashbills use considerably more than just 51 percent rye.

WHEATED BOURBON

This is a term we use to describe bourbon that is made from a mashbill which contains wheat instead of rye as a small grain. There are only a few such products on the market at present; Maker's Mark and W.L. Weller are two examples of the style.

STRAIGHT CORN WHISKEY

By law, straight corn whiskey must be made using a minimum of 80 percent corn in the mashbill, and if it is aged at all, it must be aged in used or uncharred oak barrels. No corn whiskeys are covered in this book.

How to Make Whiskey

WHISKEY-MAKING REQUIRES SPECIFIC PROCEDURES AND SOME SPECIAL equipment—much like, say, ice-cream making. To make either one, the cook follows step-by-step instructions. Recipes break complicated processes into their doable parts and lead the procedure from step to step in an orderly manner. That's why we think it's the best way to explain how whiskey is made.

A RECIPE FOR BOURBON WHISKEY

We have loosely based this recipe on the methods and equipment used by Master Distiller Steve Nally at the Maker's Mark Distillery. His mashbill uses wheat, not rye, but we included rye as an option in our ingredients. Although each distillery has its own techniques, idiosyncrasies and formulas, the processes are similar at each one. The law requires notice that making whiskey without a license is illegal and punishable under federal statutes.

MAKES ABOUT 1,007 GALLONS OF UNAGED 110° BOURBON, WHICH WILL YIELD ABOUT 988 GALLONS OF 90° BOURBON AFTER 5 YEARS OF AGING

FOR THE YEAST MASH
4   ounces hops (in pellet form)
20 gallons spring water
30 pounds malted barley, ground medium-fine

| 1 | pound active jug yeast |
| 150 | gallons cooked grain mash (made from 3 parts wheat or rye, 2 parts malted barley and spring water), at 90 degrees F |

FOR THE MASH

3,940	gallons spring water
460	gallons backset (sour mash)
151¼	bushels corn, finely ground
34½	bushels wheat or rye, ground medium-fine
30¼	bushels malted barley, ground medium-fine

FOR THE FERMENTING

| 3,250 | gallons backset |

FOR DILUTION

Demineralized spring water

EQUIPMENT REQUIRED

1	double-walled, 55-gallon, stainless-steel dona tub
	Long-handled, very large wooden spoons
1	large (200-gallon) pot
1	hammer mill or roller mill
1	large (11,000-gallon) carbon-steel mash tub
1	long thermometer
1	timer
1	medium-large (9,658-gallon) cypress fermenter
1	continuous still
1	doubler
1	large (1,300-gallon) holding tank
1	hydrometer
19	standard (53-gallon) charred new oak barrels
	About 4,000 sterilized 1-liter glass bottles with tight-fitting lids or corks

1. **Prepare the yeast mash:** Combine the hops and water in the dona tub; bring to a boil over high heat. Boil until the hops are saturated and flavorful, 25 minutes. Set aside until the mixture cools to 160 degrees F, about 15 minutes.

2. Stir in the malted barley and let set until the grain is saturated, about 1½ hours. Cook over moderate heat until the temperature of the mixture registers 178 degrees.

Adjust the heat as necessary to maintain that temperature, and cook the malt for 25 minutes. Set aside until cooled to 80 degrees.

3. Stir in the jug yeast. Partially cover and set aside for 23 to 25 hours. Try to maintain the 80-degree temperature by stirring from time to time; the fermentation of the yeast mash will produce some heat.

4. Pour the 150 gallons of grain mash into a wide 200-gallon pot. Add the yeast-mash mixture and stir with a very large wooden spoon to mix well. Set aside in a warm, draft-free place to allow the yeast to double in quantity one more time in its new environment, about 3 hours.

5. While the yeast gets going, if you didn't buy your grains pre-ground, mill the grains using either a hammer mill (faster) or a roller mill (slower). The corn should be more finely milled than the rye or wheat and malted barley.

6. **Cook the mash:** Choose a carbon-steel mash tub with an 11,000-gallon capacity; typically, it would measure about 15 feet in diameter and about 4 feet deep. The latest models have several features that more old-fashioned mash tubs don't have: steam spargers (something like sprinkler heads) that inject live steam for cooking the mash and usually 3 rings of coils stacked one above the other in the base of the tub, just inside the circumference, that circulate cold water for cooling the mash. The very latest tubs have a motor-driven rake that rotates to stir the mash. If your tub doesn't have these features, use large wooden spoons and a lot of elbow grease. Pour the water into the tub. Add the backset and heat the mixture to 140 degrees. You should have about 4,400 gallons at this point.

7. **Begin the three-step method:** Add the corn and rake or stir until well combined. Bring the mixture to a boil. Adjust the heat as necessary to maintain the temperature and cook the corn until every molecule is thoroughly and completely saturated with the liquids, about 25 minutes.

8. Turn off the heat and let the mash cool to 156 degrees, about 15 minutes if you have good cold-water coils.

9. Add the wheat or rye and rake or stir until well combined. Hold at that temperature for 10 minutes.

10. Cool the mash to 148 degrees, 5 to 10 minutes if you have coils.

11. Rake or stir in the malted barley and let set until all of the grains are saturated, about 10 minutes. At this point, the mixture will smell like instant oat cereal—sweet and grain-y. The temperature will drop to about 145 degrees. Set the mash aside until cooled to 76 degrees.

12. **Add the yeast and ferment the mash:** Choose a 9,658-gallon cypress fermenter. Pour the backset into the tank and stir in the cooled mash. Add the yeast mash all at once and inject air or stir up very well. Stop stirring; the top of the mixture will be foamy. Let the mash ferment for about 3 days—yeast needs time to convert the glu-

cose in the mash into alcohol and carbon dioxide (CO_2). You'll know it's happening when you smell the distinctive acrid-vegetal odor of the CO_2. After 8 to 10 hours, the top of the mixture will look like it's bubbling at a slow boil; this is the effect of CO_2 rising to the surface. The mixture will bubble like that for about 2½ days, and since fermentation produces heat, the mixture will rise in temperature to around 90 degrees and then cool down to 78 to 80 degrees. Toward the end of the fermentation, the odor of the mixture will sharpen and the smell of alcohol will become more intrusive. The bubbling will slack off and the grains will fall to the bottom, leaving a watery-looking yellowish liquid above it. You now have beer, or distiller's beer.

13. Prepare your continuous still and doubler, taking care that you have plenty of steam for heating both of them. While the still heats, mix the beer well to redistribute the solids and heat slowly to bring the temperature up to 145 degrees. When the steam production in the still is at full force, begin pumping the beer from the fermenter into the column of the continuous still. Run the still, keeping the temperature inside the column between 178 and 196 degrees, until the alcohol component of the beer has been vaporized, has risen to a condenser, has been concentrated further during its second distillation in the doubler and has been piped into a holding tank.

14. Use a hydrometer to check the proof of the new spirit; it will be in the range of 120° to 130°. Add enough of the demineralized water to dilute it to the desired proof, no higher than 125°. Fill the barrels and seal them well. Arrange the barrels on their sides, bung holes facing up, in an unheated warehouse; store there for at least four years. Rotate the barrels after two years, if desired. Longer storage is fine too.

15. Before bottling, reduce the whiskey to the desired proof with more demineralized water. Filter the whiskey, funnel into sterilized bottles and seal well to prevent evaporation.

Distilling Whiskey

THE ART OF THE DISTILLER COMES MOST STRONGLY INTO PLAY DURING the distillation process itself. The first and the last parts of any batch (heads and tails, or foreshots and feints) contain too many impurities to make good whiskey and are, therefore, separated from the whiskey and redistilled. The experienced distiller knows when the heads finish, what part of the run will become fine spirits and when the undesirable tails begin.

American whiskeys go through two separate distillations. The distiller's beer is first distilled in a continuous still or "beer still," and then the resultant low wines are redistilled into high wines in either a doubler or a thumper. Here's a brief description of how these stills work:

Continuous stills are, in very simple terms, very tall metal chimney-like columns fitted with a series of metal baffles, each about 18 inches above the next. Each baffle is uniformly perforated with small holes, and a three-inch-tall metal standpipe protrudes above the plate. The beer, which is a very thick slurry of grains, is pumped into the still near the top of the column. It accumulates on the first baffle below the entry point and slowly drips through the perforations. Meanwhile, the depth of the beer increases; when it reaches the top of the standpipe, the beer flows down onto the next baffle below it. All the while during this process, quantities of steam are piped into the bottom of the still, and the steam, of course, rises up through the column and evaporates the alcohol, which has a lower boiling point than the water component of the beer.

The alcohol vapors rise to the top of the still, where they encounter a rectifier—a series of copper plates and other devices. Copper has the effect of removing sulfur

A NINETEENTH-CENTURY STILL

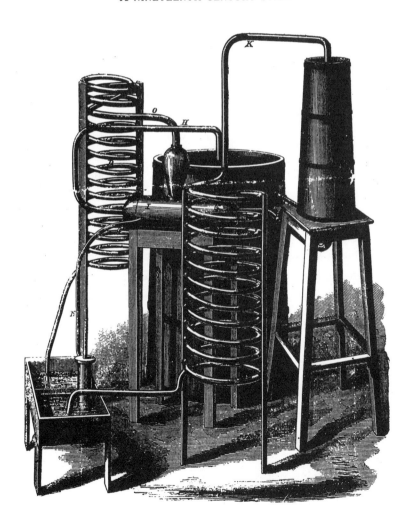

compounds from the product and thus eliminates unwanted flavors from the whiskey.

At this point, it's time for the second distillation in one of two devices: a doubler or a thumper. If a doubler is being used, the vapors enter a condenser, where they are cooled back into their liquid state; this product is known as low wines. The low wines then enter the doubler, basically a huge tank, usually in the shape of a tin can with an upturned funnel on the top. The doubler is heated, and again, the alcohol in the liquid vaporizes before the water component, thus further concentrating the vapors. When these vapors are collected and condensed, they become the high wines, or new spirit.

If a thumper is being used, the vapors from the continuous still are not condensed. Instead, they are piped into a pool of hot water in the bottom of the thumper. The vapors bubble through the water, creating quite a racket—hence "thumper"—and, just as with the doubler, the alcohol vaporizes first and leaves the still as concentrated vapors. The vapors are then collected and condensed into high wines.

Congeners and Fusel Oils

ALL DISTILLED SPIRITS CONTAIN MINUSCULE AMOUNTS OF IMPURITIES called congeners that are essentially the flavor components of the spirit. It's regrettable that these components are termed "impurities," since without them, whiskey would be very bland. Don't let the terminology put you off; congeners are absolutely essential in good whiskey.

If a spirit leaves the still at a high proof, it will bear fewer congeners and produce a lighter style of whiskey. Distilling the whiskey to a lower proof, therefore, is more desirable if the aim is to produce a heavier-bodied whiskey.

Fusel oils are a subcategory of congeners that are present in tiny amounts in beverage alcohol. During whiskey maturation, fusel oils combine with acids in the whiskey to form esters, which in turn add flavor to the final aged product. However, this takes time, and if fusel oils are present in too great a quantity, they can result in a "banana-like" flavor. The art of making fine whiskey is largely one of balancing every last ingredient in every step of production.

The Filtering Process for Tennessee Whiskeys

FEW DRINKERS REALIZE THAT TENNESSEE WHISKEYS ARE NOT BOURBONS. A very intelligent and worldly friend, who has been drinking Jack Daniel's for what she says is "a hundred years," took to her bed when she was told that Jack Daniel's isn't bourbon. She argued and refused to believe it but finally acquiesced when she understood that the recipes and legal requirements are similar to those set out for bourbon and that in some ways, Tennessee whiskeys are the more special and more work-intensive of the two. They experience a unique filtration process before they are aged.

Filtration via the Lincoln County Process, also referred to as the "mellowing," "leaching" or "charcoal mellowing" process, requires slowly dripping the raw whiskey through huge vats containing 10 feet of sugar-maple charcoal—between 7 and 10 days will pass before it reaches the bottom of the vat and drips out as "mellowed" whiskey. This type of filtration gives and takes: While it removes unwanted flavors (especially some of the fatty acids that Tennessee distillers don't like) and refines the whiskey, it also adds its own distinctive, often sweet and sooty, flavors to the spirit. This is the trait that most distinguishes Tennessee whiskey from bourbon. For the record, having tasted day-old Jack Daniel's Tennessee whiskey that has not gone through the Lincoln County Process alongside a sample of the same whiskey that was filtered through the leaching vats, the difference is astounding: The unfiltered spirit tastes similar to an eau-de-vie, and the mellow sweet-sootiness, characteristic of this style of whiskey, appears only after charcoal filtration.

The Lincoln County Process is both expensive and time-consuming. Both George Dickel and Jack Daniel's produce their own charcoal at or near the distillery, using exclusively sugar maple. Here's how they do it at the Jack Daniel Distillery:

• Hard Tennessee-grown sugar-maple trees are felled in the fall, when the sap is at a low point. They are cut into 4-inch-square planks, each about 5 feet long.

• These planks are then used to build "ricks," or stacks. Six planks are placed on the ground, in the open air, each about 6 inches from the next, creating a square that's 5 feet long on each side. Six more planks are placed crosswise on top of the first layer; this layering procedure continues, the planks in each layer crosswise over the layer below it, until the rick stands around 7 feet high. In practice, four such ricks are built at once, adjacent to each other on two sides, forming a large square that measures 10 feet on each side. The ricks are constructed on top of a shallow pit so that each of the four ricks tilts slightly toward the center of the formation.

• The four ricks are then set on fire while men with water hoses stand by to control the burning. If the wood were left to burn on its own, it would quickly be reduced to ashes, but by controlling the fire, charcoal is produced. If the wood were burned in covered kilns, unwanted impurities would remain in the wood, and Tennessee whiskey wouldn't taste the way it should.

• Once the charcoal is produced, it is allowed to cool. Next, it is broken into small gravel-size bits, each about ¼ inch in diameter.

• At this point, the operation moves indoors, where large mellowing vats await the charcoal. Each round metal-lined vat is about 6 feet in diameter and 12 to 14 feet deep. The entire bottom surface is lined with a wool blanket. Charcoal is added to measure 10 feet deep. Then the new spirit is chilled and piped into several narrow pipes that are anchored above the charcoal and extend at intervals across the diameter of the top of the vat. The pipes are perforated so that the whiskey drips onto the charcoal in droplets. This spirit will slowly make its way to the bottom of the charcoal, seep through the woolen blanket and collect below. The mellowing process takes about 10 days. At the end, the whiskey is ready for barreling and aging.

• There is no definite time period set for how long each vat of charcoal will retain its character. Every day, samples of the newly mellowed whiskey are tasted by a panel of experts, which decides when the charcoal in each vat needs to be replaced.

Whiskey Barrels—Coopers and Cooperage

COOPERS ARE THE SKILLED PEOPLE WHO CONSTRUCT AND REPAIR BARRELS, and cooperage is the term applied to the wares they make and the plant in which they make them.

Whiskey leaves its second distillation at 120° to 140° proof. The law requires that before whiskey can be put into barrels, it must be brought down (diluted with demineralized water) to a maximum of 125° proof or less. Further, the whiskey must be entered into charred new oak barrels. Although the regulations specify oak containers be used to age whiskey, the individual distiller is free to use whatever type of oak he desires. American distillers, however, always use the American white oak variety, since its density and the configuration of its grain prevent leakage and allow minimal evaporation, usually 7½ to 12 gallons per barrel after four years.

American white oak from cold forests is the wood of choice for whiskey barrels.

THE CONTAINER ON WHEELS

"THE BARREL HAS RIGHTFULLY BEEN CALLED 'THE CONTAINER ON WHEELS.' Because of its shape, it can be handled by one man, even though loaded with several hundred pounds. Due to its bilge, a barrel rests on a small surface when on its side, reducing friction to a minimum. On its side, the barrel responds readily to a push in any direction. Rolled, it covers distances quickly and with a minimum of effort. On an incline, it moves of its own weight. It is easily turned and guided in any direction, as it pivots on a small contact point."

—FROM *The Wooden Barrel Manual,* COMPILED BY F.P. HANKERSON, THE ASSOCIATED COOPERAGE INDUSTRIES OF AMERICA, INC., REVISED 1951, REPRINTED 1983.

The wood grain is dense because trees that live in a cold environment grow relatively slowly; a barrel made from it will be excellent for aging whiskey. Consequently, the wood used at the Blue Grass Cooperage Company in Louisville comes mainly from the chilly forests of northern Minnesota, where the trees grow at just the right rate. And if you fear ecological problems as a result of the whiskey industry's greed for new barrels, be assured that the coopers are interested in staying in business. John Gunn, quality controller at the Blue Grass plant, maintains that about three new trees are planted to replace each one that is chopped down.

Before the wood can be made into barrels, it must be dried to reduce its water content from about 40 percent to 10 to 12 percent. Step one of the drying process, which reduces the moisture to about 20 percent, is accomplished in one of two ways: Either the wood is left out in the open air for about 12 months, or it is placed in a temperature-controlled warehouse, known as a pre-dryer, for about 30 days. Wine-makers, whose wood is usually dried totally in the open air for up to three years, say that the fresh air helps enhance their barrels due to the development of a mildew that reduces astringency in the wood. To our knowledge, Maker's Mark is the only bourbon distillery that pays the higher price which

COOPERS AT WORK

a year of air-drying requires. Step two of the drying process involves placing the wood in a huge warehouse-like kiln heated to between 110 and 160 degrees F and leaving it there for a week to 10 days, or until the correct moisture level is achieved.

When the wood is at the correct moisture level, the barrels can be assembled. Generally speaking, whiskey barrels have a 53-gallon capacity and are about 34 inches high, with the top and bottom "heads" measuring about 21 inches in diameter. The circumference of the "bilge," the bulged area where the barrel is the fattest, is about 80 inches. An empty whiskey barrel weighs about 100 pounds; when full, about 500 pounds.

After the barrels are formed, they are "toasted"—each barrel, which has been moistened by steam, is placed over relatively gentle flames for about two minutes. Toasting the barrels "sets" them into shape but also has a curious effect on the wood. During toasting, starches in the wood begin to convert into sugars and are affected by the heat. These natural sugars are caramelized during the charring process and form the red layer from which the whiskey will take its color, aroma and flavor.

The other benefit of charring is that the porous charred layer allows the whiskey easier access to the red layer and also acts as a filter, taking some undesirable bitter flavors out of the whiskey. The charring is achieved by placing the barrels over flames so intense that the interior of the barrel actually catches fire. The flames roar for just under a minute, varying by a matter of seconds for differing levels of char but making a huge difference to the inside of the barrel, after which the flames are doused with water. Now the barrels are ready to mature whiskey.

The level of charring on each barrel is chosen by the distiller from a range of 1 (light char) to 4 (deep char). Only one distiller uses less than a number 3 char, and only a couple use a heavier grade. It's all a matter of style.

Aging Whiskey

MANY AMERICAN WHISKEYS ARE PUT INTO THE BARREL AT EXACTLY 125°, the highest proof allowed by law. Some distillers, however, prefer to age their whiskey at lower proofs, because their experience and experimentation have led them to think that that practice is best. Bear in mind, though, when the proof is lower than 125°, there will be more liquid, which will require more barrels to age the same original amount of whiskey. That's an expensive proposition. The whiskey-makers who do it swear it's worth the extra time and money.

As the spirit slumbers, the ambient temperature of each warehouse causes the liquid to expand and contract into and out of the wood's red layer. During aging, some whiskey evaporates into the air and becomes known as the "angel's share." American whiskey gains slightly in alcohol content as it ages, since water molecules seep through the pores of American white oak more readily than alcohol molecules. Oddly enough, Scotch whisky loses alcohol during its years in cask, mainly because of the damp atmosphere in Scotland, where the moist air seems to permeate the casks and keep them damp,

> " America owes as much to a cooper as ever she did to Columbus. "
>
> —FROM AN ARTICLE BY J.T. IN *The Barrel and Box*, JANUARY 1918.

and also because Scotch is aged in used barrels in which the pores of the wood tend to have been clogged a little while aging their previous occupant—usually bourbon.

A few distilleries produce a whiskey bottled at "barrel proof," which sometimes exceeds the 125° legal limit. This occurs when whiskey entered the barrel at 125° proof and then gained strength during aging.

Warehousing Whiskey

MOST WHISKEY WAREHOUSES ARE SIX TO NINE STORIES HIGH, ALTHOUGH some are built on just one level. It is in these "rackhouses" that the whiskey will slumber, gaining color and flavor over the years and developing its style. Barrels are usually stacked three high on each floor of the warehouse, resting on wooden racks, or ricks as they are often called, that are designed to allow air to circulate around the barrels. Some warehouses actually have pits dug into the floor so that the air can find its way beneath the bottom row of barrels.

Each distillery has its own warehousing techniques, based on a number of pertinent factors:

• The size, shape and configuration of the ricks within the warehouses and the proximity of other warehouses are somewhat important to air circulation. Warehouses in the country are usually built quite far apart; city warehouses, because of the price of

---

WHISKEY BARRELS IN THE WAREHOUSE

land, are built relatively close together. Proximity has become less important as city distilleries have added modern equipment to circulate the air.

• Warehouses can be made of masonry, wood or "metal-clad" wood. Masonry warehouses are more common in city distilleries and are easier to heat if the distillery chooses to do so; wood and metal-clad warehouses are more common in the country.

• The temperature on the top floors of the taller warehouses is much higher than the temperature closer to ground level, making the whiskey stored there age faster than the whiskey on lower floors.

• Some warehouses are heated, some have heating and cooling systems, and still others wouldn't think of going to the bother. In the coldest months, some distillers repeatedly heat and cool their warehouses, forcing the whiskey to expand and contract into and out of the wood at a time when it would usually be dormant. Some distillers believe that this process ages the whiskey faster, and it certainly has an effect on the finished product. Other warehouses may use heaters to keep the building at or above a certain temperature if the distiller believes that the whiskey ages better that way. It's all a matter of the personal style of the master distiller.

• Some distillers rotate their barrels, giving each barrel a chance to age in the high temperatures on the top floors as well as in the cooler air in the center and bottom levels. This is a very expensive and work-intensive proposition, and most whiskey-makers prefer to mingle whiskey from different floors of the warehouse to achieve a consistent product prior to bottling.

Filtering Whiskey

WHEN BOURBON REACHES BOTTLING AGE, IT IS FILTERED. GENERALLY, this practice is more for "cosmetic" reasons than to remove something awful from it. Without filtering, minute, perfectly harmless impurities can remain in the bourbon, and under certain conditions (intense cold), a dreaded "chill haze" could cloud the translucent amber spirit in the bottle. This clouding in a cold bottle of whiskey doesn't affect the flavor, but consumers don't much like the look of it—they tend to think their bourbon's gone "off." So producers filter their bourbon to remove the components that cause it. There's an excellent argument against it: Filtering removes a little flavor. However, the process is part of the art of the whiskey-maker.

Most distilleries chill the whiskey before filtration, helping the unwanted matter get a little thicker and therefore easier to filter out. Some, however, filter their whiskey at room temperature, getting rid of the chill haze without removing as much flavor. At this time, Booker's Bourbon is the only whiskey on the market that isn't filtered at all.

Barrels being charred at Blue Grass Cooperage

MAKER'S MARK DISTILLERY

CYPRESS FERMENTERS AT MAKER'S MARK DISTILLERY

BEER STILL AT GEORGE A. DICKEL'S CASCADE DISTILLERY

MAKING SUGAR-MAPLE CHARCOAL AT GEORGE A. DICKEL

BARRELS BEING STORED AT GEORGE A. DICKEL

SEALING BOTTLES OF MAKER'S MARK

BLANTON'S SINGLE BARREL BOURBON AGING

Bottling Whiskey

SINCE THE PROOF OF LIQUOR IS SLIGHTLY AFFECTED BY TEMPERATURE, prior to bottling, the distiller measures its temperature and checks the proof against a scale issued by the authorities that is based on liquor at 60°F. All bottles are thoroughly sterilized and are often put through a vacuum procedure to ensure that every last speck of dust is removed before being placed on a conveyer belt. There, the bottles jiggle along and are filled by well-calibrated machinery that funnels the correct quantity of liquor into each. In order to ensure that exactly the right amount of whiskey is in each bottle, the bottles are weighed after being filled.

Special Whiskeys

SINGLE-BARREL WHISKEY

Whiskeys bottled as "single-barrel whiskey" are the product of just one barrel of whiskey, details of which are often handwritten on the bottle's label. Usually, these whiskeys have undergone some special treatment during aging, such as being transferred to specific warehouses or kept in a portion of the warehouse where the master distiller knows his whiskey ages well.

When you buy your second bottle of any brand of single-barrel whiskey, check to see whether or not it was from the same barrel as the first. Chances are that it won't be, but the whiskeys will taste very similar to one another. This is because the master distiller samples different barrels of whiskey and picks those that he believes to be not only superior products but also of the style that he has chosen to highlight in his single-barrel offerings.

SMALL-BATCH WHISKEY

Time and time again, we have seen articles which state that small-batch whiskeys are distilled in small batches, but that's just not the case. The term "small batch" was introduced by the Jim Beam Brands Company when it unveiled its small-batch bourbons in the 1980s. Therefore, we turned to Jim Beam for a definition of the category. Here's what we were told:

"Small-batch bourbons are rare and exceptional bourbons married from select barrels from a cross section of barrels in the rackhouse [warehouse]. This ensures quality and consistency of flavor and character. Each small-batch bourbon has a unique aroma and taste which is credited to its unique recipe, aging, and proof. We do not

rotate because the small-batch process is based on marrying barrels from select levels where they can pick up distinct characteristics depending on location in the rack-house."

As in the case of single-barrel whiskeys, the expertise lies with the master distiller, who must locate and identify his most superlative whiskeys for the company's super-premium bottlings. And master distillers can be very picky—their reputations as masters of their craft depend on it.

VINTAGE WHISKEYS

Vintage whiskeys are distilled in a certain season and bottled when the master distiller believes they have reached their peak. They are chosen *after* they have aged, since nobody can accurately predict the final results. The quality of these whiskeys could be attributed to a magnificent batch of grain, the temperature variances during specific years of aging or simply because God decided that a certain batch of whiskey would mature well. Ideally, a vintage whiskey should bear the date when the whiskey was distilled and (unless there is an age statement on the bottle to give us a clue) the date on which it was bottled.

CHAPTER FIVE

DISTILLERIES

AN A TO Z GUIDE
TO AMERICAN
WHISKEY-MAKERS

THE "STATEMENT OF DISTILLERS IN 1891," A DOCUMENT
released on February 3, 1891, by *The Wine and Spirit Bulletin,* listed
a state-by-state breakdown of the number of operating grain distilleries in the United States as of January 1 of that year. Of the
779 total—an astonishing number—North Carolina led with 273,
Kentucky had 172, Georgia had 72, Pennsylvania had 62, Virginia had 51, Tennessee
had 47, and the remainder were scattered from Alabama to California, Massachusetts to
Wisconsin. In 1993, the "Directory of U.S. Distillers," issued by the Distilled Spirits
Council of the United States, listed a total of only 52 *spirits manufacturers,* which includes a mere 12 operations—nine in Kentucky, two in Tennessee and one in Virginia—
that actually produce all of the world's supply of straight American bourbon, Tennessee
whiskey and rye whiskey.

Why Do Whiskeys Taste Different From One Another?

AMERICAN STRAIGHT WHISKEYS ARE LIKE PASTA: BOTH ARE MADE FROM just a few basic ingredients, but after the "dough" is made, it can head in dozens of directions. With pasta, it's the shape you cut, any flavorings you add or whether you dry it or cook it fresh. Given a sheet of fresh-made pasta, no two cooks will treat it exactly the same way. One will want capellini, one will cut fettuccine, and still another will fill the pasta and roll it into tubes. The same is true of whiskey. Though the basics from one to the next are largely the same, it's the small individual additions or treatments that make the difference in what you taste and drink from your glass.

We do not believe that geography is a basis for differentiating among American whiskeys. Bourbons produced in, say, the Bardstown area don't differ from those made in Louisville due solely to their location. Some of the distinctions lie in the basics—the recipe, the distillation, the aging—and some are due to the human element—how the whiskey is treated, by whom and how that person brings his on-the-job and life experience to bear.

It is also important to mention the use of continuous stills in the American whiskey industry, since many people believe that the old-fashioned pot still will always outshine its more efficient descendant. Pot stills would produce a different product from the American whiskeys with which we are familiar, and the end result could be stunning. However, the fact is that not many people are familiar with the way in which American whiskey-makers *use* their stills. Continuous stills have been common in the industry for well over 100 years, and during that time, the distillers have learned their every nuance—they play those babies like violins. We have seen knowledgeable pot-still proponents reverse their position after hearing the details of how American whiskey-makers use their equipment.

THE BURDEN OF PROOF

THE TERM "PROOF" DATES from a time before scientific methods were used to measure the alcohol content of spirits. In order to show good faith when liquor was being sold, the seller would perform a ceremony that established, albeit approximately, how much alcohol the spirit contained. He mixed some liquor into a little gunpowder and held a flame to it: If it ignited, it was said to be "proved," indicating that it contained about 50 percent alcohol; if the flame fizzled out, the booze just wasn't considered strong enough to do its job.

THE TAYLOR AND WILLIAMS DISTILLERY AT THE TURN OF THE CENTURY

Whiskeys made with rye as a small grain often seem to have sharper, more peppery notes that are seldom found in those which use wheat in its place. Yeast that is propagated in dona tubs with hops added to them seems to produce whiskey with subtle nuances that are difficult to pinpoint but there all the same. Bottlings made from sour-yeast mashes have special characteristics of their own. The alcohol content matters at several points—the proof at the end of the first and second distillations, the barreling proof and the bottling proof. When and how much sour mash is added makes a difference, as does the intensity of the barrel's char and whether or not the barrels are rotated. The differences that result from these variables are tangible; at one point or another, you can taste or see or smell the effect.

Accordingly, every distillery is justifiably proud of its methods and its products, but each one wants to produce its own singular style of whiskey. The sometimes subtle procedures each follows will vary from bottling to bottling, and this is one of the reasons that some distillers are rather close-mouthed about how they work their magic.

In general, distillers have a long history of secrecy—in the seventeenth century, British distillers took an oath to "keep confidential the secrets and mysteries of distilling." On the other hand, as one master distiller said, "Nobody wants to make *my* whiskey—they want to make *their* whiskey." And with that, he went on to describe every last detail of his processes. Judge each and every whiskey by tasting it, not by the policies of the company that makes it. The true test of a whiskey is in the glass.

Confronting Whiskey Confusion

HOW IS IT THAT JUST 12 DISTILLERS PRODUCE MORE THAN 50 DIFFERENT brands of whiskeys? The history of the American whiskey industry gives an inkling to how this practice came to be. Whiskey labels and brands were purchased, stellar whiskey-makers were honored by naming a brand after them, bottlings took the name of their current or historical location, and some labels were created out of the minds of marketing mavens. Although some distilleries use more than one mashbill (grain recipe), they might bottle each whiskey they produce under more than a couple of different brand names. *This does not necessarily mean that the different bottlings contain exactly the same whiskey.* Most whiskeys, although certainly not all of the less expensive bottlings, are selected and bottled as specific brands according to the style that brand has established in the marketplace. Brands are also bottled at differing ages and proofs, making massive differences to each whiskey, and some are selected from different parts of the warehouse where they have matured into distinctive styles. Selecting these whiskeys is an art form unto itself.

One last bit of advice meant specifically for travelers: If you look at a variety of whiskey labels, you'll find some that list a distillery that is not included here. Some of these distilleries are completely fictitious and exist on paper only, and the rest are the names of distilleries that have been bought out and closed by other distillers who continue to use their name on the label. Don't travel the length and breadth of Kentucky or Tennessee looking for these places; the distilleries listed here are the only ones presently distilling all of the whiskeys in this book. Accept that this practice is part and parcel of the American whiskey business, but don't be put off by it. American distillers are producing some world-class whiskeys of which we can all be proud.

The Ancient Age Distillery

Address: The Ancient Age Distillery

The Leestown Company, Inc.

1001 Wilkinson Boulevard

Frankfort, Kentucky 40601

Phone: 502 223 7641

Tours: Yes, call for details.

Getting There: Tip: Once you see the Holiday Inn, you're only about 1 mile away. From Louisville: Go east on I-64 for 47 miles; north on US 127 for 5 miles to downtown Frankfort—US 421 (Wilkinson Blvd.).

From Bardstown (59 miles, about 1¼ hours): Go east on US 150 to the Blue Grass Parkway, then east on parkway for 37 miles. Go northeast on US 127 for 19 miles to downtown Frankfort—US 421 (Wilkinson Blvd.).

From Lexington (25 miles, about 30 minutes): Go west on I-64 for 19 miles, then northwest on US 60 for 2 miles. Go west on US 421 (Wilkinson Blvd.) for 1 mile.

Master Distiller Emeritus: Elmer Tandy Lee

Master Distiller: Gary Gayheart

Distillery Manager: Joe Darmand

Straight Whiskeys

Ancient Age Bourbon

Benchmark Bourbon

Eagle Rare Bourbon

Benchmark XO Single Barrel Bourbon

Blanton's Single Barrel Bourbon *(for export only)*

Elmer T. Lee Single-Barrel Bourbon

Hancock's Reserve Single-Barrel Bourbon

Rock Hill Farms Single-Barrel Bourbon

Mashbill (approximate): corn 80%, rye 10%, barley malt 10%

Production Notes: The Ancient Age Distillery draws its water from the Kentucky River and filters it to remove turbidity or murkiness and unwanted flavors, leaving its mineral content intact. The grains are cooked in an unusual two-step process: The corn and rye are cooked together under pressure, the mash is then cooled in huge vacuum tanks, and the malted barley is added. Both the pressure cooking and the vacuum cooling save on time and, therefore, money.

The cooked mash is transferred to huge fermenters (90,000 gallons) made of copper-bearing steel. The backset (sour mash) is introduced to the process in the fermenter, and Ancient Age is generous with it—adding enough to equal 33 percent of the total mash.

A post-Prohibition Schenley strain of dried yeast is added to the mash, and fermentation begins.

When the mash has become distiller's beer, it enters the beer still, and the low wines, which leave the still at 120° proof, are condensed before being piped into the doubler. There, they are redistilled and leave as 135°-proof high wines. The new spirit is reduced with demineralized water to 125° and then placed in #3 char barrels.

Most of the barrels age in huge masonry warehouses, each of which is 9 to 12 stories high. During the colder months, the sprightly Master Distiller Emeritus, Elmer T. Lee, heats the warehouses to 70 degrees F to force the whiskey to expand into the wood. Next, the heat is turned off so the temperature will drop and the spirit will contract from the wood. Every time he goes through this procedure, the whiskey takes flavors from the red layer in the barrel, and Lee swears it ages the whiskey faster.

Barrels of what will become Blanton's Single-Barrel Bourbon are given special treatment. They are aged in a separate four-story warehouse that is devoted solely to them. This warehouse is constructed of metal-clad wood and is the only heated metal-clad warehouse in Kentucky. The Blanton single-barrel bourbon is treated with kid gloves throughout its aging; metal-clad buildings are very expensive to heat.

While all of the regular bourbons from Ancient Age are filtered at room temperature, the single-barrel bottlings are chill-filtered and bottled in a special bottling room. One at a time, a cask of the aged single-barrel bourbon is dumped into a small processing tank, where it is chilled to below 30 degrees. It is filtered, transferred to another small vessel and then brought back to room temperature. Finally, it is reduced to bottling proof and funneled into its bottle. One barrel of Blanton's produces about 20 dozen 750-ml bottles and therefore will require 240 of the handwritten Blanton's labels. Each one details its bottling date, its barrel number, its warehouse and the number of the rick it sat on during aging. Skeptics who think "it can't be from just one barrel" need to watch this operation—it will change their minds.

Ancient Age's single-barrel process is interesting. Although Lee selects the whiskeys that will be bottled as Blanton's and as his eponymous Elmer T. Lee Bourbon, Gary Gayheart, the Master Distiller (*not* Emeritus), determines the other single-barrel offerings. All of the single-barrel bourbons from the Ancient Age Distillery are tasted by panels of tasters *after* Lee and Gayheart have made their selections, and nothing is bottled until everyone agrees on its worthiness.

• Elmer T. Lee drinks his Elmer T. Lee Bourbon on the rocks with an equal amount of water added. He also enjoys the occasional Manhattan.

• Gary Gayheart drinks his Rock Hill Farms Bourbon on the rocks with just a splash of water.

The Barton Distillery

Address: The Barton Distillery
Barton Brands, Ltd.
1 Barton Road
Bardstown, Kentucky 40004
Phone: 502 348 3991
Tours: No regularly scheduled tours for sightseers. People with a special interest in whiskey or distilleries may call for appointments.
Getting There: From downtown Bardstown: Go west on Stephen Foster (US 62) to Barton Road; turn left and drive ½ mile.
Master Distiller: Jerry O. Dalton, Ph.D., officially titled "Chief Chemist Quality Control Distillery Operations Manager."

Straight Whiskeys
Very Old Barton Bourbon
Kentucky Gentleman Bourbon
Ten High Bourbon
Colonel Lee Bourbon
Tom Moore Bourbon
Barclay's Bourbon
Mashbill (approximate): corn 75%, rye 15%, barley malt 10%

Production Notes: Jerry Dalton is a chemist and a statistician, and he relies on a mix of science, the five senses and a touch of Tao Te Ching—the Taoist philosophy which maintains that life should conform to the underlying pattern of the universe—to produce Barton's whiskey.

A small percentage of the water used at the Barton Distillery comes from a nearby spring. The rest is from a 22-acre spring-fed body of water known as Teur's Lake. The yeast strain used here dates to the 1940s and is stored and propagated in a central bank away from the plant. The mash is cooked at atmospheric pressure in a one-step process that doesn't require differing temperatures for each ingredient; a total of about 20 percent backset (sour mash) is added, some to the mash tubs and some to the steel fermenters.

After fermentation, the distiller's beer is pumped into the beer still; the low wines leave the still at 125° proof and are condensed before entering the doubler. The high wines leave the doubler at 135° proof, and the new spirit is diluted to 125° proof before being put into #3-char barrels for aging.

The warehouses at Barton are not heated, and therefore, the whiskey expands into and out of the red layer according to seasonal temperature fluctuations. The barrels are rotated only if Dalton deems that some need to be moved to a different area to produce the style of whiskey consistent with Barton's products.

Before bottling, Barton's whiskey is chilled to 18 to 22 degrees F for a minimum of 12 hours. It is filtered and reduced to bottle proof with demineralized water.

• Jerry Dalton drinks his Very Old Barton Bourbon on the rocks and says, "I never spill a drop."

The Jim Beam Distillery

Address: Jim Beam's Visitor's Center and Distillery
Clermont, Kentucky 40110
Note: Jim Beam also owns a second distillery in nearby Boston, Kentucky. The Boston facility is not open to the public.
Phone: 502 543 9877
Tours: Tours are available of Jim Beam's American Outpost. No tours of the distillery itself are available. Call for details.
Getting There: From Louisville (27 miles, 33 minutes): Go south on I-65 for 24 miles to Exit 112 (the Bardstown/Bernheim Forest exit); go east (left) on state route 245 for 1½ miles. Jim Beam's American Outpost will be on your left.

From Bardstown: Go northwest on state route 245, heading toward I-65; Jim Beam will be on your right, across the road from Bernheim Forest.
Master Distiller Emeritus: Booker Noe
Assistant Distiller: Jerry Summers, officially titled "Assistant Distillery Manager" acts as the hands-on distiller at the Clermont plant.
Straight Whiskeys
Jim Beam Bourbon
Old Taylor Bourbon
Old Crow Bourbon
Old Grand-Dad Bourbon
Booker's Small-Batch Bourbon
Knob Creek Small-Batch Bourbon
Baker's Small-Batch Bourbon
Basil Hayden's Small-Batch Bourbon
Jim Beam Rye Whiskey
Old Overholt Rye Whiskey
Mashbill: Mashbills, like many of the details of Jim Beam whiskeys, are closely kept proprietary secrets. Based on tasting and various knowledgeable sources, we believe that the distillery probably uses three different mashbills to produce its whiskeys—one

for the straight rye whiskeys, one for Old Grand-Dad and Basil Hayden's and a third for all of the other bottlings. Hearsay has it that the Old Grand-Dad recipe calls for more rye grain than any other bourbon on the market.

Production Notes: The water for the whiskeys made at the Beam Clermont plant is drawn from a nearby spring-fed lake. The grains are hammer-milled and then cooked at atmospheric pressure, along with some backset, in the traditional three-step method. The mash is fermented in stainless-steel tanks, where it is mixed with an extraordinary amount of backset—about 41 percent of the entire mash, according to Jerry Summers.

The jug yeast Beam uses is a post-Prohibition strain that is grown on the premises, with some hops added to the dona tubs. The distiller's beer is distilled in the beer still, leaving as low wines at about 123° proof. The spirit is condensed, piped into a doubler and redistilled to about 125° proof, the strength at which it is put into barrels for aging.

The Beam distillery—and Wild Turkey— are the only two American whiskey distilleries that specify barrels with the heaviest char available—#4. The whiskey is aged in all-wood and metal-clad wooden warehouses, and sometimes, if the distiller deems it necessary, the barrels will be rotated.

The barrels earmarked to become Booker's Bourbon, however, are aged without disturbance in the "center cut," or prime middle space, of certain warehouses and are left to age in that one choice spot. After aging, the whiskey for all of the regular bottlings is chilled and then filtered through activated carbon. Once again, the exception is Booker's, which, at this time, is the only unfiltered bourbon on the market.

• Booker Noe drinks his eponymous Booker's Small-Batch Bourbon with ice and lots of water. He calls it Kentucky Tea.

• Jerry Summers drinks his Jim Beam black label (or Knob Creek) neat, sometimes with a water chaser.

A TYPICAL DAY AT BEAM

* 8,000 bushels of grain are mashed
* 40,000 proof gallons of whiskey are produced
* 600 new barrels of whiskey are stored
* 600 aged barrels are prepared for bottling
* 75 tons of distillers' dry grain are produced
* 17,000 cases of whiskey are bottled and shipped

—FROM ONE OF THE JIM BEAM BROCHURES

The Bernheim Distillery

Address: The Bernheim Distillery
1701 West Breckinridge/P.O. Box 740010
Louisville, Kentucky 40210-7410
Tours: Not at this time.
Master Distiller: Edwin S. Foote
Straight Whiskeys

RYED BOURBONS:

Old Charter Bourbon
I.W. Harper Bourbon
James E. Pepper Bourbon (for export only)
Mashbill (actual): corn 86%, rye 6%, barley malt 8%

WHEATED BOURBONS:

W.L. Weller Bourbon
Old Fitzgerald Bourbon
Rebel Yell Bourbon
Kentucky Tavern Bourbon
Mashbill (actual): corn 75%, wheat 20%, barley malt 5%

THE SECRET OF THE FIVE KEYS

FAMED DISTILLER AND RACONTEUR PAPPY VAN WINKLE WROTE AN ARTICLE describing the five secrets to "Old Fitzgerald's authentic, old-fashioned flavor and bouquet." A few nuggets of Pappy's wisdom from the original article:

1. We mash our grains in open tubs without pressure or haste to unlock the full rich flavor of nature's wholesome grains.
2. We season our fermenters with a portion of the previous day's run to maintain an unbroken chain of uniformity and flavor.
3. We permit our fermenting tubs to ripen at the slow, natural sour-mash pace to develop the full flavor of authentic Kentucky bourbon at its old-fashioned best.
4. We gently distill, then redistill at a "flavor proof" which permits the natural bourbon flavors to be carried over to the finished product.
5. We age our whiskey in airy open-rick warehouses where Time and Nature alone mellow it to oak-ripened excellence.

THE BOTTLING CIRCLE AT THE OLD FITZGERALD DISTILLERY

Production Notes: The Bernheim Distillery—the youngest of them all, at only three years old—is outfitted with the most up-to-date equipment imaginable. In the control room, color monitors display every part of the distillation process. With just a touch on the screen, workers can bring up a display of what is going on at that precise moment in a grain silo, a mash tub, a fermenter, the beer still or the thumper.

All of the whiskeys made at this distillery use Louisville city water that is treated and filtered to make sure that fluorides and unwanted flavors are removed but vital minerals are left intact. The Bernheim Distillery produces two distinct styles of whiskey: the Bernheim recipe, which contains rye, and the Weller recipe, which uses wheat.

Both mashes are cooked at atmospheric pressure in the traditional three-step method with some backset (sour mash) added to the mash. The mash is then transferred to stainless-steel fermenters, where more backset is added, bringing the amount up to 25 percent of the total mash. The dried yeast used at the Bernheim plant is an old Schenley strain that was developed during or just after Prohibition.

The fermented mash is pumped into the beer still and leaves as vapors, which are bubbled through a thumper. The high wines distill out at 140° proof in the case of the ryed whiskeys and at 130° proof when the wheated whiskeys are being made. The ryed whiskeys are diluted to 125° proof before being entered into barrels; the wheated whiskeys are entered at 112°. Both types of whiskey age in barrels bearing a #3 char.

The ryed bourbons age in heated eight-to-twelve-story brick warehouses right at the Bernheim plant. With one exception, the wheated bourbons are taken down the road to the old Stitzel-Weller distillery (not currently in operation) and aged in unheated metal-clad warehouses that stand seven stories high. Barrels of wheated bourbon that will become Kentucky Tavern Bourbon are shipped to Owensboro, Kentucky, where they are aged in unheated metal-clad warehouses in the countryside. A certain amount of barrel rotation goes on at the Bernheim Distillery; new whiskey always starts its aging on the top floor of the warehouse and is moved down as it matures and newer barrels arrive.

The Bernheim Distillery uses two filtration methods: The ryed bourbons are chill-filtered; the wheated bourbons are filtered at room temperature.

•Ed Foote drinks his Old Fitzgerald on the rocks.

The Early Times Distillery

Address: The Early Times Distillery
The Brown-Forman Corporation
850 Dixie Highway/P.O. Box 1080
Louisville, Kentucky 40201
Phone: 502 585 1100
Tours: No regularly scheduled tours for sightseers. People with a special interest in whiskey or distilleries can call for an appointment.
Master Distiller: Lincoln Henderson
Note: Both Early Times and Old Forester labels spell the word "whisky," without the *e*.
Straight Whiskeys
Early Times Bourbon (bottled for export only)
Old Forester Bourbon
Mashbills: Early Times (actual): corn 79%, rye 11%, barley malt 10%
Old Forester (actual): corn 72%, rye 18%, barley malt 10%
Production Notes: The Early Times Distillery uses Louisville city water that is treated and filtered to make sure fluorides and unwanted flavors are removed, but vital minerals are left intact. Both bourbons made at the Early Times Distillery go through the same processes, differing only in their mashbills. The grains are cooked under pressure, using the traditional three-step method. The cooked mash is transferred to car-

bon-steel fermenters where backset (sour mash) is added, making up 20 percent of the total mash.

The yeast used at Early Times is a post-Prohibition strain of jug yeast that is propagated in dona tubs and soured by lactic bacteria to produce the distillery's signature sour yeast mash. After fermentation, the distiller's beer is pumped to the beer still and the resultant vapors are bubbled through a thumper, producing high wines that are condensed into 140°-proof new spirit. This spirit is diluted to 125° before being transferred to #3-char barrels. At this point, the barrels are ready to undergo Henderson's signature aging process.

The masonry warehouses at Early Times stand seven stories tall and are heated. When the temperature in the warehouse falls to 60 degrees F, Henderson turns on the heat, raises the temperature to 75 to 80 degrees and maintains that level for about a week. The warmth drives the whiskey into the red layer in the barrel, where it gains flavor and color. Next, he turns the heat off, and for the following two to three weeks, the whiskey is allowed to contract back into the barrel. Henderson believes his process negates the need to rotate barrels; it is repeated constantly throughout the cooler months. He claims that when treated to this process, the resulting four-year-old whiskey tastes as though it has been aging for six or seven years. Both bourbons undergo filtration through activated carbon at room temperature; neither is chill-filtered.

• Lincoln Henderson drinks his bourbon on the rocks—four ice cubes to two ounces of Old Forester.

A SPECIAL BOTTLING

THE OLD PRENTICE DISTILLERY

The Four Roses Distillery

Address: The Four Roses Distillery
1224 Bonds Hill Road
Lawrenceburg, Kentucky 40342
Phone: 502 839 3436
Tours: No regularly scheduled tours for sightseers. People with a special interest in whiskey or distilleries can call for an appointment.
Master Distiller Emeritus: Ova Haney
Master Distiller: Jim Rutledge
Straight Whiskeys
Four Roses Straight Bourbon *(bottled for export only)*

Mashbills: Mashbills are a closely kept, proprietary secret.

Production Notes: The Four Roses Distillery uses no fewer than 12 different recipes to make its whiskey. Several mashbills and individual yeast strains are employed. The straight bourbons produced here are a result of mingling the different whiskeys to achieve a consistent product for each bottling.

The water at the Four Roses Distillery comes from various natural sources. The grains are cooked using the three-step method. The cooked mash is then transferred to the fermenters (14 cypress and 6 stainless steel), and one of the yeast varieties is added. The cypress fermenters are not whitewashed, as is the norm; Four Roses relies on traditional steam cleaning to keep unwanted bacteria out of these vessels.

A total of 25 percent of the mash at Four Roses is made up of backset (sour mash), and the yeast strains are propagated in dona tubs and soured by lactic bacteria to produce the distillery's signature sour yeast mash. The fermented mash is pumped to the beer still, leaving as 132°-proof low wines that are condensed and then redistilled in a doubler. The resultant 143°-proof high wines are diluted to 120° proof and then entered into casks at #3½ char.

The whiskey is aged on six-barrel-high ricks in single-story, unheated, metal-clad warehouses located nearby in Cox's Creek. Since the temperatures within a one-level warehouse vary only slightly from the bottom to the top, rotation is unnecessary. Before bottling, the whiskey is chilled to about 20 degrees F, held at that temperature for 18 hours and then filtered.

• Ova Haney drinks his bourbon on the rocks with a splash of water.

• Jim Rutledge drinks his bourbon on the rocks.

Heaven Hill Distillery

Address: Heaven Hill Distilleries, Inc.

Highway 49, Loretto Road/P.O. Box 729

Bardstown, Kentucky 40004-0729

Phone: 502 348 3921

Tours: Yes, weekdays only; large groups by special arrangement.

Getting There: From Bardstown: Go east on Stephen Foster (US 62) to state route 49. Turn right (south) and drive about 2 miles.

Master Distiller: Parker Beam

Assistant Distiller: Craig Beam

Straight Whiskeys

Heaven Hill Bourbon

Evan Williams Bourbon

Elijah Craig Bourbon

Henry McKenna Bourbon

J.T.S. Brown Bourbon

J.W. Dant Bourbon

Mattingly & Moore Bourbon

Pikesville Rye Whiskey

Mashbills: Bourbons (actual): corn 75%, rye 13%, barley malt 12%

Rye (actual): rye 65%, corn 23%, barley malt 12%

Production Notes: Heaven Hill draws its water from two spring-fed lakes near the distillery, but the water used to propagate the jug yeast that was brought to this plant by Earl Beam in the 1950s comes from a different spring. Hops are used in the propagation method, creating a yeast mash that has become part of the distillery's signature. The grains are cooked under pressure, with a little backset (sour mash), using the traditional three-step method. The cooked mash is then transferred to the fermenters (four cypress and 27 stainless steel), where the hopped yeast mash and more backset (totaling 25 percent of the entire mash) is added.

The fermented mash is pumped into the beer still and leaves as 125°-to-130°-proof low wines vapors. They are condensed and then go to the doubler for the second distillation. The high wines leave the doubler at about 138° proof, are diluted to 125° proof and sealed in #3-char barrels for aging.

The unheated metal-clad warehouses at Heaven Hill are 9 to 12 stories high. The barrels are not rotated; instead, the distillery mingles whiskeys from various levels of the warehouses to produce a consistent style. After aging, the whiskey at Heaven Hill is chill-filtered before bottling.

THE DANT STATION DISTILLERY IN 1955

• Both Parker and Craig Beam drink their bourbon on ice with a splash of water, just the way Parker's father, Earl Beam, drank it. "He used to turn the cold water on and give his whiskey glass a fast pass under the water," said Craig. "We want to taste the whiskey—not the water."

Maker's Mark Distillery

Address: Maker's Mark Distillery
Loretto, Kentucky 40037
Phone: 502 865 2099
Tours: Yes, call for details.
Getting There: From Bardstown: Go east on Stephen Foster (US 62) to state route 49; turn right and follow 49 into Loretto. Follow state route 52 to Star Hill Farm—you can't miss the signs.
Master Distiller: Steve Nally
Note: The Maker's Mark label spells the word "whisky," without the *e*.
Straight Whiskey
Maker's Mark Bourbon
Mashbill (actual): corn 70%, wheat 16%, barley malt 14%
Production Notes: A small spring on the property provides the water used to make Maker's Mark Bourbon; this same water is demineralized and used to bring the aged whiskey down to bottling proof. Since the flow of the spring is barely enough to meet demand, all other water used for any purpose at Maker's Mark is pumped in, at considerable expense, from the local water supply. The grains are cooked, along with some backset (sour mash), at atmospheric pressure, using the traditional three-step method. The cooked mash is transferred to the fermenters (some cypress and some stainless steel), where more backset is added, totaling 32 percent of the entire mash.

The yeast strain used at Maker's dates to pre-Prohibition days, making it one of if not *the* oldest yeast strain currently being used by any distillery. It is propagated using the traditional dona-tub method along with some hops that add to the character of the bourbon. The fermented mash is pumped to the beer still, and the resultant low wines leave the still at 120° proof. They are condensed before being added to the doubler for the second distillation, and the high wines leave the doubler at 130° proof. The new spirits are then diluted to 110° proof—with the demineralized version of the same spring water that was used to make the mash—before being put into #3 char barrels for aging.

The barrels for Maker's Mark are made entirely from wood that has been air-dried for one full year—a considerable addition to production costs. Bill Samuels Jr. notes that "it reduces the astringency of the tannins in the wood." Each barrel is rotated in Maker's Mark's unheated three-to-seven-story warehouses so that every barrel of whiskey spends time in the relative heat of the top floors and the cooler temperatures lower down. The distillery prefers to allow natural seasonal temperature variances to expand the whiskey into and out of the red layer, where it gains color and flavor. After aging, the bourbon is filtered at room temperature before being brought down to bottle proof (again with the demineralized spring water used to dilute it for aging). When running at full capacity, the Maker's Mark Distillery can produce only 38 barrels of bourbon— just two small batches—a day.

• Bill Samuels Jr. drinks his Maker's Mark on the rocks with a splash of water—or in a Manhattan cocktail.

• Steve Nally drinks his Maker's Mark on the rocks with a splash of water.

The A. Smith Bowman Distillery

Address: A. Smith Bowman Distillery
One Bowman Drive
Fredericksburg, Virginia 22408-7318
Phone: 703 373 4555
Tours: Yes, call for details.
Master Distiller: Joseph H. Dangler
Straight Whiskey
Virginia Gentleman Bourbon
Mashbill (actual): corn 65%, rye 20%, barley malt 15%
Production Notes: Although the bottles of Virginia Gentleman currently in the stores were produced entirely at this plant, the distillery has, for the past few years, commissioned its low wines from distilleries located elsewhere. This product of the first distillation process is prepared especially for Bowman and made strictly according to Bowman's approved recipe.

When the low wines (between 130° and 135° proof) arrive in Virginia, they are put into a doubler for a secondary distillation and leave as high wines at between 145° and 150° proof. The high wines are then diluted to 125° with demineralized water before being entered into #2-char barrels; A. Smith Bowman is the only distillery that uses less than a #3 char in its barrels, and this, no doubt, is significant to the whiskey. The barrels are aged, stacked three to four high—on pallets rather than ricks—in one-story brick warehouses. Since all of the barrels rest on one floor, rotation is unnecessary. The warehouses at Bowman are heated as necessary so that during the colder months a constant temperature of about 52 degrees F is maintained. After aging, the whiskey is diluted to bottle proof, then chilled and filtered with activated carbon before being bottled.

• Joe Dangler drinks his Virginia Gentleman Bourbon on the rocks.

The Wild Turkey Distillery

Address: The Wild Turkey Distillery
Boulevard Distillery & Importers, Inc.
Highway 1510, Box 180
Lawrenceburg, Kentucky 40342
Phone: 502 839 4544
Tours: Yes, call for information.
Getting There: From Louisville (56 miles, 1 hour, 10 minutes): Go east on I-64 for 42 miles, then south on state route 151 for 7 miles. Go south on US 127 for 4 miles, then east on US 62 to the distillery.

From Lexington: Go west on US 60 to Versailles, then west on US 62 to the distillery.

From Frankfort (18 miles, 25 minutes): Go south on US 127 for 16 miles, then east on US 62 to the distillery.

Master Distiller: Jimmy Russell
Straight Whiskeys
Wild Turkey Bourbon
Wild Turkey Kentucky Spirit Single-Barrel Bourbon
Wild Turkey Rare Breed Small-Batch Bourbon
Wild Turkey Rye Whiskey
Mashbills: Bourbon (approximate): corn 75%, rye 13%, barley malt 12%
Rye (approximate): rye 65%, corn 23%, barley malt 12%
Production Notes: The water at the Wild Turkey Distillery comes from a nearby spring-fed lake in a huge limestone quarry. The grains are cooked at atmospheric pressure using the traditional three-step method with a little backset (sour mash) added. The cooked mash is then transferred to the fermenters (9 cypress, the rest of them stainless steel), where more backset is added to amount to over 33 percent of the total mash.

The yeast at this distillery is propagated in dona tubs, and the yeast mash is soured by the addition of lactic bacteria. (The cypress fermenters are not whitewashed but steam cleaned.) The fermented mash is pumped to the beer still and leaves as low wines at 110° to 114° proof. The low wines are condensed, put through a second distillation in a doubler and result in high wines at 120° to 125° proof. Before being barreled, the spirit is diluted to 105° to 107° proof. Wild Turkey and Jim Beam are the only two distilleries that specify barrels with a #4 char.

THE OLD JOE DISTILLERY IN THE EARLY 1900s

The barrels are then placed into metal-clad warehouses and rotated periodically so that each cask gets its share of relative heat on the top floors and cooler air at ground level. The warehouses are not heated; the distiller prefers to let natural seasonal temperature variances expand the whiskey into and out of the red layer, where it gains color and flavor. On one warehouse's ground level, the barrels are stacked only two high instead of three high. Master Distiller Jimmy Russell says experience taught him that for whatever reason, circulation was poor on that particular floor. His remedy was practical; he removed a layer of barrels.

After aging, Wild Turkey's whiskey is diluted to bottle proof with demineralized water, and most of it is filtered at room temperature; only the 80°-proof Wild Turkey is chill-filtered.

• Jimmy Russell drinks his bourbon neat or on the rocks but notes: "I have no objection to other folk adding whatever mixers they like to Wild Turkey."

The Jack Daniel Distillery

Address: Jack Daniel Distillery
Lynchburg, Tennessee 37352
Phone: 615 759 4221
Tours: Yes, call for details.
Getting There: From Nashville (86 miles, 1¾ hours): Go south on I-24 for 60 miles, then west on state route 55 for 26 miles; follow the signs.

From Chattanooga (80 miles, 1½ hours): Go north on I-24, then southwest on state route 55; follow the signs.
Master Distiller: Jimmy Bedford
Straight Whiskeys
Jack Daniel's No. 7 Brand Tennessee Sour Mash Whiskey
Gentleman Jack Rare Tennessee Whiskey
Mashbill (actual): corn 80%, rye 8%, barley malt 12%
Production Notes: The water used to make Jack Daniel's comes from Cave Spring at The Hollow, right next to the distillery. The grains are cooked at atmospheric pressure using the traditional three-step method; the mash is then transferred to stainless-steel fermenters where backset (sour mash) makes up 20 percent of the total mash. The strain

A SQUARE INCH OF THE HOLLOW

IN THE 1950S THE JACK DANIEL DISTILLERY FORMED AN ASSOCIATION CALLED THE Tennessee Squires. This "club" was established to reward people who had demonstrated loyalty to Jack Daniel's Whiskey; those named to the group would receive an unrecorded square inch of land in The Hollow, Lynchburg, Tennessee, and occasional correspondence. Journalist Tom Bentley wrote about his experience as a Tennessee Squire in the *San Francisco Chronicle* in 1989. First of all, after being named a Squire and receiving the deed to his land, he got a letter from the local hardware store in Lynchburg advising him of various supplies they had available that he might want to purchase in order to keep his one square inch of land cultivated. Shortly afterward, he was informed by the same store that his land was full of worms suitable for fishing. Bentley generously gave his rights to the worms to the storekeeper, Mr. Clayton Tosh.

After that, Bentley received photographs of Tennessee countryside, local poetry, a recording of authentic hill-country folk songs, a twist of Moore County chewing tobacco, letters about an outbreak of rabies in the area and advice on how to pick pokeberry shoots on his property—all important issues to any dedicated Tennessee Squire.

of dried yeast used at the Jack Daniel Distillery was reputedly commissioned from a baker in Memphis in 1938.

The fermented mash is pumped to the beer still and produces low-wine vapors that are bubbled through a thumper, leaving as high wines at about 140° proof. The new spirit is then chilled to about 60 degrees F and filtered, literally drop by drop, following the Lincoln County Process, in one of the distillery's mellowing vats. Each vat contains 10 to 12 feet of sugar-maple charcoal, and by slowly dripping through it, the Jack Daniel's gains the sooty sweetness that is characteristic of Tennessee whiskeys. At the bottom of the filtration tank is a woolen blanket that the whiskey must pass through before being collected. The filtered spirit is diluted to 118° proof with demineralized water and put into #3-char barrels for aging.

DANIEL AND MOTLOW

Each of Jack Daniel's 48 aging houses holds over one million gallons of whiskey. The seven-story buildings are not heated; the company prefers to allow natural conditions to help the whiskey expand into and out of the wood. The barrels are not rotated; instead, whiskeys aged in the relatively hot temperatures at the top of the warehouse are mingled with others from the center and the bottom to achieve consistency in the whiskey. Before bottling, Jack Daniel's is brought down to proof by the addition of demineralized water and filtered using traditional—not the Lincoln County Process—means. Gentleman Jack Rare Tennessee Whiskey is the exception, since it also undergoes one more filtration through sugar-maple charcoal after aging.

• Jimmy Bedford drinks his Jack Daniel's Tennessee Whiskey on the rocks.

George A. Dickel's Cascade Distillery

Address: The Cascade Distillery
George A. Dickel & Company
Cascade Hollow
Tullahoma, Tennessee 37388
Phone: 615 857 3124
Tours: Yes, call for details.
Getting There: From any direction: Take I-24 to junction 105; go south on route 41; turn right onto state route 4291 toward Blanton Chapel Road and follow signs to the distillery or Normandy Dam; pass through the town and go 1 mile farther to the distillery.

From Lynchburg (13 miles, 20 minutes): Take state route 55.

Master Distiller: Jennings D. Backus (who is also the distillery manager and likes to be called by his middle name, David)

Note: The Dickel label spells the word "whisky," without the *e*.

Straight Whiskey

George A. Dickel's Tennessee Sour Mash Whisky

Mashbill (approximate): corn 80%, rye 12%, barley malt 8%

Production Notes: The Cascade Distillery uses limestone-filtered water from the nearby Cascade Spring to make its whiskey. The grains are cooked, with a little backset (sour mash) at atmospheric pressure, using the traditional three-step method. The mash is then transferred to stainless-steel fermenters, and more backset is added to make up over 25 percent of the total mash. The dried yeast used at Dickel is the same strain it has used since the distillery was rebuilt in 1958. According to Backus, this particular yeast produces fewer fusel oils than most others.

The fermented mash is pumped to the beer still to produce low wines of about 110° proof. After condensation, they are redistilled in a doubler, creating high wines at about 130°. The whiskey is then chilled before undergoing the distinctive Tennessee charcoal mellowing process.

The Cascade Distillery has its own version of the Lincoln County Process. It places wool blankets at both the bottom and the top of the mellowing vats, surrounding the 10 feet of sugar-maple charcoal. The chilled new spirit is poured onto a shallow perforated steel disk that sits above the top blanket, and the whiskey slowly drips through the holes, distributed evenly over and throughout the entire batch of sugar-maple charcoal. The mellowing vats at Cascade are filled to capacity before any whiskey is allowed to drain out of the bottom, ensuring that every shard of charcoal is utilized to its fullest extent. The charcoal is changed when Backus, after tasting samples, deems the old batch nearly exhausted.

The George Dickel whiskey is diluted to 115° proof before it is entered into #3-char barrels for aging. The barrels are stacked six high on ricks in the one-story warehouses that overlook gorgeous Tennessee scenery. A ventilation system keeps humidity to a minimum. Barrel rotation is unnecessary, since the temperature variances between the top and the bottom barrels are minimal. Heat is used, if need be, only to maintain a minimum temperature of 55 degrees F. The whiskey is chill-filtered, using conventional methods, before bottling.

• David Backus drinks his George Dickel on ice, cut 50/50 with water.

• Ralph Dupps, former master distiller, also drinks his Dickel on ice with water.

DICKEL HAS USED THE SAME YEAST STRAIN SINCE 1958

CHAPTER SIX

WHISKEY COCKTAILS

I N *The Fine Art of Mixing Drinks*, PUBLISHED IN 1952, HOME-bartending expert David A. Embury described whiskey as "a grouchy old bachelor that stubbornly insists on maintaining its own independence and is seldom to be found in a marrying mood." He had a point—whiskey could never compete with rum, vodka or gin in a mixability race. However, with the right combination of ingredients, a little forethought and a steady pouring hand, a host of delicious cocktails and mixed drinks can be created with good straight American whiskeys. If you hold a party in a glass and invite whiskey along, it will be the one guest that no one forgets.

Good bartenders, like good Boy Scouts, are always prepared. For the recipes included here, and for all of the cocktails you mix, a few homemade ingredients can make the difference between an ordinary drink and an extraordinary creation. We urge you to make these simple syrups, julep syrups and bitters in advance so that they are ready and waiting whenever you need them; all of them will last indefinitely.

POTIONS, COCKTAILS AND MIXED DRINKS

Tips for Mixing Drinks

IN DRINK-MAKING TERMS, A "TWIST" IS A STRIP OF CITRUS PEEL THAT USUALLY has at least some of the inner white pith still attached—not just the colored zest that's often used in cooking. When you pull the skin off an orange so that you can eat the segments out of hand, the peel you're removing has excellent twist potential. Cut the peel into 1½-by-½-inch strips; each of these can be used as a twist. Though twists are often regarded as mere garnishes, they contribute greatly to the flavor of a cocktail—oils are trapped in the colorful outer peel, and when the strip is twisted, some of the citrus oils are released over the top of the drink. Here's exactly how to do it:

• Hold one end of the twist between the thumb and forefinger of each hand, with the colorful outer skin facing down; bring the twist close to the surface of the drink, and gently twist it, releasing the oils onto the top of the drink. Next, rub the colorful side of the twist around the rim of the glass, then drop it into the drink.

• If a drink calls for chilled glasses and you don't keep them in your freezer, set each glass in the sink, fill it with ice cubes, and add cold water until the water spills over the sides of the glass. Let stand for at least 1 minute, or as long as possible while you are fixing the drink. Pick up the glass by the rim, and shake it for about 10 seconds so that the iced water spills over the outside of the glass. Pour out the ice and water, take hold of the base of the glass, and shake out any excess water.

• When making a straight-up cocktail, such as a Manhattan, the drink needs time to incorporate a bit of water from the melting ice. Stir it for at least 30 seconds unless the recipe calls for a "brisk" stir, in which case, four or five times around the glass should do it.

• Once bottles of vermouth have been opened, always store them in the refrigerator. Like all wines, vermouth will oxidize fairly quickly if left at room temperature; keeping it cold helps.

Bar Supplies

BEFORE YOU START MIXING AND MUDDLING, CHECK YOUR BAR PANTRY. YOU'LL want to make sure you have a stock of "bar basics." Here's a checklist:

• **Angostura bitters**: Made from secret ingredients, this product was first created in 1824 as an appetite stimulant for Simón Bolivar's troops, who were suffering from fevers in the jungles of South America. In cocktails, bitters serve as an agent that brings the other ingredients together in harmony.

• **Peychaud bitters**: Originally concocted by apothecary Antoine Amedie Peychaud in New Orleans toward the end of the eighteenth century, Peychaud bitters are made from secret ingredients, and although the product serves the same purpose as Angostura, each is entirely different from the other. Peychaud bitters can be hard to come by in some areas but can be ordered directly from the manufacturer. Call or fax Rebecca Green at 504 831 9450 (fax 504 831 2382), or write for details: The Sazerac Company, Inc., 803 Jefferson Highway, New Orleans, LA 70121.

• **Absinthe substitute** (Pernod, Ricard or Herbsaint): Absinthe was outlawed by most countries during the first two decades of the twentieth century, when it was rumored that it drove people to insanity (Van Gogh was an absinthe drinker). Wormwood was the herb that the authorities decided was the offensive ingredient in absinthe, although since most bottlings were very high in alcohol, it's more probable that consumers were merely drinking too much. Pernod, Ricard and Herbsaint are wormwood-free absinthe substitutes.

• **Fresh lemons**: For juice and twists—don't forget to wash them.

• **Maraschino cherries**: For a proper Manhattan.

• **Superfine sugar**: This sugar dissolves quickly and easily in cocktails. Substitute Simple Syrup (facing page) if you have no superfine sugar.

• **Sugar cubes**: For use in the TVFN Champagne Cocktail (page 288) or whenever the sugar should be allowed to dissolve slowly.

• **Grenadine**: Grenadine used to be made from pomegranates, although most brands are now simply colored sugar water (check the ingredients on the bottle). This product adds color (red) and sweetness to cocktails and mixed drinks.

• **Club soda or seltzer.**

Simple Syrups

THESE SYRUPS ARE EXCELLENT ADDITIONS TO YOUR REFRIGERATOR "PANTRY." They sweeten cocktails, iced tea or lemonade without your having to dissolve the sugar, and if you need to whip up a fruit sorbet, they are a blessing in a bottle. Concentrated Simple Syrup should be reserved for drinks, such as the Mint Julep (page 273, 274), in which you want to add sweetness without diluting the bourbon too much.

SIMPLE SYRUP	CONCENTRATED SIMPLE SYRUP
MAKES 2½ CUPS	MAKES 2½ CUPS
2 cups water	2 cups water
1 cup sugar	2 cups sugar

1. Combine the water and sugar in a small saucepan over moderate heat. Stirring constantly, bring the mixture to a simmer; do not boil. Continue stirring until the sugar dissolves and the syrup is completely clear, 3 to 6 minutes.

2. Remove the pan from the heat, and set the syrup aside to cool. Pour into a sterilized bottle, cap and store in the refrigerator. The syrup will keep indefinitely.

Basil or Mint Julep Syrup

I N ORDER TO MAKE THE TENNESSEE BASIL JULEP (PAGE 275), YOU WILL NEED some Basil Julep Syrup. It's an easy concoction to prepare, and we recommend that you start a batch just as soon as spring is in the air and the basil is young. If you like very minty Mint Juleps or if you want to make the drink after the mint season is over, substitute Mint Julep Syrup for the simple syrup in the Mint Julep recipes that appear later in this chapter.

MAKES 2½ CUPS

1 cup firmly packed basil or mint leaves, washed

2 cups water

1 cup sugar

1. Tie the herb leaves into a piece of dampened cheesecloth.

2. Combine the water and sugar in a small nonreactive saucepan over moderate heat. Add the bundle of herb leaves and bring the mixture to a simmer. Stir frequently to make sure the sugar completely dissolves. Reduce the heat to very low, cover the pan, and simmer for 15 minutes.

3. Remove the pan from the heat, and let cool, still covered, to room temperature, about 1½ hours.

4. Remove the bundle of herbs and squeeze to extract any liquid. Pour the syrup into a sterilized bottle, cap and store in the refrigerator. The syrup will keep indefinitely.

Orange Bitters #4

I**F YOU ENJOY MANHATTANS, TRY JUST ONE WITH THESE BITTERS, AND YOU** will find that your time making this ingredient was well spent. This recipe is the fourth and most successful of an ongoing experiment we began in 1992, after we used up our last bottle of DeKuyper Orange Bitters and discovered that the product was hard to locate. The recipe is loosely adapted from guidelines set down in *The Gentleman's Companion—Volume II—Exotic Drink Book* by Charles H. Baker Jr. (Crown Publishers, 1946). You should note that it requires about a month to prepare; however, the process isn't work-intensive, it just takes time and a moment or two to shake the jars daily. Most of the ingredients can be found in herbalist or health-food stores, and if you can't get grain alcohol in your state (availability is subject to state laws—ask at your liquor store), simply substitute a high-proof (100°) vodka.

WARNING:

These bitters have a very high alcohol content and should *not* be consumed undiluted. They should be used in only small quantities—just drops at a time—in cocktails and mixed drinks. During preparation, remember that beverage alcohol is highly flammable, and be sure to work well away from any heat source.

MAKES ABOUT 2¼ CUPS

8	ounces dried orange peel, finely minced
1	teaspoon cardamom seeds (removed from about 1 ounce of cardamom pods)
1	teaspoon coriander seeds
1	teaspoon quassia, broken into fine pieces
½	teaspoon powdered cinchona bark
½	teaspoon caraway seeds
¼	teaspoon gentian, broken into small chunks (about ¼" diameter)
2	cups 190°-proof grain alcohol or 2½ cups 100°-proof vodka
⅓	cup sugar

1. Place the dried peel, cardamom seeds, coriander seeds, quassia, cinchona bark, caraway seeds, gentian and grain alcohol or vodka into a wide-mouth 2-quart glass jar with a tight-fitting lid. If you are using grain alcohol, add ½ cup water. Push down on the ingredients to soak them with the liquids. Seal the jar and shake well. Set aside in a cool place.

2. Shake the jar vigorously once a day for 14 days.

3. Strain the liquid through a sieve lined with a double layer of dampened cheese-cloth into a clean 2-quart jar. Gather the ends of the cheesecloth around the solids and squeeze tightly to extract as much liquid as possible; seal the jar well and set the alcohol aside in a cool place. Transfer the solids to a mortar or sturdy bowl.

4. Pulverize the solids with a pestle or wooden spoon until the seeds break up and the mixture has the texture of grainy mustard.

5. Scrape the mixture into a nonreactive saucepan. Add 3½ cups water and bring to a boil over moderately high heat. Reduce the heat to low, cover the pan, and sim-mer for 10 minutes. Remove the pan from the heat, and let cool, still covered, to room temperature, 1 to 2 hours.

6. Pour the cooled mixture into the original jar that contained the alcohol. Tightly cover and set aside in a cool place.

7. Vigorously shake the jar of herbs and spices once a day for 7 days.

8. Strain the herb-and-spice mixture through a sieve lined with a double layer of dampened cheesecloth. Discard the solids. Pour the liquid into the jar of alcohol.

9. Pour the sugar into a small nonstick saucepan and set over moderately high heat. Cook, stirring constantly, until the sugar melts and caramelizes to dark brown, about 5 minutes. Remove the pan from the heat and let cool for 2 minutes.

10. Pour the sugar into the alcohol-and-water mixture. If the sugar solidifies, don't worry—it will soon dissolve. Seal the jar, shake well, and set aside in a cool place where it won't be disturbed. Let set until the sediment settles to the bottom, 7 to 10 days.

11. Skim off any scum that has risen to the surface. Carefully pour the clear liquid into a large measuring cup, leaving any sediment behind in the jar. Measure the bit-ters; there should be about 1½ cups. Add ¾ cup cold water (or a measure equal to half of the bitters) and mix well to combine.

12. Pour the bitters into a bitters bottle (a thoroughly washed and sterilized Worces-tershire sauce bottle has the correct type of shaker top). Cover and shake well. Store the bitters indefinitely in a cool, dark cupboard or bar shelf.

The Manhattan

THE MANHATTAN COCKTAIL WAS CREATED IN THE 1870S AT NEW YORK City's Manhattan Club when Lady Jenny Churchill, the Brooklynite who became Winston's mother, held a banquet in honor of Samuel J. Tilden, the lawyer responsible for prosecuting the Tweed Ring in the late nineteenth century. This cocktail is a true classic, but unfortunately, it is often made in haste with no thought to its intricacies.

The dilemma often confronted when making a Manhattan lies in determining how much sweet vermouth should be used. In the thirties, the proportions were two parts whiskey to one part vermouth, and that works very well with straight rye whiskey and heavier bourbons, such as Wild Turkey or Old Grand-Dad. However, if using a wheated bourbon, such as Maker's Mark or Rebel Yell, try using a bit less vermouth—experiment until you find proportions that suit both your palate and your favorite whiskey.

Although blended whiskey can be used in a Manhattan, and it makes a fine drink, straight bourbon or rye is the better choice. Either will make a powerful difference. Whichever whiskey you choose, though, do not use Tennessee whiskey in a Manhattan—it just doesn't work. Also, most important, make sure to add a few dashes of Orange Bitters #4 or Angostura bitters. Without any bitters at all, a Manhattan is no more than a decent mixture; with them, it is a dazzling cocktail that will bring a sparkle to the eyes and put a slick step back into a pair of tired dancing feet.

2½	ounces bourbon or rye whiskey
½ to 1½	ounces sweet vermouth (depending on your taste and the choice of whiskey)
3	dashes Orange Bitters #4 (page 269) or Angostura bitters
1	maraschino cherry

Chill a stemmed cocktail (martini) glass. Pour the whiskey, vermouth and bitters into a mixing glass half-filled with ice cubes. Stir well to blend and chill. Strain the mixture into the cocktail glass; garnish with the maraschino cherry.

The Mint Julep

THE MINT JULEP IS THE ARISTOCRAT OF MIXED DRINKS: IT CALLS FOR STYLE, grace, wit, patience and ritual. No other cocktail has been the subject of so many arguments—or sealed as many firm friendships—as this perfect union of fresh aromatic mint and fine Kentucky bourbon. Resplendent in a frosted sterling-silver julep cup, the Mint Julep is a creation that brings wisdom to fools, turns wallflowers into the life and soul of the party, makes the clumsy graceful, the weak strong, and brings sophistication and charm to the most ill-mannered lout. The complexity of the Mint Julep lies mainly in the simplicity of its ingredients.

The word "julep" is a derivation of the Persian word *gulab* or the Arabic *julab*, both terms for "rose water." In seventeenth-century England, the term was used to describe sweetened medicines and sweetened drinks in general. The Mint Julep, however, is an all-American concoction. According to *The Mint Julep*, an excellent book by Richard Barksdale Harwell, although juleps were consumed in the United States as early as the 1700s, the first printed mention of mint being used in them was in a book published in 1803, describing a julep as "a dram of spirituous liquor that has mint in it, taken by Virginians of a morning." In our experience, if you need a shot of liquor "of a morning," you certainly don't have the patience to make a good Mint Julep.

The thorny problem with Mint Juleps is its all-American individuality. Every person swears his or hers is best and all of the rest are wrong. Bill Samuels Jr., president of the Maker's Mark Distillery, has a marvelous though idiosyncratic recipe that calls for picking the mint during a three-week window of opportunity in April—when it is no more than six inches tall—gathering only the light-colored leaves into a T-shirt and tying it closed. Next, the T-shirt is placed into a large receptacle full of Maker's Mark, where it is actively and vigorously bashed with a mallet to release the oils from the mint. The T-shirt is removed and wrung out. The bourbon is then strained and sweetened with concentrated simple syrup. Bashing that T-shirt with a mallet brings up the most debated point in julep-making circles: Should the mint leaves be crushed or not?

H.L. Mencken, renowned critic and wit, was a devoted crusher of mint leaves when he made his juleps, which led one of his friends to say, "Any guy who'd crush the leaves would put scorpions in a baby's bed." Some people agree, preferring to leave the mint out of the drink itself but garnishing it with a huge bouquet of the herb and serving it with short straws that force the drinker to get his or her head into the mint. A "bouquet" should contain at least six stems of mint, each bearing a minimum of six good-size leaves. If the stems of mint are cut immediately before garnishing the drink, they will "bleed" a certain amount of flavor into the glass, and when the flavors of the sweetened bourbon meet the mint at the back of your throat, you will see the bluegrass of Kentucky before your very eyes.

Sterling-silver julep cups are, of course, the drinking vessel of choice for Mint Juleps. However, tall collins glasses (16-ounce capacity for these recipes) can be used, or you might want to order some small metal bar shakers from a restaurant supplier. These metal shakers are ideal, since a thin layer of ice forms on the outside of the shaker in less than a minute.

Crushed ice is the one ingredient in a Mint Julep that often stops people from making it in the first place. Even worse, some use ice cubes to make the drink—and that is not a Mint Julep. If you don't own an ice crusher, wrap ice in a lint-free tea towel and bash it with a rolling pin or small mallet until the ice is very finely crushed. The towel will absorb the water as the ice melts, and the resultant crushed ice should be "snow-like."

Here are two recipes for the Mint Julep: the first uses mint as an aromatic garnish, the second is of the Mencken school.

Mint Julep #1

3   **cups finely crushed ice**

3   **ounces bourbon**

1   **ounce Concentrated Simple Syrup (page 267)**

1   **bouquet of fresh mint, the stems cut short
      at the last possible moment**

1. Fill a julep cup, small metal shaker or tall 16-ounce glass two-thirds full with the crushed ice. Add the bourbon and syrup, and stir briefly to blend.

2. Pack the glass with more crushed ice so that the ice domes slightly over the rim. Garnish with the mint bouquet, and insert 2 or 3 short straws so that the ends barely reach over the top of the mint.

3. Let the drink stand until a thin layer of ice forms on the glass, about 1 minute. Serve with a cocktail napkin to catch the condensation.

Mint Julep #2

1   ounce Concentrated Simple Syrup (page 267)
6   medium to large mint leaves, plus 1 bouquet of fresh
     mint, the stems cut short at the last possible moment
3   cups finely crushed ice
3   ounces bourbon

1. Place the syrup and the 6 mint leaves in a julep cup, metal shaker or tall 16-ounce glass. Lightly bruise the mint leaves with the back of a spoon (if you press too hard, some bitterness will find its way into your drink).

2. Fill the glass two-thirds full with the crushed ice. Add the bourbon and stir briefly to blend.

3. Pack the glass with more crushed ice so that the ice domes slightly over the rim. Garnish with the mint bouquet, and insert 2 or 3 short straws so that the ends barely reach over the top of the mint.

4. Let the drink stand until a thin layer of ice forms on the glass, about 1 minute. Serve with a cocktail napkin to catch the condensation.

Tennessee Basil Julep

AN ARTICLE THAT APPEARED IN *True* MAGAZINE IN 1954 CLAIMED THAT Jack Daniel used to make himself "Tansy Juleps" with his Tennessee sour mash. He dissolved a small amount of sugar in water, bruised a few tansy leaves in the glass, topped the mixture off with Jack Daniel's Whiskey and liked to "sit back, drinking something he made all himself, looking over his rolling acres, a gentleman at peace with both man and his Maker." Since tansy (a bitter, aromatic herb that is sometimes used in northern European and British cuisine) is somewhat hard to come by, this version uses basil. The "bouquet" of basil should be big—at least six stems, each with a minimum of six good-size leaves.

3	cups finely crushed ice
3	ounces Tennessee whiskey
1	ounce Basil Julep Syrup (page 268)
1	bouquet of basil, the stems cut short at the last possible moment

1. Fill a julep cup, metal shaker or tall 16-ounce glass two-thirds full with the crushed ice. Add the Tennessee whiskey and syrup, and stir briefly to blend.

2. Pack the glass with more crushed ice so that the ice domes slightly over the rim. Garnish with the basil bouquet, and insert 2 or 3 short straws so that the ends barely reach over the top of the basil.

3. Let the drink stand until a thin layer of ice forms on the glass, about 1 minute. Serve with a cocktail napkin to catch the condensation.

The Old-Fashioned

THE OLD-FASHIONED WAS FIRST CONCOCTED AT THE PENDENNIS CLUB IN Louisville, Kentucky, where one of the regular customers was a retired Civil War general who didn't care much for the taste of straight whiskey. (In Kentucky, disliking bourbon is tantamount to treason.) To accommodate the veteran, the bartender at the club added a little sugar, a couple dashes of bitters and a few drops of branch water to the whiskey, unknowingly creating the Old-Fashioned for the old-timer. This version calls for the addition of a maraschino cherry and a slice of orange—feel free to omit the fruit if you desire.

½	orange slice
1	maraschino cherry, stem removed
3	dashes Orange Bitters #4 (page 269) or Angostura bitters
1	teaspoon water
½	teaspoon superfine sugar
2½	ounces bourbon

In an old-fashioned glass, combine the orange slice, cherry, bitters, water and sugar. Using the back of a teaspoon, muddle the ingredients, dissolving the sugar and mashing up the fruit somewhat. Fill the glass with ice cubes, add the bourbon and stir gently.

The Sazerac

THIS DRINK HAS STOOD THE TEST OF TIME. ACCORDING TO *Famous New Orleans Drinks & how to mix 'em* by Stanley Clisby Arthur (Pelican Publishing Company, 1989 [originally published in 1937]), it was first concocted in the mid-nineteenth century by Leon Lamothe, a bartender in New Orleans. The original drink called for brandy as its base; however, in time that changed to rye whiskey, and now the Sazerac is usually made with bourbon. One ingredient, though, hasn't changed and remains absolutely indispensable to making a decent Sazerac—Peychaud bitters.

2	teaspoons absinthe substitute (Pernod, Ricard or Herbsaint)
½	teaspoon superfine sugar
3	dashes Peychaud bitters
1	teaspoon water
1	cup finely crushed ice
2½	ounces bourbon
1	lemon twist

1. Pour the absinthe substitute into an old-fashioned glass and swirl it around to coat the glass; pour out any excess.

2. In another old-fashioned glass, muddle together the sugar, bitters and water with the back of a spoon until the sugar dissolves.

3. Fill the first glass with crushed ice.

4. Add the bourbon to the muddled mixture and stir gently; pour into the ice-filled glass. Garnish with the lemon twist.

Bourbon Crusta—Simplified

THIS IS A VARIATION ON A CLASSIC COCKTAIL THAT'S LITTLE KNOWN TODAY. According to Professor Jerry Thomas, author of *The Bon Vivant's Companion or How to Mix Drinks*, 1934 (originally published as *The Bar-tender's Guide* in 1862), the Crusta was invented by a celebrated Spanish caterer by the name of Santina. It has gone through many incarnations since its creation, and today, the drink is normally served with the spiral-cut peel of a whole orange—a practice that proves a bit daunting to those not handy with a paring knife. This version is a little simpler.

2	ounces bourbon
½	ounce triple sec
½	ounce maraschino liqueur
½	ounce fresh lemon juice
2	dashes Orange Bitters #4 (page 269; if you didn't make this, don't substitute other bitters, use a twist of orange peel as a garnish instead)

Chill a stemmed cocktail (martini) glass. In a shaker half-filled with ice cubes, combine the bourbon, triple sec, maraschino liqueur, lemon juice and bitters. Shake well. Strain into the cocktail glass.

Bourbon Milk Punch

GARY'S FIRST BOURBON MILK PUNCH WAS PREPARED FOR AN OLD FRIEND, Don Lamb, a rare and wonderful character from the Upper East Side of Manhattan, who, during the 1970s and 1980s, made his living behind the bar. This drink was Don's hangover cure, and he swore by its healing properties. We like to serve it at the start of a brunch—its spicy-sweetness and decent kick of bourbon starts conversation flowing quickly.

2	ounces bourbon
4	ounces milk
1	teaspoon superfine sugar
¼	teaspoon vanilla extract
¼	teaspoon grated nutmeg
¼	teaspoon ground cinnamon

In a shaker half-filled with ice cubes, combine all the ingredients. Shake well and pour into a large glass.

Whiskey Toddy for Two

HERE'S A SIMPLE TODDY FOR A COLD WINTER NIGHT OR TO WARM YOU up on an early-spring evening on the patio when you want to stay outside a little longer. We don't sweeten the drink as a rule, but if you wish, a dash of honey or simple syrup can help make the "medicine" go down easily. The Szechuan peppercorn in this toddy helps clear a stuffed-up head, while the other spices (and the whiskey) make for a drink with lots of flavor when your taste buds aren't quite up to par.

1	small piece (1") vanilla bean, bruised
1	cinnamon stick (3"), broken
2	whole cloves
1	Szechuan peppercorn, bruised
2	cups water
4	ounces bourbon, rye or Tennessee whiskey
2	lemon twists

1. In a small nonreactive saucepan, combine the vanilla bean, cinnamon stick, cloves and peppercorn with the water. Bring to a boil over high heat. Reduce the heat to moderately low, cover, and simmer for 10 minutes.

2. Strain the mixture; discard the solids. Divide the liquid between 2 large mugs; add 2 ounces of the whiskey to each mug. Garnish each with a lemon twist.

The John Collins

A CLASSIC DRINK—THE BOURBON COUSIN TO TOM. CONTROVERSY ABOUNDS as to which of these drinks came first, and as with most cocktail lore, the truth is hard to verify. However, although it seems more likely that John came before Tom, since it is made with American whiskey rather than British gin and since mixed drinks are certainly more American than British. At least one early-twentieth-century book lists the drink as a Tom Collins Whiskey. If you make this drink with Tennessee whiskey, it becomes a Jack or George Collins, depending on whether your favorite brand of Tennessee sour mash is Jack Daniel's or George Dickel.

3	ounces bourbon or Tennessee whiskey
1	ounce fresh lemon juice
1	teaspoon superfine sugar
3	ounces club soda or seltzer
1	maraschino cherry
1	orange slice

In a shaker half-filled with ice cubes, combine the whiskey, lemon juice and sugar. Shake well and pour into a collins glass. Add the club soda or seltzer and stir. Garnish with the cherry and orange slice.

The Whiskey Sour

MANY PEOPLE SEEM TO THINK THAT WHISKEY SOURS ARE STRICTLY FOR blue-haired old ladies, but nothing could be further from the truth. The simplicity of the drink coupled with its thirst-quenching, lip-puckering qualities make it more of an "adult" lemonade in our eyes, although it shouldn't be consumed in copious quantities. When the weather is warm and your thoughts turn to sun-drenched beaches, try it.

2½	ounces bourbon, rye or Tennessee whiskey
1½	ounces fresh lemon juice
½	teaspoon superfine sugar
1	orange slice
1	maraschino cherry

In a shaker half-filled with ice cubes, combine the whiskey, lemon juice and sugar. Shake well and strain into a whiskey sour glass; garnish with the orange slice and cherry.

Alphabet Soup

S IMPLY NAMED FOR THE INITIAL LETTER OF ITS THREE INGREDIENTS—*A*, *B* and *C*—this cocktail works well as the first drink for an evening with friends. The curaçao heightens the fruitiness of a well-aged bourbon and adds sophistication to younger bottlings, and the bitters bring the ingredients together in a perfect marriage. When you serve Alphabet Soup to guests, remind them of what Bertie Wooster said to Jeeves as he requested a cocktail: "Pour me a desperate measure."

2	dashes Angostura bitters
2	ounces bourbon
½	ounce curaçao

Chill a stemmed cocktail (martini) glass. Pour the bitters, bourbon and curaçao into a mixing glass half-filled with ice cubes. Stir well to blend and chill. Strain the mixture into the cocktail glass.

Appetizer No. 4

I N 1934, PATRICK GARVIN DUFFY, A PRE- AND POST-PROHIBITION BARTENDER who claimed to have brought the highball to America in 1895, published a book called *The Official Mixer's Guide*. Although some of his bartending philosophies are disputable—"I cannot too much deplore the custom which has become prevalent of late of free and general conversation between bartenders and patrons"—the book does include some marvelous drinks. This is a variation on Duffy's Appetizer No. 3.

2	ounces bourbon
½	teaspoon Cointreau
3	dashes Peychaud bitters
1	lemon twist

Chill a stemmed cocktail (martini) glass. Pour the bourbon, Cointreau and bitters into a mixing glass half-filled with ice cubes. Stir well to blend and chill. Strain the mixture into the cocktail glass.

The Fay Rye Cocktail

NAMED FOR KING KONG'S FIRST LADYLOVE, THIS COCKTAIL IS OUR HYBRID of a Sazerac and a Manhattan. We highly recommend using the orange bitters if you made them—they marry well with the absinthe substitute and give the drink a gentle fruitiness. Don't let this cocktail sit too long; it's a far better drink when well chilled. As famed restaurateur Trader Vic is reputed to have said, "Drink it back while it's still laughing at you."

2	ounces rye whiskey
1	ounce sweet vermouth
1	teaspoon absinthe substitute (Pernod, Ricard or Herbsaint)
3	dashes Orange Bitters #4 (page 269) or Angostura bitters
1	maraschino cherry

Chill a stemmed cocktail (martini) glass. Pour the rye whiskey, vermouth, absinthe substitute and bitters into a mixing glass half-filled with ice cubes. Stir well to blend and chill. Strain the mixture into the cocktail glass; garnish with the maraschino cherry.

Remember the Maine

T HIS IS A VARIATION ON A DRINK DETAILED IN CHARLES H. BAKER JR.'S *The Gentleman's Companion,* a wonderful book, first published in 1939, in which Baker wrote, "Taken sanely and in moderation whisky is beneficial, aids digestion, helps throw off colds, megrims [migraines] and influenzas. Used improperly the effect is just as bad as stuffing on too many starchy foods, taking no exercise, or disliking our neighbor." Wise words indeed. Baker insists that this drink be stirred clockwise and briskly.

1½	ounces bourbon
¾	ounce sweet vermouth
2	teaspoons cherry brandy
½	teaspoon absinthe substitute (Pernod, Ricard or Herbsaint)
2	dashes Orange Bitters #4 (page 269) or Angostura bitters

Chill a stemmed cocktail (martini) glass. Pour the bourbon, vermouth, cherry brandy, absinthe substitute and bitters into a mixing glass half-filled with ice cubes. Stir briskly—clockwise—to blend and chill. Strain the mixture into the cocktail glass.

The "60 Minutes" Cocktail

IT WAS 6:55 ON A PARTICULARLY COLD SUNDAY NIGHT. A SAZERAC COCKTAIL seemed the proper antidote, but the cupboard was bereft of absinthe substitute. Thus we invented this drink, topping it off with club soda so that it would last through the entire hour of watching Morley Safer and company. Since then, the cocktail has become part of our Sunday-evening ritual, when we refuse to answer the telephone and curl up in bed to savor the last few hours of the weekend.

1	teaspoon superfine sugar
1	teaspoon water
3	dashes Peychaud bitters
2½	ounces bourbon
3	ounces club soda or seltzer

In an old-fashioned glass, muddle together the sugar, water and bitters until the sugar dissolves. Add ice cubes almost to the top of the glass, pour in the bourbon and club soda or seltzer. Stir and serve.

The Stump Lifter

HERE ARE TWO VERSIONS OF A DRINK THAT PACKS A POWERFUL PUNCH. A stranger told us about it during a discussion about cocktails in the New York Ritz-Carlton bar, where Norman Bukofzer holds court from behind the mahogany. We figured that anyone with enough sense to frequent Norman's domain must have a modicum of taste, so we tried it. The hard-cider variation is a favorite, and the second recipe makes a wonderfully refreshing summertime drink.

STUMP LIFTER #1

2   ounces bourbon

3   ounces hard cider

In an old-fashioned glass almost filled with ice cubes, combine the bourbon and cider. Stir well.

STUMP LIFTER #2

2   ounces bourbon

5   ounces apple juice

In a collins glass almost filled with ice cubes, combine the bourbon and apple juice. Stir well.

Sugarbuttie Cocktail

THOUGH SOME PEOPLE ARE STRINGENT "DON'T-MIX-THE-GRAPE-AND-THE-grain" believers, this particular combination is delightful. "Sugarbuttie" is a Lancashire, England, term of endearment and, literally translated, means "sugar sandwich." The drink was concocted by Mardee and named for her by Gary.

1½   ounces bourbon

1   ounce tawny or ruby port

Pour both ingredients into an old-fashioned glass full of ice or into an empty snifter for a soothing after-dinner potion. Stir to blend.

The TVFN Champagne Cocktail

NOTED FOOD AND WINE JOURNALIST DAVID ROSENGARTEN NAMED THIS drink when Gary concocted it for a New Year's Eve segment on the Television Food Network. It's merely a variation on the Champagne Cocktail, which sometimes includes a dash of Cognac. This version is strictly a bourbon drink—don't try it with Tennessee whiskey or straight rye; the results just don't compare. Serve it at black-tie functions or whenever you feel you deserve a treat. Although a decent bottle of Champagne is preferable, there's no need to use the best in the house.

1	sugar lump or cube
3	dashes Peychaud bitters
½	ounce bourbon
6	ounces Champagne
1	lemon twist

Place the sugar lump into the bottom of a Champagne flute and add the bitters and bourbon. Slowly pour in the Champagne. Garnish with the lemon twist.

The Ward Eight

ACCORDING TO WILLIAM GRIMES, IN HIS MARVELOUS BOOK *Straight Up or On The Rocks*, this cocktail was created on election eve in 1898 at the Locke-Ober Café in Boston. The idea was to commemorate the victory—albeit one day early—of a man who was running for the State Legislature from the eighth ward. It seems that everyone was pretty sure of the results. (The name "Ward Eight" has also been used to describe a gin Martini with a couple of twists of orange peel.)

If you don't have Orange Bitters #4, don't substitute any other kind of bitters; just use a twist of orange peel instead of the lemon twist. This drink is wonderfully robust, fruity and refreshing.

2	ounces rye whiskey or bourbon
1	ounce fresh lemon juice
½	ounce fresh orange juice
1	teaspoon grenadine
2	dashes Orange Bitters #4 (page 269)
1	lemon twist

Place all of the ingredients into a shaker half-filled with ice cubes. Shake vigorously and pour into an old-fashioned glass. Garnish with the lemon twist.

Whiskey Tching

THE RELATIVELY NEW CHINESE LIQUEUR CANTON GINGER MIXES PERFECTLY with bourbon, rye or Tennessee whiskey and is named for the Chinese dynasty that, according to the bottle, first concocted ginger liqueur (it's actually spelled *qing*, but we anglicized it for easier pronunciation). For a drier version of this drink, use 2½ ounces whiskey to ½ ounce liqueur, stir over ice, and strain into a chilled, stemmed cocktail (martini) glass.

1½	ounces bourbon, rye or Tennessee whiskey
1	ounce Canton Ginger Liqueur
1	lemon twist

In an old-fashioned glass almost filled with ice cubes, combine the whiskey and ginger liqueur. Stir well, garnish with the lemon twist, and serve.

Christmas Knight Tennessee Punch

MAKES 16 TO 20 SERVINGS

DUE TO A SERIES OF WILD AND WONDERFUL HAPPENSTANCES, IN DECEMBER 1994, we found ourselves breaking bread with the one and only Gladys Knight and her daughter, Kenya Newman. To the best of our knowledge, neither Gladys nor Kenya drinks whiskey or any other beverage alcohol—during our dinner with them, they sipped on a nonalcoholic potion of cranberry and apple juices. However, we had such a lovely time with these delightful women that we felt compelled to commemorate the evening by concocting an apple-cranberry punch. It's served hot, tastes great with or without the Tennessee whiskey and is the perfect grog for cold-weather parties when your guests can decide whether or not to partake of some sour mash.

This punch, minus the whiskey, can be made in advance and kept in the refrigerator for up to one week. Simply reheat the mixture to almost boiling, in the microwave or on the stovetop, just prior to serving. It is also ideal for non-drinkers if you omit the whiskey.

2	teaspoons vegetable oil
2	medium oranges, halved
20	whole cloves
2	quarts unsweetened apple juice
1½	quarts cranberry juice cocktail
1	vanilla bean, split
1	teaspoon grated nutmeg
1	teaspoon ground allspice
1	teaspoon ground cinnamon
½	teaspoon ground cardamom
½	teaspoon ground cumin
1	liter bourbon or Tennessee whiskey
	Orange slices, for garnish

1. Preheat the oven to 375 degrees F.

2. Line a baking sheet with aluminum foil and lightly coat the foil with the vegetable oil. Stud each orange half with 5 of the cloves. Place the oranges, cut sides down, on the baking sheet. Roast for 1 hour, or until lightly browned.

3. Pour the apple juice and cranberry juice into a large nonreactive stockpot—be sure it's not made of uncoated aluminum. Set the pot over high heat, add the roasted oranges, the vanilla bean and all of the spices, and bring the mixture to a boil. Reduce the heat

to low, cover, and simmer for 30 minutes.

4. Strain the mixture through a fine sieve, discarding the last few ounces if they contain sediment. (If you are preparing the punch ahead of time, let cool to room temperature, about 2 hours. Pour the punch back into the bottles that held the cranberry and apple juices and refrigerate.)

5. To serve, reheat the punch to almost boiling, then ladle 5 to 7 ounces of punch into a mug. Add 1 to 2 ounces whiskey and serve. Garnish each mug with an orange slice.

Bourbon Jelly Shots

JELL-O SHOTS ARE USUALLY MADE WITH VODKA AND FLAVORED JELL-O. THE results are interesting but somewhat sophomoric, so we decided to make a variation with some decent whiskey and unflavored gelatin. These "food-drinks" are great fun at a party for adults.

MAKES 16

1	cup 80°-proof bourbon
½	cup triple sec
¼	cup plus 2 tablespoons maraschino liqueur
½	cup fresh lemon juice
¼	cup plus 2 tablespoons Simple Syrup (page 267)
½	cup cold water
2	envelopes unflavored gelatin
½	cup very hot water

1. In a large bowl, stir together the bourbon, triple sec, liqueur, lemon juice and syrup.

2. Pour the cold water into a small bowl and sprinkle the gelatin over the top. Let soften for 1 minute. Add the hot water and stir until the gelatin dissolves. Add to the bourbon mixture and stir to combine thoroughly.

3. Pour 2-ounce portions into shot glasses or small paper cups. Cover with plastic wrap and refrigerate for at least 6 hours, or until set.

4. Serve with a teaspoon so that guests can break up the gelatin and pour the shots into their mouths. The jelly shots should be allowed to melt on the tongue.

CHAPTER SEVEN

COOKING
WITH
WHISKEY

BOURBON, RYE AND TENNESSEE WHISKEYS ARE INVALUABLE IN the kitchen—any one of them can put a fancy little curve into the most straight-laced apple pie, doll up a half-pint of heavy cream or help you put a sweet shine on a country ham. But don't think it's just a matter of grabbing a bottle, running into the kitchen to pour it all over whatever is in the making and then feeling your knees "go" during dinner—that's not the way to use these ingredients at all. Like any full-flavored ingredient, whiskey takes a dab hand and a level head about how and when to use it.

Most of the recipes included here work equally well with bourbon or Tennessee whiskey. Some were designed specifically for rye—like the Rye Rye Bread (page 296). Otherwise, use what's handy or most plentiful on your shelves. Generally speaking, when choosing a whiskey for cooking, you'll want to use one at 80° proof. But if a particular specialty or higher-proof bottling or brand has captured your heart, a few recipes will profit from using it, especially those—like Roast Pork Loin with Bourbon-Steeped Prunes and Apricots (page 306) or Whiskeyed Peach Cobbler with Peach-Whiskey Potion (page 318)—that reserve some of the steeping mixture for serving on top of the finished dish. Cooking with whiskey is like cooking with wine: You'll be happiest if you cook with the type or brand that you would serve as a beverage with the dish. Don't fall into the trap of using poor-quality whiskey in foods: you'll be disappointed with the results.

Because of their inherent sweetness, American whiskeys are widely used in desserts and other sweet mixtures, and they fit in very well. The flavors tend to marry nicely with most fruits—especially citrus, apples and stone fruits like peaches and apricots. But savory dishes can also benefit from the touch of sweetness added by bourbon or Tennessee whiskey, and most any barbecue-style mixture welcomes these all-American spirits.

One last word of advice: If you plan to serve an all-bourbon menu, do it only for guests who are tried-and-true old friends who love bourbon. Otherwise, count on including just one or two dishes over the course of the meal.

THE SAVORY RECIPES

The Sweet Recipes

Rye Rye Bread

EVEN IF YOU'VE NEVER MADE A LOAF OF HOMEMADE BREAD IN YOUR whole life, the time has come to get some hands-on experience. Every once in a while, every cook or baker hits on a particular combination of ingredients that seems so basic, so downright elemental, that it's perfect. We think this one is it—rich, chewy, full of flavor and as heavenly fresh as it is for toast or crumbs.

MAKES 2 LOAVES

2	cups lukewarm (105-115-degree) water
¼	cup honey
2	tablespoons (2 envelopes) active dried yeast
2	tablespoons vegetable oil
2 to 3	cups unbleached all-purpose flour
2	cups whole wheat flour, preferably stone-ground
2	cups rye flour
2	teaspoons salt
½	cup rye whiskey, plus more for brushing the loaves
2	tablespoons caraway seeds

1. Combine 1 cup of the warm water with the honey in a large mixing bowl. Sprinkle on the yeast and stir until dissolved. Set aside for 5 to 10 minutes, or until the mixture smells sweet and yeasty. Meanwhile, oil a large mixing bowl and set it aside.

2. When the yeast mixture is ready, stir in the remaining 1 cup warm water, the oil, 1 cup of each of the 3 flours and the salt. Stir with a wooden spoon until mixed. Add the rye whiskey and the remaining 1 cup each of the whole wheat and rye flours. Stir well—the dough will still be sticky, moist and heavy. Sprinkle on the caraway seeds and about ¼ cup of the remaining all-purpose flour; stir until thoroughly combined.

3. Generously sprinkle a work surface and your hands with some of the all-purpose flour. Turn out the dough and begin kneading in ¼ cupfuls of the remaining flour until the dough is cohesive but still somewhat sticky. Knead—pushing the dough away from you with the heels of both hands and folding it back on itself—for 6 to 8 minutes more. The dough will be thick and spongy, heavy and coarse-textured, and it will smell absolutely heavenly. Form the dough into a flattish ball.

4. Place the dough into the oiled bowl and turn it over to coat with the oil. Cover with a double layer of heavy plastic wrap and top that with a dish towel. Set aside in a draft-free place to rise until doubled in bulk, 2 to 2½ hours. (This is not a fast-rising dough.)

ROAST PORK LOIN WITH BOURBON-STEEPED PRUNES AND APRICOTS, *page 306*

RYE RYE BREAD, *page 296*

WHISKEYED PEACH COBBLER WITH PEACH-WHISKEY POTION, *page 318*

THE OLD-FASHIONED, *page 276*   THE MINT JULEP, *page 272-274*   THE MANHATTAN, *page 271*

SOUTHERN-STYLE DERBY-PECAN PIE, *page 316*

5. Line 2 baking sheets with parchment paper. Poke the dough with your finger and turn it out on a lightly floured surface. Cut the dough in half with a sharp knife. Gently and briefly knead each half into a smooth, flattish ball. Place each loaf on a lined baking sheet. Cover each ball with a sheet of the plastic wrap and a dish towel. Set aside to rise again—usually about halfway only—for 1 hour.

6. Thirty minutes before the rising time is up, preheat the oven to 375 degrees F.

7. Slash each loaf several times across the top with a razor blade or the tip of a sharp knife. Lightly brush the top and sides of each loaf with the additional rye whiskey. Bake the loaves, switching the pan positions halfway through the baking time, for 30 to 35 minutes, or until the bottoms sound hollow when tapped.

8. Slide the parchment paper and loaves onto wire racks to cool. The bread will stay moist and chewy for several days. Wrap in plastic to store.

Smoky Bourbon-Black Bean Soup

W E HAVE GREAT DIFFICULTY—AND NO EXPERIENCE—IN PREPARING SOUP in small quantities. We don't understand the concept of "a little soup." Therefore, we make mass quantities and freeze some for busy days or give it to the neighbors. This soup is the most deserving use we know for a great smoky ham bone. We thank our friend Anna Banana Walker for freeing us of the habit of soaking black beans—it's just not necessary. Serve bowls of this with Rye Rye Bread (page 296) and sweet butter.

FOR 12 OR CONSIDERABLY MORE

1	pound black beans, picked over
1	large smoked ham bone with lots of meat left on it or 4 smoked ham hocks, well washed
16	cups (4 quarts) chicken broth or water or some of each
2	bay leaves
3	tablespoons unsalted butter or olive oil
3	large Spanish onions, chopped
4	celery ribs, halved lengthwise and sliced
4	skinny carrots, scraped and thinly sliced
2	tablespoons hot sauce
3	tablespoons dried oregano
2	teaspoons ground cumin
1	teaspoon freshly milled black pepper
	Coarse salt
⅔ to 1	cup bourbon, plus additional tots of bourbon, for serving

1. You'll need a 12-quart stockpot or other huge pan to start this recipe, but you can divide the soup between 2 smaller pans later on, if necessary. In the big pot, combine the beans, the ham bone or hocks, broth or water and bay leaves. Bring the mixture to a boil over high heat. Reduce the heat to low, cover, and simmer for 2½ hours.

2. Toward the end of the 2½ hours, heat the butter or oil in a large sauté pan over moderate heat. Add the onions, celery and carrots and sauté until limp, about 10 minutes.

3. Spoon out a few black beans and taste for tenderness. If they are soft and flavorful, remove the ham bone or hocks to a large plate. If the beans are not yet tender, cover and cook for 20 minutes longer. Add the hot sauce, oregano, cumin and pepper to the soup. Scrape the vegetable mixture into the pot. Sprinkle on about 1 teaspoon of coarse salt and stir in. Cover and simmer over low heat.

4. When the ham bone or hocks are cool enough to handle, remove the meaty bits. Stir the meat and the bourbon into the soup. Taste for salt and adjust as necessary. Cover the pot and simmer over low heat for 1 hour longer. This soup is very forgiving—you can cook it for 2 hours if you want. Remove and discard the bay leaves.

5. Ladle the soup into bowls and top each with a tot—say, 1 scant tablespoon—of bourbon.

"Manhattan" New England Clam Chowder

THERE WE WERE, SIPPING MANHATTANS AT A SEAFOOD RESTAURANT WE love, discussing just how well made our drinks were and waiting for our food to arrive. When it did—one bowl of New England clam chowder and one bowl of a thick seafood bisque—the bourbon-on-the-brain idea hit: If a jot of sherry improves lobster bisque, shouldn't the sweetness of the Manhattan be just right for chowder? We each poured a bit of the drink atop our soup. It was a fabulous combination—to the nose and the palate—and one that deserves a try.

FOR 6 TO 8

4	ounces thick-sliced smoked bacon or salt pork, finely diced
6	large boiling potatoes, peeled and cut into small cubes
2	large Spanish onions or 3 to 4 large Vidalia or other sweet onions, chopped
2	celery ribs, halved lengthwise and sliced
2	cups whole milk or clam broth
3	cups shucked fresh clams in their juice
4	cups half-and-half, heated until hot (do not boil)
½	cup bourbon
3	tablespoons sweet vermouth
	Salt and freshly milled black pepper

1. Place the bacon or salt pork in a large nonreactive saucepan and set over moderate heat. Sauté until lightly browned but not yet crisp, about 4 minutes. Add the potatoes, onions and celery and sauté until the onions and celery are limp, about 8 minutes. Reduce the heat to low and pour in the milk or broth. Cover and cook until the potatoes are tender, about 15 minutes.

2. While the soup simmers, drain the clams, reserving their juice. Line a sieve with a double layer of dampened cheesecloth and strain the clam juice to remove any bits of sand. If the juice seems at all gritty, rinse the cheesecloth and strain again. Chop the clams.

3. When the potatoes are tender, add the clams and their juice to the saucepan. Cook for 2 minutes. Add the hot half-and-half and bring just to a simmer; do not let the mixture boil. Get ready to serve the soup as soon as it is just hot—it won't wait without overcooking the clams.

4. Meanwhile, combine the bourbon and sweet vermouth in a small pitcher or creamer. Season the chowder with salt and pepper to taste. Ladle into soup plates and pour a noggin of Manhattan mixture on each serving. Pass the remaining Manhattan at the table.

Roast Pork Loin with Bourbon-Steeped Prunes and Apricots

W E LOVE PORK, BOURBON AND APRICOTS, AND WE LIKE PRUNES—ESPECIALLY with pork. This is the simplest and tastiest thing we do with them. Follow Step 1 right now—even if you have no intentions of making this for a month or more.

FOR 6 TO 8

10	prunes, rinsed
10	dried apricots, rinsed
2	cups bourbon or Tennessee whiskey
12 to 18	small red or white new potatoes, scrubbed
2	boneless pork loins (about 4 pounds total weight)
	Salt and freshly milled black pepper
6	celery ribs, cut into 1½-inch lengths
6	skinny carrots, scraped and cut into 1½-inch lengths
3 to 4	cups apple cider or apple juice

1. In a jar, combine the prunes, apricots and bourbon or Tennessee whiskey, taking care that the fruit is completely covered with the liquor. Set aside for at least 24 hours or up to 1 month—the longer the better.

2. Place the potatoes in a large saucepan and add cold water to cover by 2 inches. Bring to a boil over high heat. Reduce the heat to moderately low and parboil the potatoes until half-cooked, 8 to 14 minutes, depending on their size. Drain well.

3. Preheat the oven to 350 degrees F. Set a roasting rack in each of 2 roasting pans.

4. Place each pork loin, fat side up, on a cutting board. Using a sharp knife, slice each loin lengthwise, through the thicker of the 2 long sides, cutting three-fourths of the way through to the other side to semi-butterfly it. Remove some of the plumped prunes and apricots from the whiskey. Starting at least ½ inch from one end of 1 loin, line up prunes end to end in a single row. Close the meat over the fruit and tie at 1-inch intervals with kitchen string. Use the same method to stuff the remaining loin with the apricots; tie with string. Reserve the whiskey.

5. Sprinkle both pork loins with salt and a generous amount of pepper. Place a loin, fat side up, on each roasting rack. Divide the celery, carrots and potatoes between the roasting pans; pour 1½ to 2 cups of the cider or apple juice into each pan.

6. Roast until the pork registers 170 degrees on a meat thermometer, about 1 hour. (Take care that the thermometer is in the thickest part of the meat, not stuck into a prune or an apricot.)

7. Meanwhile, strain 1½ cups of the whiskey used to steep the fruit into a gravy boat.

8. Remove the pork loins to a platter and let rest for 10 minutes. Mound the vegetables on a serving platter. Pour the cooking juices over them. Slice the pork and transfer slices with each of the fruit stuffings to warmed dinner plates. Serve at once, letting each diner ladle some of the fruit-flavored whiskey over the pork. (If you have any fruit left over, tuck it into a chicken cutlet or pork chop.)

Braised Julep Lamb Shanks
with Cannellini Beans

THE BIG, FAT, SOFT CANNELLINI BEANS MAKE A WONDERFUL PILLOW FOR the braised lamb shanks, but if you can't find them, use any other meaty bean that pleases you. The aromas of this dish are guaranteed to make you starving hungry.

FOR 4

⅓	cup unbleached all-purpose flour
2	teaspoons freshly milled black pepper
1	teaspoon coarse salt
4	large lamb shanks (each about 1 pound)
2	tablespoons unsalted butter
2	tablespoons olive oil
2	large Spanish onions, chopped
2	garlic cloves, minced
1	tablespoon dried basil
1½	teaspoons dried oregano
½	teaspoon ground cinnamon
1	pound dried cannellini beans, picked over and soaked overnight
2	bay leaves
1	bottle (750 ml) dry red wine
¾	cup bourbon
½	cup chopped fresh mint leaves

1. Combine the flour, pepper and salt in a bag and shake to mix well. One at a time, add a lamb shank and toss to coat well; shake off any excess.

2. Preheat the oven to 350 degrees F.

3. Choose a large, heavy nonreactive casserole or Dutch oven that has a tight-fitting lid and is large enough to hold the shanks in a single layer. Add the butter and oil and set over moderately high heat until the fats begin to shimmer. Add the lamb shanks and brown, turning as necessary, on all sides. (This can take a while because they're lumpy and have lots of sides to deal with—8 to 10 minutes should do it.) Remove the shanks to a plate.

4. Add the onions and garlic to the casserole and sauté over moderate heat until limp, 8 to 10 minutes.

5. Sprinkle on the basil, oregano and cinnamon and stir well. Drain the beans and add them to the onions; stir well to combine. Toss in the bay leaves; pour in the wine and bourbon and stir to mix. Return the shanks to the casserole, nestling them into the beans a bit; cover the casserole. Place in the oven and braise for 2½ to 3 hours, until the lamb is almost falling off the bones and the beans are tender and creamy.

6. Taste and adjust the seasonings as necessary. Remove and discard the bay leaves. Sprinkle the chopped mint over the shanks and beans and serve directly from the casserole.

Bourbon Baked Beans

THE NEATEST THING ABOUT OVEN-BAKED BEANS IS THAT THEY ARE SO LOW-maintenance: Combine the ingredients and put them in the oven—no sautéing required. We like these made with cider or apple juice but plain old tap water will suffice. Whatever you do, though, don't forget the bourbon—these beans like to drink.

FOR 6 TO 8

1	pound navy or pea beans, picked over and soaked overnight
2	large Spanish onions
3	garlic cloves, minced
½	cup packed brown sugar (light or dark)
⅓	cup unsulphured molasses
¼	cup prepared mustard
2	tablespoons dry mustard
1	tablespoon ground cinnamon
⅔ to 1	cup bourbon
4 to 5	cups apple cider, apple juice or water
2	smoked ham hocks, rinsed, or 4 ounces thick-sliced smoked bacon, cut into 1-inch squares
	Rye Rye Bread crumbs (page 296; optional)

1. Pour the soaked beans into a saucepan, add water to cover by 2 inches and bring to a boil over high heat. Reduce the heat and cook for 30 minutes. They won't be done at all, but that's all right.

2. Meanwhile, preheat the oven to 350 degrees F.

3. Drain the beans and pour them into a large bean pot, heavy casserole or Dutch oven. Add the onions, garlic, brown sugar, molasses, mustard, dry mustard and cinnamon. Stir to mix well. Pour in the bourbon and 3 cups of the cider, apple juice or water. Tuck the ham hocks or smoked bacon into the beans.

4. Cover the pot and bake for 1 hour.

5. Stir the beans and add 1 cup more cider, apple juice or water, if needed. Cover and continue baking for 3 hours more. Stir and check the liquid every hour, adding more if necessary.

6. When the beans are almost tender, uncover the pot and bake for about 1 hour more. These beans are especially good if you sprinkle the top with a layer of Rye Rye Bread crumbs.

Sour-Mash Stewed Tomatoes (Kentucky Panzanella)

S ERVE THIS SIDE DISH HOT, AT ROOM TEMPERATURE OR CHILLED—IT'S GOOD all three ways. The vegetables stay crisp since the whole mixture cooks only long enough to melt the sugar and mingle the flavors. Also, this dish makes an excellent "instant salad"—just spoon it over some fresh-torn lettuces and endive.

FOR 6 TO 8

2	cans (each 28 ounces) Italian plum tomatoes, with their juices, chopped
1	Spanish onion, chopped
1	large celery rib, diced
½	red or green bell pepper, diced
3	tablespoons packed brown sugar (light or dark)
1½	teaspoons ground coriander
1	teaspoon celery seeds
1	teaspoon ground cinnamon
½	teaspoon ground ginger
	Hot sauce (optional)
⅓	cup bourbon or Tennessee whiskey
	Salt and freshly milled black pepper
4 to 5	slices stale or dried bread, cut into 1-inch cubes

1. Combine the tomatoes with their juices, the onion, celery and bell pepper in a large nonreactive saucepan over moderately high heat. Stir in the brown sugar, coriander, celery seeds, cinnamon and ginger and bring to a bubble. Cook for 5 minutes. Remove the pan from the heat.

2. Stir in hot sauce, to taste. Stir in the bourbon or Tennessee whiskey. Season with salt and pepper, to taste. Add the bread cubes and stir until moistened. Serve at once, let cool to room temperature, or cover and chill.

Sun-Dried Tomato-Whiskey Ketchup

THOUGH THIS MAKES A SEXY-TASTING KETCHUP, WE'VE ALSO USED IT AS A marinade for pork and chicken and ribs, stirred it into baked beans and jazzed up some fresh tomato soup with a dollop of it. Thinned with a cup of chicken stock and with some mushrooms added, it's a pasta sauce that has a flavor all its own.

MAKES 5 TO 6 CUPS

1	cup dry sun-dried tomato bits
1	cup bourbon or Tennessee whiskey
1	can (28 ounces) crushed Italian plum tomatoes, with their juices
1	Spanish onion, chopped
¼	cup packed light brown sugar
1½	teaspoons chili powder
¼	teaspoon ground cumin
¼	teaspoon ground allspice
¼	teaspoon ground cinnamon
	Salt and freshly milled black pepper, to taste

1. Combine the sun-dried tomato bits and bourbon or Tennessee whiskey in a jar. Cover and shake well. Set aside overnight.

2. Combine the steeped sun-dried tomato mixture with all of the remaining ingredients in a heavy nonreactive saucepan. Bring to a simmer over moderate heat. Reduce the heat to low and cook until very thick and most of the liquid evaporates, 45 to 55 minutes. Remove from the heat and set aside to cool to lukewarm.

3. Working in 2 batches, ladle some of the mixture into a blender and puree until relatively smooth. Pour into hot, clean glass bottles or jars and let cool to room temperature. Cover and refrigerate. Stored in the refrigerator, the ketchup will keep for 1 month.

Bourbon-Honey-Mustard Sauce

H ERE'S ANOTHER ALL-PURPOSE SAUCE—GREAT AS A GLAZE FOR HAM, BUT also wonderful over broiled or roasted chicken and potatoes, as a condiment on sandwiches, in salad dressing, in barbecue sauce or as a dip for raw vegetables.

MAKES ABOUT I CUP

½   cup honey
4   tablespoons dry mustard
¼   cup bourbon or Tennessee whiskey
1   tablespoon yellow or brown mustard seeds, crushed

1. Combine all of the ingredients in a small bowl and stir until well blended. Use immediately or set aside to allow the flavors to blend.

2. Pour the mixture into a jar and tightly cover. Refrigerate until needed. Use cold, at room temperature or warmed. The sauce will keep for at least 2 weeks.

Bourbon Barbecue Sauce

Oven-barbecued chicken tastes—and smells—great when smothered in this simple sauce. Your racks of ribs will thank you for it too. Use it indoors as a cooking medium for meaty fish fillets or outdoors over virtually anything you want to grill.

MAKES 1½ TO 2 QUARTS

1	tablespoon vegetable oil
1	large Spanish onion, chopped
3	garlic cloves, minced
2	cans (each 28 ounces) Italian plum tomatoes, with their juices, chopped
1	can (6 ounces) tomato paste
⅓	cup packed light brown sugar
¼	cup maple syrup
¼	cup prepared mustard
2	tablespoons Worcestershire sauce
2	tablespoons chili powder
2½	teaspoons ground cumin
2½	teaspoons ground coriander
1	teaspoon celery seeds
1½	teaspoons salt
1½	teaspoons freshly milled black pepper
¼	teaspoon ground allspice
¾	cup bourbon or Tennessee whiskey

1. Warm the oil in a large nonreactive saucepan or sauté pan over moderate heat. Add the onion and garlic and sauté until just softened, about 5 minutes.

2. Stir in all of the remaining ingredients. Bring the sauce to a simmer. Reduce the heat to low and cook, stirring from time to time, until all of the vegetables are very soft, 30 to 40 minutes. Let cool to room temperature.

3. Puree the sauce in a blender or food processor, or simply push it through a fine-mesh sieve. Bottle and store in the refrigerator; it will keep for 2 weeks.

Southern-Style Whiskey-Poppy-Seed Salad Dressing

MARDEE'S MOM, GLADYS HILGERT, LOVED POPPY-SEED SALAD DRESSING; she also loved bourbon. We're pretty sure she'd love this combination too. It makes an excellent dressing for a sweet-style coleslaw.

MAKES ABOUT ½ CUP

2	tablespoons bourbon or Tennessee whiskey
1	tablespoon packed light brown sugar
2	teaspoons balsamic vinegar
2	teaspoons poppy seeds
⅓	cup canola or safflower oil
	Salt and freshly milled black pepper

Put the bourbon or Tennessee whiskey, brown sugar, vinegar and poppy seeds into a small jar. Cover and shake to blend well. Add the oil and shake until emulsified. Taste and season with salt and pepper. Cover and shake again. Set aside at room temperature until needed.

Southern-Style Derby-Pecan Pie

EVERYONE KNOWS WHAT MAKES A GOOD SOUTHERN-STYLE PECAN PIE, AND anyone who has ever been to Louisville leaves town as a big fan of Derby pie. We've put the two together—sort of. Chocolate lovers will be happy for it; if you don't like or want the chocolate, just omit it.

FOR 6 TO 8

PIECRUST

1	cup unbleached all-purpose flour
½	teaspoon salt
⅓	cup plus 1 tablespoon chilled solid vegetable shortening
2 to 3	tablespoons ice water

PIE

6	ounces semisweet chocolate, melted and cooled
4	large eggs
⅔	cup dark corn syrup
1	cup packed brown sugar (light or dark)
4	tablespoons (½ stick) unsalted butter, melted and cooled to room temperature
⅓	cup bourbon or Tennessee whiskey
2	cups pecan halves

Bourbon Whipped Cream (page 331), for serving

1. **Make the piecrust:** In a food processor or mixing bowl, combine the flour and salt. Pulse or stir to blend. Add the shortening and pulse or cut in until the mixture resembles coarse meal. Gradually add the ice water and process or stir until the pastry gathers together into a ball. Press the dough into a large flat disk and place between 2 sheets of plastic wrap. Fold the wrap over to seal. Refrigerate for 1 hour.

2. Preheat the oven to 350 degrees F. Choose a 9-inch deep-dish pie plate.

3. Smooth out the plastic wrap on the top and bottom of the pastry, but leave it covered. Roll out the pastry to an even 12-inch round. Peel away the top sheet of plastic. Invert the pie plate over the dough and flip the two at once; remove the remaining plastic wrap. Ease the pastry into the pie plate; fold under the edges along the rim and crimp decoratively.

4. **Make the pie:** Pour the melted chocolate into the bottom of the pie shell and spread into an even layer that covers just the bottom, not the sides. Refrigerate the pie shell until needed.

5. Whisk the eggs together in a mixing bowl until thick and smooth. Whisk in the corn syrup, brown sugar and melted butter until smooth. Add the bourbon or Tennessee whiskey. Stir in the pecan halves until coated.

6. Pour the filling into the chilled pie shell; place the pie plate on a baking sheet. Bake for 40 to 45 minutes, or until the filling is puffed and risen and the crust is golden brown. Let cool to room temperature on a rack. Serve with Bourbon Whipped Cream.

Whiskeyed Peach Cobbler with Peach-Whiskey Potion

BELIEVE IT OR NOT, THIS COBBLER TASTES GREAT EVEN WHEN THE PEACHES aren't superlative. The peach-whiskey potion is just that—the strained mixture of sweetened peach juices and whiskey that you soak the peaches in. Don't be a sissy when you pour some on top of the warm cobbler. Roy Finamore deserves credit for this rich cobbler dough.

FOR 6 TO 8

DOUGH

2½	cups unbleached all-purpose flour
¼	teaspoon salt
½	pound (2 sticks) cold unsalted butter, cut into bits
7 to 8	tablespoons ice water

FILLING

5 to 6	cups thick-sliced ripe fresh stoned peaches (about 7 large)
1	tablespoon fresh lemon juice
1 to 1½	cups bourbon or Tennessee whiskey
½	cup packed light brown sugar
½	teaspoon vanilla extract
	Sugar, for sprinkling (optional)

Vanilla ice cream, for serving (optional)

1. **Make the dough**: In a food processor or mixing bowl, combine the flour and salt. Pulse or stir to blend. Scatter the bits of butter over the top and pulse or cut in until the mixture resembles coarse meal. Gradually add the ice water and process or stir until the dough gathers together into a ball. Press the dough into a large flat rectangle and cover with plastic wrap. Refrigerate for 1 hour.

2. **Make the filling**: In a nonreactive bowl, toss the peaches with the lemon juice.

3. In another bowl, combine the bourbon or Tennessee whiskey with the brown sugar and vanilla. Stir to dissolve the sugar. Pour the mixture over the peaches, toss to coat well, and set aside at room temperature until needed.

4. Preheat the oven to 400 degrees F. Choose an 11-by-7-inch glass or ceramic baking dish.

5. On a lightly floured surface, roll out the dough to an even, very large rectangle,

about 22 by 16 inches. Roll up loosely and transfer it to the baking dish; ease the dough into the dish, allowing the edges to overhang the rim.

6. Using a slotted spoon, spoon the peaches into the dough, covering the bottom and mounding them a bit in the center. Sprinkle with sugar, if desired. Fold in the overhanging dough, leaving an area of peaches uncovered in the center. Place the baking dish on a baking sheet. Bake for 45 to 50 minutes, or until the fruit is lightly browned and the pastry is golden.

7. While the cobbler bakes, strain the leftover whiskey, peach juices and sugar mixture into a pitcher.

8. Serve the cobbler warm or at room temperature in shallow soup plates, with a scoop of ice cream, if desired. Drizzle some of the whiskey-peach potion over the top of each serving.

Bananas Stephen Collins Foster

WHETHER YOU DO A DRAMATIC PYROTECHNIC PERFORMANCE AT TABLEside or merely put this dessert together in the kitchen, don't skip this because it seems difficult. It's easy and tasty—a perfect pick-me-up when you're feeling like the "Old Folks at Home."

FOR 4

8	tablespoons (1 stick) unsalted butter
1	cup packed light brown sugar
⅓	cup plus 2 tablespoons bourbon or Tennessee whiskey
4	ripe bananas, peeled and halved lengthwise
½	cup pecan halves or pieces, toasted

1. In a large skillet or your prettiest flambé pan, melt the butter with the brown sugar and the 2 tablespoons bourbon or Tennessee whiskey over moderate heat. Stir until the mixture begins to bubble. Add the bananas, cut sides down, and sauté, spooning the butter mixture over them, until heated through and well coated, 4 to 6 minutes.

2. Slowly pour the remaining ⅓ cup bourbon or Tennessee whiskey down the side of the pan. Tilt the pan slightly away from you and ignite the liquor with a match, taking care not to tilt the pan too much. The whiskey will flare up and then settle down to a lowish burn. Spoon the sauce over the bananas until the flames subside.

3. Place 2 banana halves on each dessert plate and spoon some of the sauce over top. Sprinkle with some of the toasted pecans. Serve at once.

Bourbon-Pineapple Upside-Down Cake

YOU CAN MAKE THIS CAKE THE OLD-FASHIONED WAY IN A BIG CAST-IRON skillet or in any large round, square or rectangular baking dish. There is no substitution for fresh pineapple here—it's the only thing that will do.

FOR 6 TO 8

PINEAPPLE LAYER

4	tablespoons (½ stick) unsalted butter
½	cup packed light brown sugar
3	tablespoons bourbon or Tennessee whiskey
1	ripe fresh pineapple
6 to 10	pecan halves

CAKE LAYER

1	cup sugar
8	tablespoons (1 stick) unsalted butter, at room temperature
2	large eggs
1¾	cups sifted cake flour
2	teaspoons baking powder
½	teaspoon salt
¾	cup pineapple juice
¼	cup bourbon or Tennessee whiskey
2	teaspoons vanilla extract

1. Preheat the oven to 350 degrees F. Generously butter an 11-inch cast-iron skillet or a large baking dish (there's plenty of batter, so the size and shape of the dish don't matter too much).

2. **Make the pineapple layer:** Combine the butter and brown sugar in a small non-stick saucepan. Set over moderate heat and cook, stirring, until the sugar melts into the butter, 2 to 3 minutes. Remove from the heat and stir in the bourbon or Tennessee whiskey. Pour the mixture into the buttered skillet or baking dish and tilt to coat with an even layer.

3. Cut the top and bottom off the pineapple. Stand it upright on a cutting board and cut down, from the top to the bottom, slicing off the rind and eyes. Check your work—you don't want any snarly rough bits in your cake. Turn the pineapple on its side and cut into ⅔-inch-thick slices. Cut out the core from the center of each slice with the tip of

a paring knife. Decoratively arrange the pineapple rings in the prepared pan or dish, halving the slices as needed to cover the bottom. Place a pecan half, rounded side down, in the center of each ring and anywhere else there is room to sneak one in.

4. **Make the cake layer:** Beat the sugar into the butter until well mixed. Add the eggs and beat until smooth. Stir together the dry ingredients and add them in 3 parts, alternating with the pineapple juice and bourbon or Tennessee whiskey. Stir in the vanilla. The batter will be thick and smooth.

5. Pour the batter over the pineapple slices and smooth the top. Bake for 40 to 50 minutes, or until a cake tester inserted in the cake layer comes out almost clean.

6. Cool the cake in the pan on a wire rack. When completely cool, invert a platter over the top and flip the two together. The cake will "thud" onto the platter. Serve when desired.

Bourbon Bread Pudding

BREAD PUDDINGS ARE LIKE BOURBONS—THERE'S A STYLE FOR EVERYONE. Some are baked in shallow baking pans and use nearly whole slices of bread; others are made from coarse bread crumbs, and this one, like many others, uses cubes of stale bread. The type of bread you choose will alter the results from batch to batch, but this particular method works well with most types, at various stages of staleness.

FOR 10 TO 12

5	large eggs
1½	cups sugar
2	teaspoons ground cinnamon
1	teaspoon ground allspice
1½	teaspoons vanilla extract
3 to 4	cups milk (the quantity will depend on the staleness and texture of the bread)
⅔	cup bourbon or Tennessee whiskey
16-20	cups loosely packed, 1-inch cubes of stale bread (crusts removed if thick or hard)
	Warm Whiskey Sauce or Warm Whiskey Cream (page 328), for serving

1. Whisk together the eggs, sugar, cinnamon, allspice and vanilla in a large, deep bowl. Add 3 cups of the milk and the bourbon or Tennessee whiskey and whisk until well combined. Add the bread cubes and any crumbs and mix until submerged or coated with the mixture. If the liquid seems scant, add more of the milk. Set aside for 30 minutes, until the bread is softened and completely saturated.

2. Meanwhile, butter a 5-to-6-quart heatproof bowl. Preheat the oven to 350 degrees F.

3. Pour the soaked-bread mixture into the bowl, leaving about 1 inch of space at the top so the pudding can puff up without spilling over. Bake for 60 to 70 minutes, or until medium gold and crusty on top and firm to the touch.

4. Transfer the bowl to a wire rack and let cool to room temperature. Serve as is or top with Warm Whiskey Sauce or Warm Whiskey Cream.

Bourbon-Brown-Sugar Shortbread

RICH, GOLDEN SHORTBREAD WITH A TOUCH OF SOUTHERN HOSPITALITY added to it. Don't be alarmed at the rather ugly color of the batter when you scrape it into the pan; it bakes up to look just a tad darker than regular shortbread. Be sure to score it lightly into wedges before baking, since traditionally, shortbread is broken, not cut, into serving pieces.

FOR 8 TO 12

½	pound (2 sticks) unsalted butter, at room temperature
1	cup packed light brown sugar
3	tablespoons bourbon or Tennessee whiskey
1	teaspoon vanilla extract
2¼	cups unbleached all-purpose flour

1. Preheat the oven to 325 degrees F, with a rack in the upper third. Butter an 8- or 9-inch round or square cake pan.

2. In a large bowl, beat the butter until very soft and fluffy, about 2 minutes. Beat in the brown sugar until thoroughly combined. Sprinkle on the bourbon or Tennessee whiskey and vanilla and mix until incorporated. Gradually add the flour and beat until well mixed.

3. Scrape the dough into the prepared pan and pat it into an even layer. Crimp the edges or make a traditional border of thumbprints all around the edge. Prick the top all over with the tines of a fork. Score the shortbread into wedges or squares with a sharp knife, cutting just partway through the dough.

4. Bake for about 30 minutes, until puffed and very lightly browned on top. Cool in the pan on a wire rack. Break into pieces along the score lines for serving. Store in an airtight container.

Blasted Brownies

SOME OF THE WHISKEY COOKS INTO THESE BROWNIES, AND THEN YOU spike them with a little bit more.

MAKES 16

6	ounces semisweet chocolate, chopped
2	ounces unsweetened chocolate, chopped
8	tablespoons (1 stick) unsalted butter
¾	cup sifted unbleached all-purpose flour
¼	teaspoon baking soda
¼	teaspoon salt
2	large eggs
1½	teaspoons vanilla extract
¾	cup sugar
6	tablespoons bourbon or Tennessee whiskey
½	cup chopped pecans

1. In a small saucepan over moderately low heat or in a heatproof bowl in a microwave oven at medium power, heat the semisweet and the unsweetened chocolate with the butter until almost melted. Remove from the heat and stir until smooth and completely melted. Set aside to cool to room temperature.

2. Preheat the oven to 325 degrees F. Butter an 8- or 9-inch square cake pan. Stir together the flour, baking soda and salt.

3. In a bowl with an electric mixer, beat the eggs until thick and pale. Add the vanilla, sugar and 3 tablespoons of the bourbon or Tennessee whiskey and beat until well blended. Add the cooled chocolate mixture and fold together. Fold in the pecans.

4. Scrape the batter into the prepared pan and smooth the top. Bake for 25 to 30 minutes, or until a cake tester inserted about 1 inch from the edge comes out clean but still moist. Remove the pan to a wire rack and let cool to room temperature.

5. Poke small holes in the top of the brownies with a skewer. Sprinkle the remaining 3 tablespoons of liquor over the top and coax it into the holes. Let set for 1 hour.

6. Cut the brownies into small squares and serve.

Mr. Ransdell's Kentucky Bourbon Balls

T HIS RECIPE BELONGS TO MR. WILLIAM RANSDELL, FATHER OF OUR FRIEND Darren Ransdell and a native of Louisville, Kentucky. The directions reflect his way of making them—getting your hands right down into the mixture. Using paraffin to thin the chocolate and help it set is as Kentucky-traditional as the day is long. You can use whatever bourbon you prefer.

MAKES ABOUT 45 DELICIOUS CANDY BALLS

1	box (1 pound) confectioners' sugar
8	tablespoons (1 stick) unsalted butter, at room temperature
3	tablespoons Maker's Mark Bourbon
1	teaspoon vanilla extract
¼	cup finely ground pecans or walnuts
4 to 6	ounces semisweet chocolate, chopped
½	ounce paraffin, shaved or grated

1. In a bowl, use your hands to mix together the confectioners' sugar, butter, bourbon and vanilla. Add the nuts and mix very well. Roll the candy into 1-inch balls.

2. Melt the chocolate with the paraffin until smooth and well mixed. Using toothpicks, dip each ball into the chocolate mixture and transfer to waxed paper to dry.

3. Store the bourbon balls in an airtight container in a cool place.

Chocolate Tennessee Whiskey Balls

WE FELT BADLY THAT TENNESSEE DIDN'T HAVE ITS OWN EQUIVALENT of bourbon balls, so we created these. If you refrigerate these and then chop them up, they make an excellent topping for a bowl of ice cream.

MAKES ABOUT 6 DOZEN

2	cups finely ground chocolate cookie crumbs (from one 9-ounce box of Famous Wafers or other chocolate wafers)
1½	cups confectioners' sugar
¾	cup unsweetened cocoa powder
1	cup finely chopped pecans or walnuts
½	cup Tennessee whiskey
3	tablespoons light corn syrup
½	cup unsweetened cocoa powder mixed with ½ cup confectioners' sugar, for coating

1. In a bowl, combine the cookie crumbs, confectioners' sugar, cocoa and nuts and stir until uniformly mixed. Add the Tennessee whiskey and corn syrup and mix until evenly moistened and sticky.

2. Place the cocoa-and-sugar mixture in a shallow plate. Shape the chocolate mixture into ¾-inch balls and roll each one in the cocoa-and-sugar mixture. Transfer to a tin, separating each layer with a square of waxed paper. Cover and store in a cool place.

Bourbon-Pecan Ice Cream

I F THE PECANS YOU USE IN THIS ICE CREAM ARE LIGHTLY SALTED, THEY'LL ADD an extra dimension that can't be duplicated merely by adding salt to the recipe. If you don't want the nuts to get soggy, add them when you stir in the bourbon instead of earlier.

MAKES ALMOST 1 QUART

3	cups half-and-half
½	cup packed light brown sugar
¼	cup sugar
1¼	cups broken pecan pieces
3	tablespoons bourbon or Tennessee whiskey

1. Combine the half-and-half and both sugars in a food processor and whirl for 2 full minutes, or until the sugars dissolve into the cream. Stir in the pecans. If there's time, chill the mixture before freezing it.

2. Pour the mixture into an ice-cream maker and freeze according to the manufacturer's directions until moderately set but still spoonable.

3. Stir in the bourbon or Tennessee whiskey and continue freezing until the ice cream is firm. Serve as is, or spoon into a cookie-crumb crust and freeze to make an ice-cream pie.

Warm Whiskey Cream

THIS CREAM IS WONDERFUL POURED OVER ALMOST ANY DESSERT OR FLOATED on top of a cup of coffee. You'll be tempted to drink a shot of it—very tempted.

MAKES ABOUT 2 CUPS

8	tablespoons (1 stick) unsalted butter
1	cup sugar
½	cup heavy cream
¼	cup bourbon or Tennessee whiskey

1. Melt the butter in a small saucepan set over moderate heat. Stir in the sugar and mix until it partially dissolves into the butter, 2 to 3 minutes. Pour in the heavy cream and cook, stirring, until the sugar completely dissolves and the mixture thickens slightly, about 2 minutes more. Remove from the heat.

2. Whisk in the bourbon or Tennessee whiskey until well combined and slightly thickened. Serve at once.

Warm Whiskey Sauce

YOU'LL WANT THIS ONE TO TOP YOUR BOURBON BREAD PUDDING (page 322).

MAKES ABOUT 1½ CUPS

3	tablespoons unsalted butter
1	cup warm water
½	cup packed light brown sugar
¼	teaspoon ground cinnamon
¼	teaspoon ground allspice
	Pinch of salt
½	cup bourbon or Tennessee whiskey

1. Combine the butter, water and brown sugar in a small saucepan set over moderate heat. Cook, stirring, until the sugar begins to dissolve. Stir in the cinnamon, allspice and salt and cook until the sugar dissolves completely and the mixture is smooth.

2. Remove the pan from the heat, and stir in the bourbon or Tennessee whiskey. Use at once or let cool and reheat when needed. The sauce will keep for up to 1 week.

Sweet Bourbon Butter

SPREAD THIS OVER POUND CAKE, BROILED PINEAPPLE OR RAISIN TOAST. IT'S a heady treat melted over Sunday brunch waffles, too.

MAKES ABOUT ⅔ CUP

½	cup confectioners' sugar
1½	tablespoons bourbon or Tennessee whiskey
8	tablespoons (1 stick) unsalted butter, at room temperature

Combine the confectioners' sugar and bourbon or Tennessee whiskey in a small bowl. Add the butter and beat with a wooden spoon until thoroughly mixed. Use at once or spoon into a crock and refrigerate.

Bourbon-Ginger Hard Sauce

THE GINGER IS THE SECRET INGREDIENT HERE—IT MAKES AN EXCELLENT flavor combination with the whiskey, sugar and soft butter. Try a spoonful over a wedge of hot apple pie.

MAKES ABOUT ¾ CUP

½	cup packed light brown sugar
2	tablespoons bourbon or Tennessee whiskey
2	tablespoons minced crystallized ginger
8	tablespoons (1 stick) unsalted butter, at room temperature

Combine all of the ingredients in a bowl and beat with a wooden spoon until thoroughly mixed. Use at once or spoon into a crock and refrigerate.

Snockered Fudge Sauce

USE THIS SAUCE TO MAKE A HOT FUDGE SUNDAE WITH A KICK, OR POUR it over a cake to give it a rich, shiny glaze.

MAKES ABOUT 3½ CUPS

8	ounces semisweet chocolate, chopped
½	pound (2 sticks) unsalted butter
¼	cup packed light brown sugar
⅓	cup light corn syrup
⅔	cup evaporated skim milk
1	teaspoon vanilla extract
⅔	cup bourbon or Tennessee whiskey

1. In a small saucepan over moderately low heat or in a heatproof bowl in a microwave oven at medium power, heat the chopped chocolate with the butter until almost melted. Remove from the heat and stir until smooth and completely melted.

2. Stir in the brown sugar, corn syrup, evaporated skim milk and vanilla. Stir constantly until the sugar melts and the mixture is completely smooth. Add the bourbon or Tennessee whiskey and stir briefly, just until mixed in. Use at once or pour into a jar, cover, and refrigerate for up to 2 weeks.

Bourbon Whipped Cream

A MUST-HAVE FOR ALL BOURBON LOVERS—ESPECIALLY WHEN BOURBON-Pineapple Upside-Down Cake (page 320) is on the menu.

MAKES ABOUT 2 CUPS

1	cup heavy cream
¼	cup bourbon or Tennessee whiskey
2	tablespoons confectioners' sugar

Beat the heavy cream until soft peaks begin to form. Add the bourbon or Tennessee whiskey and confectioners' sugar and continue to beat until just floppy. Use at once.

OLD HEAVEN HILL SPRINGS DISTILLERY, INC.
BARDSTOWN- NELSON COUNTY, KY.

CHAPTER EIGHT

TRAVEL
AND FURTHER LEARNING

The Kentucky Derby and the Kentucky Oaks

T HE KENTUCKY DERBY IS MUCH MORE THAN A TWO-MINUTE race over a 1¼-mile racetrack. It ranks right up there with other all-American must-do experiences—Mardi Gras, the Super Bowl, Times Square on New Year's Eve, the World Series and the Indy 500—in spectacle, excitement and pure energy. Derby Day is just one small but significant part of Derby Week, an incredibly well-organized, homegrown celebration that brings out the best that Louisville, Churchill Downs and thoroughbred racing have to offer. It also is the occasion best suited to sipping mint juleps, and if you participate at all, you'll be surrounded by them everywhere you go.

The Louisville Jockey Club was founded in 1874 by Meriwether Lewis Clark, who built the Jockey Clubhouse and track on the same ground that is Churchill Downs today. On May 17, 1875, the Club sponsored the first Kentucky Derby, a race that featured 15 three-year-olds running over a 1½-mile track. The 10,000 spectators watched as "Aristides" became the first winner of what would later be called the Run for the Roses. In time, the date of the race was fixed as the first Saturday in May, and in 1895, the course was shortened to its traditional 1¼-mile distance. Churchill Downs grew into a magnificent facility, complete with the longest grandstand in the United States and twin spires that have become recognizable to racing fans the world over.

Derby Week in Louisville is as festive as the day is long. The main event of the Wednesday before the Derby is the Great Steamboat Race: Louisville's own *Belle of Louisville* versus New Orleans' *Delta Queen* in a 14-mile race on the Ohio River. Viewing is free to all from the riverfront. Locals admit that though the *Delta Queen* is the considerably larger and more powerful of the pair, somehow it manages to beat the *Belle* only every other year. Thus each of the competitors has taken possession of the Golden Antlers winner's trophy 15 times in the 30 years the race has been run. The rivalry is all in good fun and an excuse to throw a party, listen to the calliopes and get the week off to a merry start.

The Pegasus Parade is Thursday's big event, featuring a total of 95 floats, bands, clowns, horses and celebrities as it wends its way along Louisville's Broadway. Admission is free; bleacher and chair seating is available at a nominal price.

Friday is Kentucky Oaks Day at Churchill Downs. The morning hours are important to fans because the post positions for horses that will run in the Derby are chosen, marking the beginning of the major speculation among potential bettors. All of Louisville turns out for the Oaks, and the day becomes as festive an event as the Derby itself. In addition, since many locals attend the Oaks and then go to Derby Day parties, they have the chance to place bets on the Derby after the third race on Oaks Day.

The Kentucky Oaks was fashioned after the English Oaks, just as the Derby was fashioned after the English Derby at Epsom Downs. Like its English counterpart, the Kentucky Oaks is a 1⅛-mile race for distinguished three-year-old fillies, and its purse is substantial—$300,000 in 1995. Though the turnout is considerably smaller than the attendance on Derby Day—87,383 versus the Derby's 144,110 in 1995—the crowds enjoy the full 10-race program offered at each day's meet.

Well before sunrise on the first Saturday in May, the entire city of Louisville is prepared to celebrate. The atmosphere is electric, but the city has the difficulties of the Run for the Roses completely under control. Though the gates of Churchill Downs open at 8:00 A.M., post time for the first race isn't until 11:30 A.M. The eighth race—the Kentucky Derby—doesn't run until 5:31 P.M. Pre-race brunches are popular Derby-morning affairs for those who have reserved seat tickets, while many of those who plan to watch the races from the infield area stake their claims for space early. No alcoholic beverages can be brought into the track, but all sorts of drinks are available onsite—including the Derby's traditional mint julep.

Oaks and Derby Day festivities are enlivened by the remarkable getups worn by so many Derby regulars. Ladies and gentlemen in their finest attire are there, as are some of the cleverest, funniest hats you'll ever see. Red roses and white tulips are the flowers of the day, and you'll see them—or representations of them—at every turn. The party atmosphere and excitement are palpable—Derby Day is unquestionably Louisville's finest and best day of the year.

By race time, each and every attendee is nervous. The bets are down, a $500,000 purse is at stake, and the action is about to begin. Nineteen or so of the world's best and most beautiful three-year-old thoroughbreds are raring to go. And they're off! There's silence, there's an incredible cacophony—sound seems to go in and out—as all eyes are on the horses. It's the world's longest and shortest two minutes for everyone anywhere who's watching. And so soon, it's over—the gold cup is presented, the blanket of glorious red roses is set in place, it's a happy, sad, thrilling moment that's not to be forgotten. It's the one and only Kentucky Derby, and it's an experience of a lifetime.

If you go to the Kentucky Derby, a few words to the wise can be of great help. Contact Churchill Downs for tickets well ahead of time. Book everything you'll need—hotel, airfare, car rentals and especially restaurant reservations—early, and go buy a hat. The city of Louisville will be ready and waiting with open arms. The local media, too, deserve high marks for their coverage of Derby Week activities. Every event is remarkably well documented; the newspapers are full of good advice, maps, hints and "survival tactics" of all sorts, and the television coverage is virtually continual on Friday and Saturday. Even if you aren't invited to join friends who will be watching the race from Millionaire's Row, you'll be up to date on everything that's going on everywhere.

Bourbon Country: Louisville

LOUISVILLE WAS FOUNDED IN 1778, WHEN GEORGE ROGERS CLARK LEFT A band of settlers in the area after bringing them there along with militia that he led on to fight the British for the land northwest of the Ohio. The following year, the settlers named their new home Louisville in honor of King Louis XVI of France, who aided the American colonies in their fight against the British. In 1830, upon completion of a canal that circumvented the seasonally impassable rapids that made up the Falls of the Ohio, Louisville was assured of growing success as a port. Its location, Kentucky's highest point along the Ohio River, placed it at an ideal port position between Pittsburgh and the Mississippi River. Nowadays, visitors strolling along the Riverfront Plaza/Belvedere can gaze at the Louisville Falls Fountain, the world's largest floating fountain. This wonderful sight, located mid-river and illuminated at night, shoots water 350 feet high in the shape of a fleur-de-lis, the city's symbol.

Visitors Information Center
400 South First Street (at First and Liberty Streets)
502 584 2121/ 800 792 5595
Kentucky Department of Travel Development
800 225 8747
Airport: Louisville International Airport (formerly Standiford Field)
502 368 6524
   Service via America West Express, American, British Airways, Continental, Delta, KLM, Northwest, Southwest, TWA, United, USAir, ValuJet.

Tourist Attractions

Belle of Louisville
The Wharf, Fourth Street and River Road
502 574 2355
   Cruise on the Ohio River in a 1914 steamship, complete with an authentic calliope. Afternoon and evening cruises from Memorial Day through Labor Day.

Star of Louisville
Starship Landing
151 West River Road (under the Second Street Bridge)
502 589 7827
   A cruise ship offering lunch, dinner and moonlight cruises, year-round.

Churchill Downs
700 Central Avenue at South Fourth Street
502 636 4400
   Established in 1874, Churchill Downs is America's oldest continuously operated racetrack and home of the Kentucky Derby (the first Saturday in May) and the Kentucky Derby Museum. The spring meet starts on the last Saturday in April and runs through early summer. The fall meet runs from the end of October through Thanksgiving weekend.

Old Louisville
   South of downtown Louisville lies an elegant residential neighborhood with an eclectic mixture of Victorian Gothic, Romanesque, Italianate, Queen Anne and Beaux-Arts architecture.

Actors Theater of Louisville

This Tony Award-winning regional theater is much lauded for mounting new plays and supporting modern playwrights. Call 502 584 1205 for information and schedules.

Getting Around Town

The Toonerville II Trolley
502 585 1234

Free rides on Fourth Avenue from the Galt House, near the riverfront, to the Brown Hotel and Theater Square at Broadway. The trolleys make frequent stops along the way and are equipped with wheelchair lifts. Operates 7:30 A.M. to 11 P.M. on weekdays; 9:30 A.M. to 11 P.M. on Saturdays.

Museums

The Colonel Harland Sanders Museum
1441 Gardiner Lane
502 456 8353

Situated in the Kentucky Fried Chicken Headquarters. Free admission. Open Monday through Thursday, 8:30 A.M. to 4:30 P.M.; Friday 8:30 A.M. to 3 P.M.

The Filson Club
1310 South Third Street
502 635 5083

Established in 1884 and named for John Filson, author of *The Discovery, Settlement, and Present State of Kentucke*, 1784, the club contains over 50,000 books, maps and pictures pertaining to Kentucky history and genealogy.

Kentucky Derby Museum
704 Central Avenue (at Churchill Downs racetrack)
502 637 7097

Historical exhibits surrounding the Kentucky Derby, a 360-degree multi-media show and tours of Churchill Downs (weather permitting). Don't miss this.

CHURCHILL DOWNS IN THE 1800S

Muhammad Ali Museum
Louisville Galleria (temporary location)
502 583 6770

Newly opened (May 1995) tribute to the life and career of boxing champion Muhammad Ali, a native of Louisville.

J.B. Speed Art Museum
2035 South Third Street
502 636 2893

The state's largest and oldest art museum has a broad-based permanent collection and features many changing exhibits. Admission is free.

Bourbon Country: Clermont

Bernheim Arboretum and Research Forest
Clermont, Kentucky 40110
502 955 8512
Getting There: Take state route 245, one mile east of I-6. The Arboretum is just 15 miles from Bardstown, on the way to Bardstown if traveling from Louisville.

Fourteen thousand acres of land with hiking trails, lakes, picnic areas and a nature museum. The land was donated by I.W. Bernheim, creator of I.W. Harper Bourbon.

Jim Beam's Visitor's Center and Distillery
Clermont, Kentucky 40110
502 543 9877
Getting There: From Louisville (27 miles, 33 minutes): Go south on I-65 for 24 miles to Exit 112 (the Bardstown/Bernheim Forest exit), then east (left) on state route 245 for 1½ miles. Jim Beam's American Outpost will be on your left.

From Bardstown: Go northwest on state route 245, heading toward I-65; Jim Beam will be on your right, across the road from Bernheim Forest.

Tours are available of Jim Beam's American Outpost, where sightseers can watch a film of a distillery tour, tour the Regal China Museum, the Hartman Cooperage Museum, a warehouse and a gift shop. No tours of the distillery itself are available. Call for details.

Bourbon Country: Bardstown

BARDSTOWN WAS FOUNDED ON PART OF THE 1,000-ACRE TRACT GRANTED to David Bard by Governor Patrick Henry of Virginia. It became the county seat when Nelson County was formed in 1784. Here, you will find many quaint bed-and-breakfasts, a number of motels and a marvelous collection of helpful, friendly people—all close to the biggest clutch of whiskey distilleries in Kentucky. Four of them—Barton, Jim Beam, Heaven Hill and Maker's Mark—are within short drives of this picturesque town. Two others—Wild Turkey in Lawrenceburg and Ancient Age in Frankfort—are less than an hour away.

Bardstown-Nelson County Tourist and Convention Commission
107 East Stephen Foster Avenue (P.O. Box 867)
Bardstown, Kentucky 40004
502 348 4877/800 638-4877

Area Attractions

Heaven Hill Distillery
Highway 49, Loretto Road (P.O. Box 729)
Bardstown, Kentucky 40004-0729
502 348 3921
Getting There: From Bardstown: Go east on Stephen Foster (US 62) to
state route 49. Turn right (south) and drive about 2 miles.

Heaven Hill offers two free 30-minute tours to visitors on weekdays
only. As always, it's best to reserve space early—especially if you are part
of a group.

Maker's Mark Distillery
Loretto, Kentucky 40037
502 865 2099
Getting There: From Bardstown: Go east on Stephen Foster (US 62) to
state route 49; turn right and follow 49 for about 20 miles, all the way
into Loretto. Follow state route 52 to Star Hill Farm—you can't miss the
signs.

Maker's Mark offers six tours a day Monday through Saturday and
three afternoon tours on Sunday. The 45-minute walking explorations
depart from the Visitor's Center, meander over the grounds and through
the buildings of the distillery and warehouses and return to the Gift
Gallery. As Tour Director Donna Miles is sure to inform you, "No samples are allowed—you just have to breathe deeply while you're walking
around." Tours are free.

In-Town Attractions

The Oscar Getz Museum of Whiskey History and
The Bardstown Historical Museum
Spalding Hall
114 North Fifth Street
Bardstown, Kentucky 40004

502 348 2999

A must-see museum filled to overflowing with Oscar Getz's personal collection of whiskey artifacts and documents. A real treat that shouldn't be missed.

My Old Kentucky Home State Park
501 East Stephen Collins Foster Avenue
Bardstown, Kentucky 40004
502 348 3502/800 323 7803

Federal Hill, the house on this property, was owned by the Rowan family, cousins of Stephen Collins Foster's father. Foster visited several times, and *My Old Kentucky Home,* the song that brings tears to the eyes of any Kentuckian, was written about this stately home, now a museum and open to the public.

My Old Kentucky Dinner Train
602 North Third Street
502 348 7300

All aboard for a two-hour lunch or dinner trip in restored 1940s dining cars.

St. Joseph Proto-Cathedral
310 West Stephen Collins Foster Avenue
502 348 3126

The first Catholic cathedral west of the Allegheny Mountains.

The Stephen Foster Story
Highway 150, Drama Drive (P.O. Box 546)
Bardstown, Kentucky 40004
800 626 1563 or 502 348 5971

A musical retelling of a year in the life of famed composer Stephen Collins Foster, performed outdoors by a cast of 60 in period costume. Saturday matinees and rainy-day performances are indoors. Nightly June 4 through Labor Day.

Horse Country: Lexington and Frankfort

LEXINGTON AND FRANKFORT, LOCATED JUST 26 MILES APART, MARK THE heart of the Bluegrass Region, the world-famous area known for its thoroughbred horse farms. Both cities offer historic attractions as well as locations that are near to much of the best Kentucky has to offer.

Greater Lexington Convention and Visitors Bureau
800 84-LEX-KY

Lexington Airport: Bluegrass Airport

Frankfort/Franklin County Tourist and Convention Commission
800 960 7200

Area Attractions

The Ancient Age Distillery/The Leestown Company
1001 Wilkinson Boulevard
Frankfort, Kentucky 40601
502 223 7641
Getting There: Tip: Once you see the Holiday Inn, you're only about
1 mile away.
From Louisville: Go east on I-64 for 47 miles, then north on US 127 for
5 miles to downtown Frankfort—US 421 (Wilkinson Blvd.).
From Bardstown (59 miles, about 1¼ hours): Go east on US 150 to the
Blue Grass Parkway, and east on the parkway for 37 miles. Go northeast
on US 127 for 19 miles to downtown Frankfort—US 421 (Wilkinson
Blvd.).
From Lexington (25 miles, about 30 minutes): Go west on I-64 for 19
miles, then northwest on US 60 for 2 miles. Go west on US 421 (Wilkinson Blvd.) for 1 mile.

Tours of the Ancient Age Distillery are offered free of charge and depart on the hour from Monday through Friday between 9:00 A.M. and 2:00 P.M. Don't miss the gift shop—there's always a little something you'll want to take home as a treat. Groups of 10 or more should call ahead for reservations.

The Wild Turkey Distillery
Highway 1510, Box 180
Lawrenceburg, Kentucky 40342
502 839 4544

Getting There: From Louisville (56 miles, 1 hour, 10 minutes): Go east on I-64 for 42 miles, then south on state route 151 for 7 miles. Go south on US 127 for 4 miles, then east on US 62 to the distillery.
From Lexington: Go west on US 60 to Versailles, then west on US 62 to the distillery.
From Frankfort (18 miles, 25 minutes): Go south on US 127 for 16 miles, then east on US 62 to the distillery.

Wild Turkey offers free 1¼-hour tours four times a day, Monday through Friday. Large groups can make special arrangements. Check in at the Visitor's Center across the road from the distillery; chances are good that you'll be offered an edible treat. The distillery is closed to visitors for the last two weeks of July and the first week of January.

Other Attractions

Keeneland
P.O. Box 1690
Lexington, Kentucky 40592-1690
800 456 3412 or 606 254 3412

Keeneland is the other of Kentucky's two premiere thoroughbred race tracks. Located six miles outside Lexington, Keeneland runs just two short meets every year: in April and in October. The Blue Grass Stakes—an important pre-Derby "prep" race—is the major event of the spring, and the Spinster Stakes precedes the Breeders' Cup races in the fall.

Kentucky Horse Park
4089 Iron Works Pike
Lexington, Kentucky 40511
606 233 4303

The first park devoted to horses, this working farm features 1,032 acres and over 40 different breeds. Attractions include two museums, two films, a walking farm tour, a horse-drawn tour and a beautiful memorial to the famous racehorse Man o' War. Open year-round.

Tennessee Whiskeys:
Nashville, The Athens of the South

NASHVILLE RANKS WAY UP THERE AMONG THE FRIENDLIEST, THE MOST festive and the most community-minded cities we've ever experienced. And Nashville is an experience—an exhilarating one, filled with history, culture, beauty, brains, fun for one and all and music, music, music. You don't have to love country music to love Nashville; it's a city that sings every style of music ever invented, and it surrounds you everywhere you go. Whether you're meandering around Centennial Park, staring at its full-scale replica of the Parthenon or, indoors, gazing at the incredible 42-foot-high sculpture of Athena Parthenon or wandering the corridors of the art museum that's housed there, you will be amazed at the open friendliness offered by one and all. And certainly, if you venture to the massive Opryland complex—for a meal, a round of live concerts and/or to enjoy the amusement-park rides, you will feel right at home with your Tennessee kin.

Nashville Convention & Visitors Bureau
161 Fourth Avenue, North
Nashville, Tennessee 37219
615 259 4730; Tourism Hotline: 615 259 4700

Nashville Department of Tourism Information Line
615 259 4747

Tennessee Tourism Development
615 741 2158

Area Attractions

Barbara Mandrell Country
1510 Division Street
Nashville, Tennessee 37203
615 242 7800 or 800 969 7800
    A look at Barbara Mandrell's family and career, including a recording studio where you can "sing along" and make your own recording.

Belle Carol Riverboat Company
106 First Avenue South
Riverfront Park
Nashville, Tennessee 37201
800 342 2355 or 615 244 3430

Daytime sightseeing cruises, evening dinner excursions and late-night party cruises on the Cumberland River featuring live Nashville entertainment. Cruises depart from the Nashville Old Steamboat Dock, four blocks from the downtown Convention Center.

The Country Music Hall of Fame and Museum
4 Music Square East
Nashville, Tennessee 37203
615 255 5333

Exhibits include The Grand Ole Opry—The First 65 years and Elvis's Solid Gold Cadillac. Don't miss this interesting and enjoyable museum— it's a must.

Belle Meade Plantation
5025 Harding Road
Nashville, Tennessee 37205
615 356 0501

Visit this 1853 Greek Revival mansion that was once the centerpiece of a 5,300-acre plantation. Handicapped-accessible except on the second floor of the mansion.

The Parthenon
Centennial Park
West End and 25th Avenues
Nashville, Tennessee 37201
615 862 8431

A must-do on any trip to Nashville. Visit the world's only reproduction of the Greek Parthenon, featuring Athena Parthenon—the tallest indoor statue in the Western world—a reproduction of the original Parthenon interior and various galleries. The museum also features plaster castings of the London Museum's famed Elgin Marbles.

Broadway Dinner Train
108 First Avenue South
Nashville, Tennessee 37201
800 274 8010 or 615 254 8000
Take a 2½-hour train ride while enjoying a four-course meal. Live entertainment in two lounge cars; "passenger only" rides available in the "Spirit of Tennessee" car.

Car Collectors Hall of Fame
1534 Demonbreun Street
Nashville, Tennessee 37203
615 255 6804
Go see one of Elvis's Cadillac, Louise Mandrell's MG, the Bat Mobile (from the TV series) and many more famous cars (48 in all).

Grand Ole Opry House
2804 Opryland Drive
Nashville, Tennessee 37214
615 889 3060
Visit the world's largest broadcast studio, where country music stars perform every weekend on the nation's longest-running live radio show.

The Grand Ole Opry Museum, Roy Acuff Museum and Minnie Pearl Museum
2802 Opryland Drive
Nashville, Tennessee 37214
615 889 6611
Exhibits at the Grand Ole Opry Museum include tributes to Country Music Hall of Fame members such as Patsy Cline, Little Jimmy Dickens and Jim Reeves; the Roy Acuff Museum features memorabilia of the "king of country music"; and the Minnie Pearl Museum pays tribute to the fabled country music comedienne.

Nashville on Stage
2806 Opryland Drive
Nashville, Tennessee 37214
615 889 6611
Some of country music's top names perform here, including Tanya Tucker, Tammy Wynette, Johnny Cash and the Oak Ridge Boys.

Opryland

2802 Opryland Drive

Nashville, Tennessee 37214

615 889 6611

Another must-do. A musical theme park featuring country music shows, 24 rides and a petting zoo. Don't miss a stroll thorugh the Opryland Hotel's breath-takingly beautiful Cascades.

Ryman Auditorium and Museum

116 Fifth Avenue North

Nashville, Tennessee 37219

615 889 6611

This former home of the Grand Ole Opry reopened in 1994 after under-going massive renovations. Many concerts and shows are performed here and the exhibits include a section that details the history of the Ryman.

Tennessee State Museum

505 Deaderick Street

Nashville, Tennessee 37243

615 741 2692

Exhibits trace the state's history from prehistoric Native Americans into the early twentieth century.

Wildhorse Saloon

120 Second Avenue North

Nashville, Tennessee 37201

615 251 1000

A necessary stop, the Wildhorse features a 3,300-square-foot dance floor and a full-service restaurant. Don't just stand around tapping your toe, get out there and dance.

Opryland USA River Taxis

615 889 6611

Travel from the Opryland complex to Nashville's Riverfront (or vice versa) on the Cumberland River.

Nashville Trolley Company

615 242 4433

Trolleys leave Riverfront Park every 15 minutes and travel through downtown Nashville and Music Row.

24-Hour Information Hotline

615 244 9393

Information on weather, entertainment, events and sports scores.

Tennessee Whiskey Country: Lynchburg and Tullahoma

B OTH LYNCHBURG AND TULLAHOMA ARE TINY TOWNS IN THE MIDDLE OF Tennessee walking horse country. Between the two of them, they produce all of America's Tennessee whiskeys. Both towns are small, but be sure to leave yourself time to take in all of the local attractions.

Lynchburg Chamber of Commerce

Welcome Center

615 759 4111

Tullahoma Chamber of Commerce

615 455 5497

Area Attractions

The Jack Daniel Distillery

Highway 55 (P.O. Box 199)

Lynchburg, Tennessee 37352

615 759 4221

Getting There: From Nashville (86 miles, 1¾ hours): Go south on I-24 for 60 miles, then west on state route 55 for 26 miles; follow the signs. From Chattanooga (80 miles, 1½ hours): Go north on I-24, then southwest on state route 55; follow the signs.

Don't look for a drink of Jack Daniel's at the distillery; there's none to be had in the whole dry county. However, for free one-hour tours of the distillery (from 8 A.M. to 4 P.M. daily) and shopping in a score of stores around the Lynchburg town square, you're in the right place. Enjoy.

George A. Dickel's Cascade Distillery
1950 Cascade Hollow Road (P.O. Box 490)
Tullahoma, Tennessee 37388
615 857 3124

Getting There: From any direction: Take I-24 to junction 105; go south on route 41; turn right onto state route 4291 toward Blanton Chapel Road and follow signs to the distillery or Normandy Dam; pass through the town and go 1 mile farther to the distillery.
From Lynchburg (13 miles, 20 minutes): Take state route 55.

George A. Dickel's Cascade Distillery offers free tours Monday through Friday from 9:00 A.M to 3:00 P.M. You'll start your visit at the old-fashioned Miss Annie's General Store and proceed around the distillery and the beautiful grounds of the Cascade Hollow property. Be sure to keep an eye out for the wool blankets used at the top and bottom of the charcoal-filtering tanks.

Miss Mary Bobo's Boarding House
P.O. Box 78
Main St. (three doors west of the Moore County Jail)
Lynchburg, Tennessee 37352
615 759 7394

Call now for "Mid-Day Dinner" reservations at this world-famous, absolutely charming Lynchburg institution. Southern hospitality is defined by Miss Bobo's—diners are served family-style meals seated at large tables and presided over by a charming hostess who is unfailingly adept at the art of conversation and making guests comfortable. You'll revel in great home-style Southern cooking, and you'll want to stay—for every meal, or maybe even forever. Don't miss this fabulous experience.

Whiskey Societies and Newsletters

HERE'S A LIST OF SOME CLUBS AND NEWSLETTERS THAT YOU MAY WANT TO consider to broaden your whiskey knowledge and to keep updated on new bottlings, etc.

The Kentucky Bourbon Circle
P.O. Box One
Clermont, Kentucky 40110-9980
For free membership, call 1-800-652-2472 or write for details and include the name of your favorite bourbon, whether you are interested in attending bourbon tastings and how you heard about the Kentucky Bourbon Circle.

Single-Barrel Bourbon Society
P.O. Box 1031
Louisville, Kentucky 40201
Free membership, write for details.

The Bourbon Country Reader
3712 North Broadway
Box 298
Chicago, Illinois 60613
Send a stamped, self-addressed envelope for a free issue and subscription details.

F. Paul Pacult's Spirit Journal
421-13 Route 59
Monsey, New York 10952
Subscription $49 per year. This excellent newsletter deals with all manner of spirits, beers, ports, sherries, etc.

Malt Advocate
3416 Oak Hill Road
Emmaus, Pennsylvania 18049
This magazine deals with beers and whiskeys of all types. Call 610 967 1083 or write for subscription rates.

A GLOSSARY OF
WHISKEY TERMS

Backset: Liquid strained from the mash after its primary distillation. Sometimes referred to as **Sour mash** or **Setback**.

Barrels: In American whiskey terms, closed wooden casks constructed from oak. The interiors are charred over open flames, and the barrels are then used to age whiskey.

Beading: The bubbles that form on top of whiskey in a bottle after the bottle has been shaken. Large bubbles denote high proof.

Beer: Usually called **Distiller's Beer**—fermented **Mash** ready to be distilled.

Beer still: A **Continuous still** used to distill **Low wines** from **Distiller's beer**.

Blended whiskey: **Straight whiskey** blended with neutral grain spirits, often with the addition of coloring and flavor enhancers.

Bourbon (straight): A whiskey made from a **Mash** containing at least 51 percent corn, distilled out at a maximum of 160° proof, aged at no more than 125° proof for a minimum of two years in charred new oak barrels and bottled at a minimum of 80° proof. If the whiskey is aged for less than four years, its age must be stated on the bottle. No coloring or flavoring may be added to any straight whiskey.

Charcoal mellowing: Filtration, before aging, of Tennessee whiskey through a minimum of 10 feet of sugar-maple charcoal. Also known as **Mellowing, Leaching** or the **Lincoln County Process**.

Charring: The process that sets fire to the interior of barrels for less than one minute and creates a layer of charred wood that allows the whiskey access to the **Red layer**. Distillers can choose from four levels of char.

Chill haze: A term used to describe the "cloudiness" that appears in cold whiskey when the whiskey has undergone either a light filtration or no filtration at all. There is nothing wrong with a whiskey that bears a chill haze.

Congeners: Impurities, such as esters and fusel oils, that are present in minuscule amounts in beverage alcohol and develop into rich flavors in the final, aged product.

Continuous still: Also known as a Coffey still but referred to as the **Beer still** by American whiskey distillers, who use it to distill **Low wines** from **Distiller's beer**.

Corn whiskey: A whiskey made from a **Mash** containing a minimum of 80 percent corn and, if it is aged at all, is aged in used or uncharred oak barrels.

Distillation: Purifying the liquid part of a mixture by a series of evaporation and condensation processes.

Distiller's beer: The fermented **Mash** that is transferred from the **Fermenter** to the **Beer still** for the first **Distillation**.

Dona tub: A vessel in which jug yeast is grown to produce enough **Yeast** to ferment a whole batch of **Mash**. Pronounced "DOE-nee" or "DOE-nuh."

Doubler: A large copper still, looking somewhat like a small water tank with an upturned funnel on top, used to distill **High wines** or new spirit from **Low wines**.

Doublings: The spirit produced by a secondary **Distillation**. Often called **High wines**.

Feints: The last section of **High wines** to exit the **Doubler** or **Thumper**; this spirit is high in impurities and is sent back to the still for redistillation. Sometimes called **Tails**.

Fermenter: A large vessel, made of metal (usually steel) or cypress, where the mash receives yeast and backset and is fermented to create distiller's beer.

Foreshots: The first quantity of the high wines to exit the doubler or thumper; this spirit is high in impurities and is sent back to the still for redistillation. Sometimes referred to as **Heads**.

Fusel oils: A subcategory of **Congeners**. Fusel oils are alcohols with a higher molecular weight than beverage alcohol that are present in minuscule amounts in beverage alcohol and add flavor to the product during aging. The presence of excess fusel oils, however, leads to a "banana" flavor in whiskey.

Heads: The first quantity of the **High wines** to exit the **Doubler** or **Thumper**; this spirit is high in impurities and is sent back to the still for redistillation. Sometimes called **Foreshots**.

High wines: The final spirit produced by the secondary **Distillation**. At this point, it is ready for aging. Sometimes called **Doublings**.

Hopped yeast mash: A **Mash** flavored by cooked **Hops** in which **Yeast** is propagated.

Hops: A member of the mulberry family, hops, in pellet form, are sometimes used to flavor the **Yeast mash** in a **Dona tub**.

Leaching: Filtration, before aging, of Tennessee whiskey through a minimum of 10 feet of sugar-maple charcoal. Also known as **Mellowing**, **Charcoal mellowing** or the **Lincoln County Process**.

Lincoln County Process: The filtration of Tennessee whiskey, before it is aged, through a minimum of 10 feet of sugar-maple charcoal. Sometimes called **Mellowing**, **Charcoal mellowing** or **Leaching**.

Low wines: Technically, spirits with too low a proof to be aged. In American whiskey-making, the term describes spirits produced by a primary **Distillation**. Sometimes called **Singlings**.

Malt: Malted grain. In American whiskey-making, the grain is almost always barley.

Malted barley: Barley that has been partially germinated and then heated or roasted to stop the germination. Malted barley (or any malted grain) contains enzymes not present in unmalted grains that convert starches into the fermentable sugars on which **Yeast** feeds.

Mash: The cooked grains from the mash tub.

Mash tub: A large metal vessel in which the grains are cooked prior to being transferred to the **Fermenter**.

Mashbill: The grain recipe used to make whiskey.

Mellowing: Filtration, before aging, of Tennessee whiskey through a minimum of 10 feet of sugar-maple charcoal. Also known as **Charcoal mellowing**, **Leaching** or the **Lincoln County Process**.

Mingling: The process in which straight whiskeys from a number of **Barrels** are mixed together in order to achieve a consistent style of **Straight whiskey**.

Proof: Measurement of beverage alcohol on a scale, in America, of 200. A 100°-proof spirit contains 50 percent alcohol.

Rackhouse: The building in which whiskey is aged, sometimes called the **Warehouse**.

Red layer: A layer of caramelized wood sugars that is formed when **Barrels** are toasted and charred.

Ricks: The wooden structures on which **Barrels** of whiskey rest during aging. Also— tall stacks of sugar-maple planks that are burned to produce the charcoal through which Tennessee whiskey is filtered.

Rye whiskey (straight): A whiskey made from a **Mash** containing at least 51 percent rye, distilled out at a maximum of 160° proof, aged at no more than 125° proof for a minimum of two years in charred new oak **Barrels** and bottled at a minimum of 80° proof. If the whiskey is aged for less than four years, its age must be stated on the bottle. No coloring or flavoring may be added to any **Straight whiskey**.

Setback: Liquid strained from the **Mash** after the primary **Distillation**. Sometimes called **Backset** or **Sour mash**.

Single-barrel whiskey: Whiskey drawn from one **Barrel** that has not been mingled with any other whiskeys.

Singlings: An old moonshiner term for **Low wines**.

Small grains: The grains other than corn used in the production of American whiskey.

Small-batch whiskey: A product of mingling select barrels of whiskey that have matured into a specific style.

Sour mash: A term used to describe **Backset**.

Sour-mash whiskey: Whiskey made from a **Mash** to which **Backset** has been added in the **Fermenter**.

Sour-yeast mash: A **Mash**, usually of corn and rye, which is "soured" by the addition of lactic bacteria.

Spent beer: The residue of **Mash** taken from the **Beer still** after the first **Distillation**.

Stillage: The residue of **Mash** taken from the **Beer Still** after the first **Distillation**.

Straight whiskey: A whiskey made from a **Mash** containing at least 51 percent of any grain, distilled out at a maximum of 160° proof, aged at no more than 125° proof for a minimum of two years in charred new oak **Barrels** and bottled at a minimum of 80°

proof. If the whiskey is aged for less than four years, its age must be stated on the bottle. No coloring or flavoring may be added to any straight whiskey.

Sweet mash: A **Mash** of grains that is fermented using fresh yeast only, without the addition or help of any **Backset**.

Tails: The last section of **High wines** to exit the **Doubler** or **Thumper**; this spirit is high in impurities and sent back to the still for redistillation. Sometimes called **Feints**.

Tennessee whiskey (straight): Whiskey made from a **Mash** of at least 51 percent corn, distilled out at a maximum of 160° proof, filtered through a minimum of 10 feet of sugar-maple charcoal, aged at no more than 125° proof for a minimum of two years in charred new oak **Barrels** and bottled at a mimimum of 80° proof. The sugar-maple filtration is not a legal requirement for Tennessee whiskey, but describes the way in which present-day Tennessee whiskeys are made. No coloring or flavoring may be added to any **Straight whiskey**.

Three-step method: A phrase that we use to describe the traditional practice of cooking the grains. This involves cooking corn at a high temperature, allowing the **Mash** to cool a little before the rye or wheat is added and cooked and then allowing it to cool some more before adding and cooking the **Malted barley**.

Thumper: A **Doubler** containing water through which **Low-wine** vapors are bubbled to produce **High wines**.

Toasting: The process of heating the staves of a barrel over a gentle flame in order to form the shape of the barrel and convert starches into sugars that will form the **Red layer** during the charring process.

Vintage whiskey: Whiskey that is the product of one particular season of **Distillation** that has matured particularly well.

Warehouse: The building in which whiskey is aged, sometimes referred to as the **Rackhouse**.

Wheated bourbon: A term that we use to describe bourbon that is made from a **Mashbill** that contains wheat instead of rye grain.

Whiskey: A spirituous liquor distilled from a fermented mash of cooked grains.

Yeast: A living organism that feeds on fermentable sugars, transforming them to beverage alcohol, **Congeners**, carbon dioxide and heat.

Yeast mash: When jug yeast is grown in **Dona tubs**, cooked grains, known as a yeast mash, are usually used as the growing medium. A yeast mash may be "sweet" or "sour." The introduction of **Hops** into this process produces a product that we refer to as a **Hopped yeast mash**, which is not usually soured.

BIBLIOGRAPHY

Abraham Lincoln: His Speeches and Writings. Edited with critical and analytical notes by Roy P. Basler. New York: Da Capo Press, 1946.

Ade, George. *The Old-Time Saloon.* New York: Old Town Books, 1993.

The Anti-Saloon League Year Book, 1910. Compiled and edited by Ernest Hurst Cherrington. Westerville, Ohio: The Anti-Saloon League of America Publishers, 1910.

Baker, Charles H. *The Gentleman's Companion.* New York: Crown Publishers, 1946.

Brown, George Garvin. *The Holy Bible Repudiates Prohibition.* Louisville, Kentucky: George Garvin Brown, 1910.

Brown, John Hull. *Early American Beverages.* New York: Bonanza Books, 1966.

Crockett, Albert Stevens. *The Old Waldorf-Astoria Bar Book.* New York: A.S. Crockett, 1935.

Crowgey, Henry G. *Kentucky Bourbon—The Early Years of Whiskeymaking.* Lexington, Kentucky: The University Press of Kentucky, 1971.

Dabney, Joseph Earl. *Mountain Spirits, A Chronicle of Corn Whiskey from King James' Ulster Plantation to America's Appalachians and the Moonshine Life.* New York: Charles Scribner's Sons, 1974.

Dalton, Judy H. *The Origins of Barton Bourbon.* An unpublished paper.

The Distilled Spirits Industry, 2—Alcohol—The Beverage Industry's Part in the War Effort. New York: Allied Liquor Industries, Inc., 1944.

Documents of American History. Volume 1. 9th edition. Edited by Henry Steele Commager. Englewood Cliffs, New Jersey: Prentice-Hall, 1973.

Downard, William L. *Dictionary of the History of the American Brewing and Distilling Industries.* Westport, Connecticut: Greenwood Press, 1980.

Duffy, Patrick Garvin. *The Official Mixer's Guide.* New York: Alta Publications, Inc., 1934.

Earle, Alice Morse. *Home Life in Colonial Days.* (Written in 1898.) Stockbridge, Massachusetts: The Berkshire Traveller Press, 1974.

Elliot, Sam Carpenter. *The Nelson County Record, An Illustrated Historical & Industrial Suppliment, 1896.* Bardstown, Kentucky: The Record Printing Company, 1986. Reprinted from original in Nazereth Archival Center, Nazereth, Kentucky.

Embury, David A. *The Fine Art of Mixing Drinks.* 2nd edition. New York: Garden City Books, 1952.

Fortune. July 1951.

Fortune. May 1936.

Fortune. November 1933.

Fulmer, David. *Barrels & Bottles & Tennessee Jugs.* Lynchburg, Tennessee: Lynchburg Hardware & General Store, no date.

Getz, Oscar, with the collaboration of Irv. Blow. *Whiskey—An American Pictorial History.* New York: David McKay Company, Inc., 1978.

Gilbert, Martin. *American History Atlas.* New York: Macmillan,1968.

Green, Ben A. *Jack Daniel's Legacy.* Nashville, Tennessee: Rich Printing Co., 1967.

Grimes, William. *Straight Up or On The Rocks—A Cultural History of American Drink.* New York: Simon & Schuster, 1993.

Grun, Bernard. *The Timetables of History.* 3rd New Revised Edition, based on Werner Stein's *Kulturfahrplan,* © 1946, 1963 by F.A. Herbig Verlagsbuchhandlung. New York: Simon & Schuster/Touchstone, 1991.

Harwell, Richard Barksdale. *The Mint Julep*. Charlottesville, Virginia: University Press of Virginia, 1975.

Hibbs, Dixie. *Nelson County Kentucky: A Pictorial History*. Norfolk, Virginia: The Donning Company, 1989.

Jackson, Michael. *The World Guide to Whisky*. Topsfield, Massachusetts: Salem House Publishers, 1987.

The Kentucky Encyclopedia. Editor in Chief, John E. Kleber. Lexington, Kentucky: The University Press of Kentucky, 1992.

Kroll, Harry Harrison. *Bluegrass, Belles, and Bourbon—A Pictorial History of Whiskey in Kentucky*. New York: A.S. Barnes, 1967.

Langdon, William Chauncy. *Everyday Things in American Life 1776-1876*. New York: Charles Scribner's Sons, 1941.

The Lincoln Reader. Edited and with an introduction by Paul M. Angle. New Brunswick, New Jersey: Rutgers University Press, 1947.

The Living Lincoln, The Man, his mind, his times, and the war he fought, reconstructed from his own writings. Edited by Paul M. Angle and Earl Schenck Miers. New York: Barnes & Noble Books, 1955.

Lockhart, Sir Robert Bruce. *Scotch, The Whisky of Scotland in Fact and Story*. London, England: Putnam, 1959.

MacLean, Charles. *The Mitchell Beazley Pocket Whisky Book*. London, England: Reed Consumer Books, 1993.

McCreary, Alf. *Spirit of the Age, The Story of Old Bushmills*. Belfast, Northern Ireland: The Universities Press, 1983.

McDonald, General John. *Secrets of the Great Whiskey Ring*. Chicago: Belford, Clarke & Co., 1880.

McFeely, William S. *Grant, A Biography*. New York: W.W. Norton & Company, 1981.

McLaughlin, Jack. *Jefferson and Monticello, The Biography of a Builder*. New York: Henry Holt and Company, 1988.

A Memorial History of Louisville. Volume 1. Edited by J. Stoddard Johnston. Chicago: American Biographical Publishing Company, 1896.

The New York World Telegram. May 10, 1944.

Newsweek. December 28, 1942.

The Official Price Guide to Bottles. 3rd edition. New York: The House of Collectables, 1987.

The Oxford Book of Royal Anecdotes. Edited by Elizabeth Longford. Oxford, England: Oxford University Press, 1989.

Panati, Charles. *Extraordinary Origins of Everyday Things*. New York: Perennial Library, Harper & Row, 1987.

Pearce, John Ed. *Nothing Better In The Market*. Louisville, Kentucky: Brown-Forman Distillers Corp, 1970.

Playboy. January, 1981.

Rice, Arnold S., John A. Krout & C.M. Harris. *United States History to 1877*. 8th edition. New York: HarperCollins, 1991.

Rice, Patricia M. *Altered States, Alcohol and Other Drugs in America*. Rochester, New York: The Strong Museum, 1992.

Sante, Luc. *Low Life, Lures and Snares of Old New York*. New York: Farrar Strauss and Giroux, 1991.

Stephen, John, M.D. *A Treatise on the Manufacture, Imitation, Adulteration, and Reduction of Foreign Wines, Brandies, Gins, Rum, &c. and all kinds of Domestic Liquors based on the French System.* Philadelphia: published for the author, 1860.

This Was America. True Accounts of People and Places, Manners and Customs, as recorded by European Travelers to the Western Shore in the Eighteenth, Nineteenth, and Twentieth Centuries. Edited and with an introduction and commentary by Oscar Handlin. Cambridge, Massachusetts: Harvard University Press, 1949.

Thomas, Professor Jerry. *The Bon Vivant's Companion, or How to Mix Drinks.* Edited and with an introduction by Herbert Asbury. New York: Grosset & Dunlap, 1934.

Time Almanac of the 20th Century. CD-ROM, Compact Publishing, Inc.: 1900s Highlights; 1920s Highlights; February 27, 1933; December 11, 1933; November 6, 1944; March 6, 1950; March 9, 1962; July 17, 1964; September 16, 1966; November 14, 1983.

Trader Vic. *Bartender's Guide.* New York: Garden City Books, 1948.

True. 1954 (issue number illegible).

Whiskey Paper. Edited by Robert E. Snyder. Amarillo, Texas: Snyder Research Center, 1980.

Willkie, H.F. *Beverage Spirits in America—A Brief History.* New York: The Newcomen Society of England, American Branch, 1949.

Wilson, James Boone. *The Spirit of Old Kentucky.* Louisville, Kentucky: Glenmore Distilleries Company, 1945.

GENERAL INDEX

Page numbers in **boldface** indicate photographs or illustrations.

RECIPE INDEX

Page numbers in **boldface** indicate photographs.

ILLUSTRATION AND PHOTOGRAPHY CREDITS

The Bettmann Archive: 9, 14, 16, 18, 26-27, 34, 36, 39, 42, 49, 54, 57, 63, 65, 67, 68, 69, 70, 72, 88, 262.

Courtesy of Brown-Forman Corporation, Louisville, Kentucky: 75, 171, 173, 221, 249.

Clark Capps: 106, 225-232.

Culver Pictures: 51.

Courtesy of the Heaven Hill Distillery Archives, Bardstown, Kentucky: 124, 143, 332.

Courtesy of the Jack Daniel Distillery, Lynchburg, Tennessee: 98, 121, 123, 259, 292.

Courtesy of George A. Dickel's Cascade Distillery, Tullahoma, Tennessee: 261.

Courtesy of the Filson Club Historical Society, Louisville, Kentucky: 24, 76, 77, 79.

Courtesy of the Oscar Getz Museum of Whiskey History, Bardstown, Kentucky: 5, 22, 23, 44, 83, 127, 132, 162, 182, 217.

Courtesy of the Kentucky Derby Museum, Louisville, Kentucky: 338.

Becky Luigart-Stayner: 297-300.

Courtesy of the Seagram's Four Roses Distillery Archives, Lawrenceburg, Kentucky: 10, 134, 148, 204, 236, 250, 257.

Courtesy of United Distillers North American Archives:
    Glenmore Collection: 202, 239.
    I. W. Harper Collection: 138, 139, 253.
    Old Fitzgerald Collection: 167, 223, 247.
    Rebel Yell Collection: 185.

Courtesy of J.P. Van Winkle and Son, Louisville, Kentucky: 187.